*Für Kurt im Sommer 2000.
Deine Kibi*

The Finnlines Fleet

1947–1997

Copyright © Matti Pietikäinen and Finnlines Ltd

Published in Finland by Finnlines Ltd, Helsinki

ISBN 952-90-9115-X

Printed and bound by Gummerus Kirjapaino Oy,
Jyväskylä 1998

Matti Pietikäinen

THE FINNLINES FLEET

1947–1997

50 YEARS AT YOUR SERVICE

LIST OF VESSELS MANAGED BY

Oy Baltic Chartering Ab in 1947–1954
Oy Finnlines Ltd in 1954–1989
FG-Shipping Oy Ab from 1989 on

Contents

	Page
Fifty Years	3
Preface	4
Acknowledgements	5
Photograph Acknowledgements	6
A Brief History	7
Ships Managed by Baltic Chartering/Finnlines/FG-Shipping	29
Owners of the Ships Managed by Baltic Chartering/Finnlines/FG-Shipping	31
Sponsors of the Vessels	34
Fleet List Notes	36
Abbreviations Used in the Fleet List	37
Fleet List	38
Other Ships Connected with Finnlines Having the Prefix "Finn" in Their Names	242
Sources and Bibliography	246
Index of Ship Names	248

Fifty Years

In Finland, shipping is a must. Finland is an island seen from the transport point of view. Most of Finland's tonnage was lost during and after World War II. So the means of transportation were severely diminished. As presented elsewhere in this book, Finnlines was founded to enable post-war rebuilding of Finland. The heavy weather conditions in Finland did also from the very beginning make additional demands on Finnish ships. Ice-strengthened vessels are vital for Finland and this has created an excellent technical skill in both ship construction and ice navigation.

After World War II, Finland was in urgent need of vessels able to carry Finnish forest industry products. The vessels then purchased and later on built were fitted for this. But later on the needs diversified. All this can be seen also from the list of our fleet.

In the 1970s Finnlines was the pioneer of roro traffic. The roro line then opened from Finland to Germany is still being in strong growth and generating advanced solutions for new generations of vessels, which naturally reflect the development of Finnish foreign trade and its diversion into several other areas than paper industry. Behind the roro concept is also the logistic thinking as an integrated part of the JOT (just on time) philosophy.

Shipping is depending on the framework created by the Government. In this respect Finland has seen both hard times and good times. The outflagging boom in the 1980s threatened the Finnish flagged fleet as a whole. Fortunately measures were taken by legislation and most of the fleet was saved at that time. However, long-term shipping strategy cannot be dependent on short-term governmental measures. That is why the Finnlines group has diversified into other shipping related activities and that is also why the company continuously follows up the development of the conditions for shipping elsewhere in Europe.

Finnlines as well as the entire shipping community of Finland are extremely grateful to Mr. Matti Pietikäinen, the outstanding expert on the history of Finnish ships. Without his enthusiastic work, this book would never have been published. Looking back at the history of Finnlines' fleet, and knowing our strong position today, I am looking forward to a bright future for our group and its fleet.

Antti Lagerroos
President and CEO
Finnlines Ltd

Preface

It has been a great pleasure to prepare this fleet list of the ships managed by Oy Baltic Chartering Ab, Oy Finnlines Ltd and FG-Shipping Oy Ab. It has also been a special challenge to study all these ship biographies, as I have lived all my life very close to Finnlines and have been able to follow the progress of this prominent shipping company, which is now passing the 50th anniversary milestone.

My first memories of Finnlines vessels date back to 1948, when ss Kalle was lying from January to June at Katajanokka shipyard in Helsinki for repairs. Another reminiscence from the year 1948 is the first arrival of ss Pankakoski in August at her home port, Helsinki. I went to the West Harbour to see her discharging the record cargo of 3,562 tons coffee from Colombia. It goes without saying that they were great days for a schoolboy to see the first visits to Helsinki of the new liners Finntrader in 1951, and Finnpulp and Finnsailor in 1953. At that time I decided that my future career will be within shipping. Already in the 1960s I had a chance to get an inside view of Finnlines as the office manager of the head office. During the past years I have been able to make many memorable trips on board Finnlines vessels, viz. on ms Hansa Express in September 1964, on ms Finnhansa in April 1966, on ms Finnfellow in December 1972, on gts Finnjet and ms Olau Finn in May 1982, on ms Capella av Stockholm in September 1987 and on ms Finnmerchant in May 1989, just to mention some of them. From 1980 on I have had a chance to follow closely the activities of Finnlines and FG-Shipping as the manager of Thomesto Maritime Business.

I wrote a first version of a Finnlines fleet list already in the 1960s and it was published in 1967 in connection with the 20th anniversary. Ten years later I updated the fleet list and it was printed as "A Review of Oy Finnlines Ltd's Activities 1947–1977". In other words this book is a result of a compiling work that has continued for decades.

However, the present list is more detailed than the earlier versions and there is now included one special feature never before seen in fleet lists. As a sponsor has a prominent role in naming ceremonies, I consider she cannot be neglected even in a fleet list. Therefore plenty of work has been done to reveal all their names. I hope this will arouse interest in this book even among female readers.

Ships are not only vehicles. They have their lives with happy days as well as with reverse things. All those days of every Finnlines vessel are told in the following fleet list with short notes, but behind them there are varied fates.

Helsinki in August 1997

Matti Pietikäinen

Acknowledgements

I would like to thank all those persons who have contributed to the fact that we now have in hand a complete 50th anniversary fleet list of the ships managed by Oy Baltic Chartering Ab, Oy Finnlines Ltd and FG-Shipping Oy Ab. I greatly appreciate the opportunity afforded to me by the direction of Finnlines Ltd and especially Mr. Antti Lageroos, President and CEO of Finnlines Ltd, and Mr. Lars Trygg, Vice President of Finnlines Ltd.

I like to express my warm thanks to all those who have willingly helped me in the compilation of this fleet list. First of all I am greatly indebted to Mr. Rolf Sundström and Mr. Olavi Pylkkänen, retired presidents of Oy Finnlines Ltd and FG-Shipping Oy Ab who have helped me in tracing names of the sponsors. I also wish to express my special gratitude to Mrs. Solveig Beckman of Finnlines Ltd for her help in translation of the text, to Mr. Raimo A. Wirrankoski, Mr. Bengt Sjöström and Mr. K. Brzoza for proof reading with utmost accuracy my manuscripts and for many important amendments and corrections made by them, and to Mr. Petri Sipilä who has spent so much of his valuable time in the Guildhall Library studying Lloyd's Voyage Records and Weekly Casualty Reports. Many others have also made priceless contributions in their own field to this fleet list, viz.:

Pekka Aarnio
Liisa Aho
Lasse Alhonen
Harold Appleyard
Asko Arkkola
Dag Bakka Jr
J. Robert Boman
Piero Costa
Nils-Erik Eklund
Ilmari Elo
Alvit Fernandez
Bernt Fogelberg
Erik Hag
Matti Hakala
William Hultgren
Nils Jacobsson
Robert Jansson
Sten Johansson
Tomas Johannesson

L. J. Jouhki
Heikki Jäntti
Jorma Kaipio
Marja Kalli
Taru Kaplin
Seppo Ketola
Trond Kittilsen
Tatu Korhonen
Bert Kruidhof
Juhani Lares
Peter Lesch
Guy Lindroos
Stig Löthner
Jaakko Mattila
Keijo Mehtonen
Sixten Norrgrann
Christer Nyberg
N. A. Pappadakis
Hans Pedersen
Kari Peltonen
Ritva Punta
Anneli Salminen
Wm. A. Schell
Reinhart Schmelzkopf
Antonio Scrimali
Joachim Stahl
Marko Stampehl
Pirkko Stewen
Søren Thorsøe
Lena Tontti
Leena Vakkilainen
Tom Waselius
Kurt Winqvist
Kari Wuorimaa

If any name is missing, the omission is not intentional, and I tender my apologies.

Last, but by no means least, I like to thank my wife, Raili, for her encouragement and good natured forbearance during this work that has affected our family life during so many years.

Matti Pietikäinen

Photograph Acknowledgements

Illustrations come from many sources, and I like to thank the many photographers and collectors acknowledged beneath their pictures. The aim has been to select the best photograph(s) of each ship and to show the various liveries and appearances. The photographs have been credited to their photographer (Photo by …) or the collection from which they were obtained (Photo from …), the photographer having the highest priority.

I am indebted to the following photographers:

Aeromarine
Airfoto
K. Brzoza
Krister Bång
Michael Cassar
Nereo Castelli
Farabee's Studio
F.H. van Fijk
Bernt Fogelberg
FotoFlite
Erik Hag
F.W. Hawks
Hede Foto
Richard Hildebrand
Esa Hänninen
Lars Helge Isdahl
Dirk Jankowsky
Tomas Johannesson
P-E. Johnsen
Seppo Kaksonen

Klaus Koszubatis
Stig Löthner
Foto Martin
Rolf Mieritz
Kari Mäkirinta
Studio B. Möller
Didier Noirel
Aulis Nyqvist
Holger Nyström
H.-J. Reinecke
Kari Riutta
Selim San
Sea-Foto Hannu Laakso
Bengt Sjöström
Pär-Henrik Sjöström
Skyfotos
Studio-Eira
Kalevi Sundqvist
Foto Tammelin
Wm. J. Taylor
Raimo A. Wirrankoski
Bertil Zandelin

and to the following collections:

Jay N. Bascom
K. Brzoza
J. K. Byass
Krister Bång
John Clarkson
A. Duncan
FG-Shipping Oy Ab
Finncarriers Oy Ab
Tomas Johannesson
Eric Johnson
Donald Mac Fie
Neste Oy
Thomproperties Oy
Søren Thorsøe
World Ship Photo Library
Oy Wärtsilä Ab Turku

Matti Pietikäinen

A Brief History

Finland in 1947 and the Founding of Merivienti Oy and Oy Finnlines Ltd

World War II dealt very hard with the Finnish merchant fleet. There were several reasons for the dramatic decline in tonnage. Finnish ships had been sunk, or had been seized in a number of countries during the war and, finally, Finland had to surrender 104 of its best vessels to the Soviet Union as a part of its peace terms. The Finnish merchant fleet was at its lowest point in August 1945, at a mere 257,000 gross register tons. That was less than 40 per cent of the 649,000 tons of 1939.

Under the leadership of the state-owned forest industry consortium Enso-Gutzeit Oy and on the initiative of its President and CEO, Wm Lehtinen, export and import circles in Finland on April 18, 1947 founded a shipping company called Merivienti Oy. Enso-Gutzeit subscribed half the share capital, and the Finnish Social Insurance Institution the other half. The first important task of the company was to start up traffic to the North Sea. Merivienti, however, acted exclusively as the finance corporation and for the practical ship operations a majority in Oy Baltic Chartering Ab was purchased in May 1947. The constituent meeting of shareholders of another subsidiary, Oy Finnlines Ltd, was held on November 8, 1947. The purpose of this company was at the start specifically to operate a liner service to the United States. When the capital of Merivienti was to be increased, the forest industry company Veitsiluoto Oy and the wholesalers SOK, OTK, Tukkukauppojen Oy, and Keskc Oy became new shareholders in November 1947, each with a portfolio of four per cent. Subsequently, Enso-Gutzeit and the Social Insurance Institution held 40 per cent each. In 1950 the Institution sold half its shares in Merivienti to Enso-Gutzeit, which thus assumed a 60 per cent majority in the company. United Paper Mills Ltd. and the agricultural wholesaler Keskusosuusliike Hankkija became minority holders in 1954.

Inauguration and Pioneer Years of Finnlines Liner Service to the U.S.E.C.

Wm Lehtinen, of Enso-Gutzeit Oy, went to the United States in spring 1947, where he learnt that imports of woodpulp and paper from Finland had once again got off to a promising start. Merivienti Oy had been established in the meanwhile, as mentioned above, and a subsidiary of it, Oy Finnlines Ltd, had been set up to run a liner service to the United States. Six old steamships were bought that same year, three of them being rather small and suitable for the European traffic. Two of the bigger vessels, ss Hamina and ss Pankakoski, each 5,400 dwt, were old Great Lakes ships which had been converted for ocean traffic during the war, while the third one, ss Tornator of 6,800 dwt, was an old Danish liner. It was with this modest tonnage that the service to the United States was opened on February 5, 1948, when the Tornator left Rauma with a cargo of 5,776 tons of woodpulp and paper to cross the Atlantic with her destination Portland, Maine. In March 1948 Finnlines was admitted to membership of the North Atlantic Baltic Freight Conference, but in practice this did not bring in much general cargo, as half of such cargo had gone directly to Moore McCormack Lines, of the United States, due to the terms for the financing of trade between the United States and Finland.

At roughly the same time, Finland Steamship Co. Ltd. (FÅA) had started a service between Finland and the United States with two old cargo vessels. For some time, negotiations were held between Finnlines and FÅA about traffic arrangements, and efforts were made to reach a deal on traffic shares between the Swedes, the American competitor, and the Finns.

The ships of the Finnish companies were, however, too old for the demanding liner service. Both shipping lines began to acquire new, faster motor vessels. The Finnish shipyards were fully occupied with deliveries of war reparations, and all the vessels were ordered from Dutch shipyards. The first new vessel for Finnlines and Merivienti was completed in Holland in January 1951. This, ms Finntrader of 6,400 dwt, initiated a handsome series which as early as 1953 was extended by her sister ships ms Finnpulp and ms Finnsailor. Upon completion of these motor vessels, the old triad of steamers had to give way. Along with Merivienti, Enso-Gutzeit had also become a shipowner; the Finnsailor, mentioned above, was its first new vessel.

With its new tonnage Finnlines was able to offer a departure every three weeks. The vessels loaded paper, woodpulp, and other forest industry products in ports of Southern Finland for the United States where the usual discharging ports were Boston, New York, Philadelphia, and Baltimore. In addition to general cargo, the cargo on the return trips consisted of coal for Finland.

When the 8,500 dwt Finnmerchant was added to the service in 1956, and the 9,200 dwt Finnboard completed in 1958, and ms Finnbirch and ms Finnstar, purchased when fairly new, were included in the fleet in 1959, Finnlines was able to use seven ships to offer almost weekly sailings.

Apart from the United States run, Finnlines and FÅA had also competed on a U.K. service. For the purpose of rationalising, the companies signed an agreement at the end of 1960 under which Finland Steamship Co. Ltd. gave up its traffic to the United States and Finnlines its traffic from Hull to Finland.

European Traffic and the Start of a Liner Service from the U.K.

At the founding of Merivienti in 1947 six old steamships had been bought, including three of a smaller size for North Sea traffic. These vessels, the Wille of 3,350 dwt, Kalle of 4,150 dwt, and Eero of 3,500 dwt, ran primarily in tramp trade, carrying sawn goods and woodpulp from Finland to the United Kingdom and coal back. Gradually, the company also went into carrying general cargo from the U.K. to Finland, which prompted Finnlines into opening a general cargo line of its own from London and Hull to Southern Finland in March 1955. The Wille and Kalle were available for this line, as was a second-hand cargo vessel bought by Enso-Gutzeit in

ss TORNATOR discharging paper in Alexandria, Va.
Photo from FG-Shipping Oy Ab

ms FINNMERCHANT, ss FINNMASTER and ms FINNPULP simultaneously at the West Harbour in Helsinki
Photo from FG-Shipping Oy Ab

ss WILLE loading at Kotka
Photo from Matti Pietikäinen

1950, the Enso of 3,050 dwt and also ss Pamilo of 3,500 dwt, the first new ship on the European service, completed for Enso-Gutzeit in Holland in February 1954. More tonnage to provide a proper service was acquired for this service in subsequent years. The 3,500 dwt ss Finnmaid was completed in Holland in summer 1956 for Merivienti, as was ms Finnkraft of the same size at Rauma in Finland in December the same year. In 1959 Enso-Gutzeit bought the almost new Finnwood and Finnpine, each of 3,100 dwt, from Norway.

The acquisition of the new vessels led, however, to a trade war that reduced the profitability of Finnlines, FÅA, and United Baltic Corporation (UBC), specially in respect of the eastbound traffic. At the request of FÅA, negotiations on cooperation were started in autumn 1960, an agreement being signed in December, under which the Finns and UBC were to run coordinated services at the same freight rates from London to Finland. It was also agreed that Finnlines would give up its line from Hull and get 30 per cent of the line from London. But the agreement did not cover the traffic from Finland to London, this being left up to each one as they saw fit. Finnlines was also given the right to carry woodpulp in contract trade from Finland not only to the South of England but also to the British West Coast.

Opening a Passenger and Roro Cargo Service to Germany

Up to the early 1960s, the car and truck traffic to the Continent went by sea to Sweden, then overland through Sweden and Denmark. In 1959, the President and CEO of Enso-Gutzeit, Wm Lehtinen, was the first to raise the question of opening up a direct car ferry link between Finland and Germany, but others were still doubtful about the financial outcome of such a long line. However, when Rederi Ab Vikinglinjen cancelled a car ferry order in Germany because of the financial difficulties of the shipyard, a sudden opportunity arose of getting an ice-strengthened car ferry on brief delivery terms. Merivienti closed the deal with the Hamburg yard on January 18, 1962 and in two weeks time a 2,300 GRT passenger/car ferry was launched and given the name Hansa Express. Because of the difficulties of the shipyard, the ship was not completed until July 18, 1962; she went into service from Hanko to Travemünde on July 24, calling at Visby and later at Slite on Gotland. The vessel was found right away to be too small, and as early as the following winter she was lengthened at Kiel by 7.8 meters, increasing the passenger capacity from 133 to 179 berths. It was noticed that although Hanko provided the shortest voyage, the port was too small and too remote, and from September 1963 the Hansa Express consequently went over to the Helsinki – Kalmar – Travemünde route.

The experiment had proved encouraging, and in November 1963 Merivienti Oy ordered a 7,500 GRT passenger/car ferry for the Helsinki – Travemünde so-called Hansa route, from the Hietalahti shipyard of the Wärtsilä Group; and a year later Amer-Tupakka Oy ordered a sister ship from the same shipyard. Due to a devastating fire on board during the construction, the first of the ferries, given the name Finnhansa, was not completed until March 1966. The sister ship Finnpartner went into traffic on Germany via Sweden in June 1966. In addition to the transportation of passengers, this provided a convenient link for the increased volume of trucking directly to Germany.

The Hansa Express was transferred to the Copenhagen service in 1966 and renamed Finndana but, upon having completed her original purpose, she was sold to Poland the following year.

Expansion of the U.S. Liner Service

In the 1960s, new and more efficient ships were built to maintain the service to the East Coast of the United States. In 1962–1963 three motor vessels, the Finneagle, Finnclipper, and Finnforest, each 7,180 dwt, were completed at Emden, and the smaller Finnbirch and Finnstar were shifted to the Mediterranean service.

ms HANSA EXPRESS in 1962
Photo from Matti Pietikäinen

Two Finnlines vessels in 1968 at the ITO Terminal, 23rd Street, Brooklyn, N.Y.
Photo from FG-Shipping Oy Ab

The superliner FINNSAILOR
Photo from FG-Shipping Oy Ab

Furthermore, the owners of Finnlines had nine vessels built all at Turku in 1964–1965, five of them – the Finnboston, Finnhawk, Finnarrow, Finnmaid, and Finn-Enso, each 9,500 dwt – going on the U.S. liner service.

As the transport capacity of Finnlines grew, the westbound ships began to call at Hamburg from 1958 onwards and also at Bremen from 1963 to replenish their freight with general cargo. Similarly, on their return voyage they brought general cargo to Hamburg from 1959 onwards and to Rotterdam from 1963.

In the late 1960s, containers became common in the Western European and United States services. Finnlines had to be able to respond to this new challenge, and the eight newest vessels mentioned above were lengthened in 1968 and 1969 by a new section of 14.7 meters between their second and third hatches providing two special holds to carry containers. The five old liners from the 1950s had done their job and were sold off.

A new investment for the traffic to the East Coast of the United States, a series of three so-called universal superliners were built at Emden in 1971–1972. These 14,270 dwt vessels, the Finn-Amer, Finnbuilder, and Finnsailor, were real multipurpose vessels which in addition to derricks and hatches also had a stern ramp and three side doors for both roro and forklift loading. Apart from the big and fast 20-knot superliners, two semi-container vessels, the Finnboston and Finnforest, remained on the East Coast service.

In the 1970s, U.S. exports to Europe developed vigorously. At the same time, containers became the predominant transportation means in the United States. The Atlantic traffic was also adapted to container shipments on purpose-built vessels. At the same time there was a re-shuffle of traffic among the shipping lines, and old lines with conventional tonnage went out of business one after another. Finnlines actively studied various options such as cooperating with another shipping line, participating as owners of a container line, or acquiring container vessels of its own; but none of these ideas materialized. The owners of the superliners had meanwhile become dissatisfied with the results of the traffic, and Finnlines was consequently left with no other option than to decide that it was impossible to go on in such circumstances.

The company's service to the East Coast of the United States had been running for 28 years when the Finnsailor discharged her last cargo from the United States in Hamburg in 1976.

Extension of European Lines to Biscay and the Mediterranean

United Paper Mills Ltd. (UPM) was interested in exporting shipments of its own, to such an extent that it joined Merivienti as a minor shareholder and, at Rauma in 1960–1961, built the sister ships ms Simpele and ms Kaipola, which were a slight development over the Finnkraft. When Finnlines began traffic to the ports of Biscay in 1962 in conjunction with its U.K. service, carrying woodpulp and kraftliner, the first vessel on the line was ms Kaipola of UPM. Because of its deal with FÅA, Finnlines was unable to operate to the Continent while the UPM ships sailed to Rouen and other places.

At Wärtsilä in Turku, Enso-Gutzeit and UPM had four cargo ships of 3,700 dwt built for the traffic to Britain and Biscay: the Finnseal, Lotila, Rekola, and Finnfighter.

Meanwhile, Finnlines had in February 1961 opened up a line to Spain and Italy with the 3,570 dwt Kaipola, as Finnish exports of woodpulp and paper there were in steep upswing. In June 1961, the 5,800 dwt ms Finnalpino purchased from Norway, was introduced on the line and in 1962 the Finnbirch and the Finnstar, the smallest vessels on the American service, were transferred to the Mediterranean. There was a great demand for export capacity but return cargoes were not so easily available, though the vessels brought fruit from Spain and Morocco for Christmas and at other times phosphates from Tunisia to Denmark.

The Mediterranean service was, however, profitable and therefore worth developing. A new series of 8,000 dwt cargo vessels was built by Valmet in Helsinki and in 1972–73 the Finnpine, Finnwood, Finntrader, and the new Finnalpino were delivered to Merivienti Oy, replacing the older vessels.

ms FINNALPINO was named after the famous Italian Alpine soldiers
Photo from FG-Shipping Oy Ab

ms FINNROSE ex LOVISA
Photo by Börje Gustafsson

Concentration on Woodpulp Transport

Finnlines had long had problems with its carriage contracts on woodpulp exports, while the ships of Oy R. Nordström & Co Ab carried nearly 50 per cent more woodpulp than Finnlines. So Finnlines began negotiations in 1970 to augment its market share by buying up the Nordström company. The deal materialized at the end of December, and the six Nordström vessels were transferred to the management and operations of Finnlines. In spring 1971 they were given names beginning "Finn", and in November 1971 the name of the Nordström company was changed to Oy Enso-Chartering Ab. All the over-aged vessels except for one were sold abroad by 1974, but the woodpulp transports remained with Finnlines.

Finnlines in International Cruising

By chance Finnlines found itself operating ocean cruises as early as in the fall of 1965 when, after the summer and until the expiry of the charter-party, use had to be made of the Israeli ferry Nili, acquired to replace the fire-damaged Finnhansa. The Nili, under her marketing name of Helsinki Express, proceeded on the "first Finnish ocean cruise", leaving Helsinki on September 16, 1965 for Genoa via several intermediate ports. The second cruise went to the Eastern Mediterranean, and the third from Genoa to Dakar and back to Lisbon.

A Finnish ship proceeded for the first time on an ocean cruise on September 8, 1973 when the Thomesto-owned ms Finnpartner, which had been employed for the summer on the Finnlines Hansa route, at the end of the season departed from Helsinki for Malaga via Cherbourg and Lisbon. Cruises then continued to the

ms FINNPARTNER was cruising in 1973–1975
Photo from FG-Shipping Oy Ab

Easy life on board ms FINNSTAR
Photo from FG-Shipping Oy Ab

Mediterranean and the Black Sea until, with winter approaching, the Finnpartner went over to the West Coast of Africa, going all the way to Monrovia in Liberia. In the spring the vessel returned to the Baltic service but, the following fall, proceeded once again to the south. The program now contained 23 different cruises, calling at a total of 27 different ports, the remotest one being Freetown in Sierra Leone. For winter 1975–1976, a bigger ship was desirable, and the chartered passenger/car ferry ms Bore Star, completed in France in December 1975, proceeded directly from the shipyard under Finnlines colours on a cruise of Western Africa. For the summer she returned to ply the Silja Line route between Helsinki and Stockholm, but from November 1976 to May 1977 she cruised again on the West Coast of Africa.

A decision was made in 1978 to convert for ocean cruise service the passenger/car ferry Finlandia, which had been transferred to Enso-Gutzeit from FÅA in 1975; and in January 1979 the vessel, renamed Finnstar, departed from the shipyard at Turku for the familiar cruise traffic in the Mediterranean and off West Africa, with cruises all the way down to São Tomé and the Equator. But, as a result of a seamen's strike in spring 1980, the manning costs under Finnish flag rose above the profitability level, and the Finnstar had to be laid up on September 14 at Toulon. The vessel was sold the following spring, and that was the end of the Finnlines cruise program.

Liner Service to the U.S. Gulf and AGS/ACS

Upon completion of the vessels built at Turku, Finnlines had 13 ships on the American service. This provided a chance to broaden the range of operations. So in May 1965 traffic to the Gulf of Mexico was commenced, and ships began to carry newsprint to Mobile, New Orleans, Houston, and Vera Cruz in Mexico once a month. The return cargoes were also forest industry products: sawn goods and kraftliner for Britain and the European Continent. But none of the ships was specifically assigned to the route, and the ships took turns on the U.S. East Coast and Gulf of Mexico lines in accordance with available cargoes.

Early in October 1971, six of the vessels in the U.S. traffic were transferred to the Gulf of Mexico service of the company Atlantic Gulf Service Ab., or AGS, which was founded and 50/50 owned by Finnlines and Ab. Svenska Amerika Linien, a member of the

*The AGS funnel mark of ms FINN-ENSO
Photo from FG-Shipping Oy Ab*

*ms FINN-ENSO with Atlanticargo painted on
the superstructure
Photo from FG-Shipping Oy Ab*

*ms FINNEAGLE at Wallhamn
Photo from FG-Shipping Oy Ab*

Broström Group. The Finnclipper, Finn-Enso, and Finnmaid were leased directly to AGS, and the Finnarrow, Finneagle, and Finnhawk were time-chartered to Ab. Svenska Atlant Linien, a subsidiary of Svenska Amerika Linien, and from there again to AGS under the names Vasaholm, Trolleholm, and Maltesholm. At intervals of two weeks the line had sailings from Finland and Scandinavia, via the European Continent and the British Isles, to the coasts of the Southern United States, specifically to Miami and ports on the Gulf of Mexico, chiefly Tampa, New Orleans, and Houston, and also to Vera Cruz in Mexico. In addition to Finnish newsprint, the vessels carried mechanical and chemical woodpulp from Sweden to Mexico. On the return voyages, cargoes were picked up at Mobile, Tampa, and Savannah. In 1973 the Finnforest entered service with AGS as its seventh vessel.

Cooperation under the auspices of the Atlantic Gulf Service continued for a period of five years, with Finnlines terminating the agreement in the fall of 1976 because the Broström Group had started up a service in competition with AGS through its Dutch subsidiary. The operations of AGS were ended at the closing of 1976; and on January 1, 1977 the personnel of the AGS office in Gothenburg and almost the entire AGS network of agencies were transferred to Atlantic Cargo Services AB (ACS or Atlanticargo), founded and wholly owned by Finnlines. The new company continued with the same tonnage with the only difference that Finnarrow, Finneagle, and Finnhawk got their original names back.

However, the business of Atlanticargo proved to be rather unprofitable as Finnish paper cargoes were declining, and in order to step up the line's roundtrips the number of calls in the Baltic Sea were reduced from three times to once a month; but even this did not work out, and from the beginning of 1978 Gothenburg was the only port of loading in Scandinavia while further cargo was picked up thereafter at Bremen and Rotterdam. Even so, the result was not satisfactory, and a cooperating partner was sought in order to share the risk. The vigorously expanding Johansson Group from Sweden became interested, and at the start of 1979 Wallhamn AB of that group took over half the shares of ACS.

It was decided to get rid of the conventional liners, and a roro service started in summer 1979, when ACS time-chartered two cargo ferries of 14,500 dwt from Skärhamns Oljetransport AB of the Johansson Group. They were renamed Finneagle and Finnclipper, more appropriate to Finnlines, and a third roro ship was chartered and for the charter period renamed Finnrose. Through the influence of Johanssons, Wallhamn north of Gothenburg became the only port of loading for the line in Scandinavia, while Bremen and Rotterdam remained ports of call on the Continent. Port Everglades in Florida became an important port of transshipment for cargoes going to islands in the Caribbean. Due to the prevalence of roro, concentration now shifted to general cargo and somewhat away from forest industry products.

New, larger roro cargo ferries, the Finnhawk and a new Finnrose, of 18,500 dwt, were completed for Skärhamns Oljetransport already in 1980 and were leased to Merivienti for five years with a purchase option. Johanssons' new 20,700 dwt roro vessels Finneagle and Finnclipper were introduced on the line in 1981, replacing the former ships of the same names. However, the Johansson Group had expanded too violently, and financial difficulties began to trouble the cooperation as early as 1981. Consequently, Merivienti acquired the Finnhawk and Finnrose in December 1981 to ensure the continuity of the operations of Atlanticargo. Soon thereafter, in January 1982, the Johansson companies went bankrupt and ACS was again left with Finnlines and Enso-Gutzeit, which had taken over the ships from Merivienti at the end of December 1982. In addition to the Finnhawk and Finnrose, the line had a third vessel on charter, initially the Finnclipper of the bankrupt's estate and, in 1983, a German conventional cargo vessel, which was renamed Finnsailor; so traffic continued.

Early in the 1980s Enso-Gutzeit concentrated on forest industry and gave up its vessels. The last of its cargo ships, the Finnhawk and Finnrose, as well as the ACS company, were sold by Enso-Gutzeit in August 1985 in a so-called MBO deal to the Finnish management of ACS. South Atlantic Cargo Shipping N.V. in the Dutch Antilles was entered as owner of the vessels, but they sailed under the Bahamas flag. Their names remained unchanged, and the ACS office in Gothenburg continued as before but now at the management's own risk.

Liner Traffic to the Middle East

As a result of a visit to Finland by the Saudi Arabian magnate Adnan N. Khashoggi, a preliminary agreement was made in September 1976 by Khashoggi's Triad Group, Finnlines, and Valmet to start liner traffic to the Middle East. In July 1977 these companies decided to found a joint shipping line, the Saudi International Shipping Company Ltd., or Sisco. Finnlines subscribed 15 per cent of the share capital and Valmet 10 per cent, while the remaining 75 per cent was subscribed by the Resources Development Company, a Saudi Arabian company of the Triad Group. The Triad Group promised that, as a Saudi Arabian company, Sisco would have a government-guaranteed priority for import transportation to Saudi Arabia. A year went on licensing arrangements for Sisco without the business being settled. As Finnlines found it necessary to employ its semi-container ships released from Atlanticargo, it decided to start up operations of its own to the Middle East under the name of Finnlines-Sisco Middle East Cargo Services. The Finn-Enso consequently left Hamburg on September 9, 1978 for Dubai, Dammam, and Khorramshahr in the Persian Gulf. During the autumn she was followed by three other semi-container vessels from the Atlantic traffic, the Finnmaid, Finnarrow, and Finnhawk, with ports of loading in Europe including Hamburg, Rotterdam, and Antwerp and the Gulf ports of discharge Dubai, Dammam, and Kuwait and, on inducement, Abu Dhabi, Sharjah, and Umm Said/Doha. There was a departure every other week.

When it became clear that the Saudi partner would not be able to obtain an operating licence for Sisco, Finnlines gave notice in spring 1979 of termination of the agreement of cooperation. The above four semi-container vessels had made a total of 20 voyages to the Gulf in the name of Finnlines-Sisco by August 1979 when the traffic came to an end. The vessels plying the route were then sold off abroad.

Finnlines resumed the Gulf service independently in August 1979 under the name Finnlines Europe – Middle East Cargo Service and put its superliners Finn-Amer, Finnbuilder, and Finnsailor on the line. Ports of loading remained Hamburg, Antwerp, and Rotterdam, the cargoes from Finland being sent to the last-mentioned. The most common ports of discharge for the

ms FINNSAILOR at Khor al Fakkan, the Sultanate of Oman
Photo from FG-Shipping Oy Ab

superliners were Dubai, Dammam, and Kuwait. From November 1979 the return voyages called in also at Khor al Fakkan in the Sultanate of Oman, where the chartered feeder vessel Finnorient brought containers from Bombay.

There had already been experience from the Atlantic with the Johansson Group when it was decided early in March 1980 to combine forces in the Middle East traffic under the name MECS Middle East Cargo Services, (Mideastcargo). To the superliners, the OT Express Line of Johansson was able to add at first two, and later three, 15,000 dwt roro vessels which loaded also at Immingham and Leghorn and discharged at Abu Dhabi, Umm Said, and Dammam as well as at Karachi.

The line did not prove profitable under this type of cooperation either, especially as traffic was hindered by the revolution in Iran and by the Iraq-Iran war that broke out in autumn 1980. The superliners were put on sale, and in May 1981 ms Finn-Amer was the last ship to return to Hamburg where, like her sister ships, she was delivered to a buyer from Chile. But Mideastcargo was continued with Johansson's five roro vessels until November 1981.

Worldwide Contract and Tramp Shipping

Finnlines became a shareholder in the international Scanscot Consortium in March 1975, when it was able to put into traffic Thomesto's recently completed 23,323 dwt bulk carrier Finntimber. A few bulker shipping companies had founded Scanscot already in 1967, its most important cargo then consisting of forest industry products from British Columbia to the East Coast of the United States and to Europe. Because of her ice-strengthening, the most important responsibility of the Finntimber became the carrying of newsprint from Finland to Japan; but she carried a lot else, too. The ship's crew began to keep a record of ports at which the ship called

ms FINNTIMBER loading at Kemi
Photo from FG-Shipping Oy Ab

ms FINNTRADER loading at Kotka in 1986
Photo by Matti Pietikäinen

to load or discharge. They had a world map on a bulkhead on which a red-headed pin was inserted whenever a new port was reached. This went on for 12 years, until the ship was sold to Greece in 1987. There were over 150 pins by the time the map was cautiously removed and brought to the Thomesto office as a souvenir. The strangest place the Finntimber had called at was Little Cornwallis Island in Arctic Canada near the magnetic North Pole. For all those 12 years the Finntimber had been in traffic with the Scanscot freight pool, and during that period she set a Finnish record in the series of engine-driven vessels, of seven circumnavigations of the world.

From her time of completion in January 1986 until she was sold in December 1990, Thomesto's ms Finntrader, of 30,975 dwt, was also in traffic with Scanscot.

Under the Finnlines flag, several other bulk carriers also sailed as cross traders on the seven seas. Ky Jussi Ketola & Co. had two bulkers, the Finnbeaver and Finnfury of 34,995 dwt from 1978 for 10 years forward and for a few years the new 32,813 dwt Finnfalcon and Finnwhale, both completed in 1984–1985. The Puhos of 30,242 dwt owned by the Palkkiyhtymä group was managed by Finnlines from 1980 to 1993, and its new Finnwood of 30,946 dwt was introduced in December 1989 and is the only one now remaining.

Development of the European Traffic and the Establishment of Oy Finncarriers Ab

Since 1963 Finnlines had operated a limited cargo service on the line Helsinki – Travemünde/Lübeck, initially with the passenger/car ferry Hansa Express and, since 1966, by making use of the car decks of the Finnhansa and Finnpartner. As in those days the passenger traffic was almost completely restricted to the summer seasons, the expensive ferries had to be effectively employed by cargo transports during off-season. But this required rapid loading and discharging, so Finnlines developed its own Finnflow cargo handling method for moving unitized cargoes on wheels. Such experience encouraged the expansion of this model and of a cargo ferry system. A new design of vessel was developed and its prototype, ms Finncarrier, which had 1,800 lane meters, was completed at Wärtsilä's Helsinki shipyard in 1969. The slightly more developed sister ship, the ms Hans Gutzeit, was delivered in September 1972 to match the Finncarrier on the Lübeck service.

The epoch of cargo ferries also prompted the opening of a service to Britain, and in 1972 Finnlines, FÅA, and UBC founded a joint venture, Finnanglia Line Ltd, for this purpose. Ms Finnfellow, a sister ship to ms Hans Gutzeit, was completed in May 1973 and immediately began traffic to Felixstowe. The following year the new cargo ferries of UBC and FÅA went into traffic, though the port of destination was meanwhile changed to the newly finished Purfleet terminal in the lower reaches of the Thames.

The launch of ms FINNCARRIER on March 26, 1969 in Helsinki
Photo by Matti Pietikäinen

ms FINNMERCHANT
Photo by Matti Pietikäinen

Early in 1975 Finnlines and FÅA began negotiations on developing freight and passenger services. Already on June 10, 1975 a framework agreement was published for the purpose of rationalizing sea transports of importance to the Finnish economy, and for improved service for customers. To these ends, a marketing company called Oy Finncarriers Ab, owned on a 50/50 basis by Finnlines and FÅA, was founded to run the Finnlines and FÅA contract and liner services in Europe. The objective of Finncarriers was, firstly, to concentrate on the most rational management of Finnish export and import transportation; secondly, to develop expedient and economical transport systems for the country in cooperation with shipping circles and industry; and thirdly, to strengthen the position of our merchant fleet and to improve customer service. The two biggest shipping lines had resolved to improve their marketing conditions by means of consolidated cooperation in times of recession. The operations of Finncarriers began early in 1976, and Finnlines and FÅA made their vessels in the European traffic available to Finncarriers. FÅA then abandoned its passenger service between Finland and Germany, and ms Finlandia was transferred to the Finnlines fleet while ms Finncarrier became FÅA's Polaris. Finncarriers' operations were geographically divided into four traffic areas: the Baltic Sea and the West German North Sea, the Continent, the U.K. and Ireland, and the Western Mediterranean.

Early in the 1980s the shareholders of Finncarriers planned a cargo ferry of a new generation for traffic to Britain. The jumbo roro vessel Arcturus of 2,170 lane meters, ordered by Effoa, (the change of name from FÅA to Effoa was made in 1976), was completed at Rauma in June 1982 and went on the Purfleet route. However, her capacity was so big that it was decided to combine the British and Continental lines into a triangular route, calling at Rotterdam on the return. Ms Finnmerchant, a sister ship delivered to Neste Oy, made up a pair on the same route in January 1983. Effoa had a third sister ship, ms Oihonna, built at Rauma, and she went on the Lübeck route in April 1984. Finnlines then started to plan a jumbo roro vessel of the same size specifically for the Baltic Sea traffic, and ms Finnsailor was completed at Gdansk in October 1987 for Neste Oy. Her sister ship ms Finnforest was delivered to Thomesto Oy in August 1988 but was soon sold to Finncarriers and renamed Antares.

New Solutions in the Baltic Passenger Traffic

The ms Finnpartner was sold by Amer-Tupakka by the end of 1968 but the Finnhansa got a new mate on the route between Helsinki and Lübeck in another ms Finnpartner of the same size purchased by Thomesto in 1973. But, concurrently, Enso-Gutzeit was getting the designs made for the future Finnjet. The fundamental idea was

*gts FINNJET on arrival at Travemünde
Photo from Matti Pietikäinen*

*ms FINNPARTNER in October 1968 in London
Photo from FG-Shipping Oy Ab*

for the ship to make the run between Helsinki and Travemünde in 22 hours at a speed of 30 knots, doing the whole voyage including loading and discharging within 24 hours. Along with the founding of Finncarriers, Effoa had meanwhile given up its passenger traffic with Germany and sold ms Finlandia to Enso-Gutzeit in summer 1975. When the 55,000 kW gas-turbine vessel Finnjet commenced traffic in spring 1977, the Finnhansa was sold, the Finnpartner had been chartered for traffic in the English Channel, and the Finlandia had been converted into a cruise liner, the Finnstar. The oil crisis had knocked the bottom out of the original cost calculations for the Finnjet, so supplementary diesel engines were installed in 1981, for economic voyaging during off-season.

By 1982 Enso-Gutzeit had already decided to wind up its fleet but the sale of ms Finnjet to Effoa did not come about until summer 1986. When Enso-Gutzeit sold off its last vessel, this, for the time being, meant an end to the Finnlines passenger service.

Redistribution of Shipping

During the business upswing, Enso-Gutzeit had in 1970 bought up the entire capital stock of Merivienti Oy and by the end of that year had merged the company. Early in the 1980s the situation was different, and Enso-Gutzeit wanted to concentrate on its own business, the forest industry, and let others take care of the transports. In summer 1982 an agreement was made on redistributing the shipping, through which Enso sold all its vessels that had operated within the sphere of Finncarriers to Effoa and Neste Oy. At the beginning of that October, six former Enso vessels were given new names by Effoa but the four vessels transferred to Neste and the jumbo roro vessel Finnmerchant under construction retained their names beginning "Finn". After this, Enso-Gutzeit also gave up its Finncarriers shares held through Finnlines. After the transaction Finncarriers became a subsidiary fully owned by Effoa. Enso moreover sold 75 per cent of the capital stock in Finnlines, Neste buying 25 per cent of this, Effoa 25 per cent, Thomesto 15 per cent, Rautaruukki Oy six per cent, and Oulu Oy four per cent.

ms FINNFELLOW and gts FINNJET meet in the Baltic Sea
Photo from FG-Shipping Oy Ab

Another re-shuffle among the shipowners was also conducted in the 1980s. Neste Oy decided to concentrate its shipping on oil transport, and began to sell off its dry-cargo carriers. In 1986 Oy Finnlines Ltd bought the cargo ferry Finnfellow as the first vessel of its own, while the cargo vessel Finnfighter was purchased by Palkkiyhtymä Oy in 1988. The Finnmerchant and Finnsailor, Neste's last dry-cargo carriers, were sold in 1988–1989 to part-owner companies established by Finnlines, Finncarriers, and Thomesto.

Contract Services to the U.S.E.C. and F-ships Pool

Although the Atlantic liner traffic was terminated, the vessels of Finnlines did not entirely vanish from the ports on the U.S. East Coast. At the turn of 1982–1983 the owners of the so-called "Juliana" vessels formed, on the initiative of Thomesto, the F-ships pool through which the resources were consolidated, in order to

ms LOTILA
Photo from FG-Shipping Oy Ab

*ms FINNFIGHTER in ice-dress
Photo from FG-Shipping Oy Ab*

provide a more comprehensive service for contract clients. The Juliana vessels were eight special vessels with super-ice class strengthening, of 14,900 dwt, built at the Juliana shipyard in Gijon, Spain, in 1977–1981 for the transportation of forest industry products. Neste Oy, Oulu Oy, and Thomesto Oy each placed two Juliana vessels at the disposal of the pool, and Effoa – Finland Steamship Co. Ltd. nominally one Juliana vessel which in fact became engaged in the system traffic between Hamina and Bremen. Thomesto's third Juliana vessel entered the F-ships pool in 1984, upon being redelivered from her time-charter. The vessels mainly carried Transfennica paper cargoes to Philadelphia and Rautaruukki and Outokumpu steel to the United States. The return cargoes were forest industry products from Canada to Britain and the European Continent or, more recently, clay from Savannah to Sweden and Finland. Although this traffic was quite regular, it was nevertheless pure contract trade in which nothing but large consignments by specific clients were carried. In 1997 three of the Juliana vessels are still in the Atlantic traffic with the F-ships pool, as are two chartered vessels, ms Nomadic Patria and ms Nomadic Pollux, of the so-called Haugesund class, originally built for Effoa.

Special Ships and the Pusher-Barge System

Finnlines has always tried to stay up with developments. The company's research and development have concentrated on finding solutions that with a view to transportation for Finnish foreign trade will provide the best possible support for the marketing efforts of

*The pusher-barge combination RAUTA-
RUUKKI and KALLA on sea trials
Photo from FG-Shipping Oy Ab*

its clients. Numerous examples have already been given of epoch-making types of vessel, but there are many more to come.

One vessel built for demanding transport assignments was the 952 dwt chemical tanker, Finnlark, completed in 1966 at Valmet's shipyard in Helsinki for Enso-Gutzeit, in which all the tanks, pipes, and pumps were made of acid-proof steel. A year later, a special vessel, ms Tyysterniemi, designed by Finnlines for the transportation of sulphuric acid, was completed in France for Rikkihappo Oy, which today is Kemira Oy.

The pusher-barge system, planned ever since the 1970s, materialized in 1986 when the 7,780 kW pusher Rautaruukki and two barges of 14,000 dwt, ordered by Rautaruukki, were completed at the Hollming shipyard in Rauma. As a ship is productive only while at sea, it is necessary to minimise the time in port. The pusher-barge system involves two or three barges of which one is always under way with the pusher and the others are being loaded or unloaded. The most expensive unit, which also causes the highest costs, the pusher, is always busy. Furthermore, for a pusher of the Rautaruukki type, a nine-man crew will suffice, while a same-size freighter of 14,000 dwt would require twice the manning. Savings can thus be made in two ways. The very next year a similar combination was completed, the pusher Finn and the three barges Baltic, Board, and Bulk from Hollming for part owners managed by Finnlines; but these were soon sold to Rautaruukki Oy. Both combinations have now carried bulk cargoes, ore, coal, limestone, etc. for their owner in Baltic waters for a period of more than 10 years.

Voyages to Polar Waters

In their cold homeland, the Finns have grown accustomed to struggling against ice and snow. Is not Finland the only country in the world where all the harbours freeze up in a normal winter? More than 100 years have passed since Finland got its first icebreaker and winter navigation with merchant ships strengthened for navigation in ice began. Over 100 merchant vessels built to the highest I A Super or I A ice classes sail under the Finnish flag, being largely able to move without icebreaker assistance. So it is no wonder that this know-how and equipment should open up markets in waters covered by Polar ice.

The first vessel managed by Finnlines in Polar waters was the Thomesto bulk carrier Finntimber which in November 1976 called at Marmorilik, one of the northernmost ports in Greenland, to load zinc ore and lead ore. Though it is no more than 71 degrees north, which is the latitude of the North Cape, the conditions on the other side of Greenland are quite different. Icebergs are so plentiful in the Davis Straits that on a single occasion up to about 300 bigger or smaller tips of icebergs were visible from the vessel. The voyage was a success, and in December the Finntimber brought part of its cargo to Antwerp and the rest to Ykspihlaja, Finland.

Besides Greenland, the northern hemisphere has another vast and almost unsettled and unknown area, the Arctic islands of Canada. The climate of the shores of the Northwest Passage is arctically severe. The ice never leaves the Northwest Passage but in normal summers it does break up, and for a couple of months in August–September it is possible to move in the channel with the help of helicopter surveillance and ice reports. Lots of natural resources have been found in the region and, despite the difficult conditions, these attract prospecting and exploitation. In other words ice-strengthened ships are needed for these waters.

In summer 1974 Finnlines succeeded in chartering the Finnmaster, a 5,900 dwt dry-cargo carrier of Oy Enso Chartering Ab, to carry 4,500 tons of materials needed for oil drilling, such as piping and cement, to Resolute Bay in Arctic Canada north of the Northwest Passage. This strange Resolute Bay is located "on top of the world", as the Canadians use to say. The cargo was picked up late in July in New Orleans for the northbound destination. During the trip, the message came that the ice had torn away the quay at Resolute Bay, so three small barges were taken on deck from

ms FINNMASTER was the first Finnlines vessel in the Northwest Passage in 1974
Photo from FG-Shipping Oy Ab

ms FINNTIMBER berthed at Little Cornwallis Island in Arctic Canada on August 31, 1983
Photo by Jan Lindroos

Holsteinsborg in Greenland to be used as landing stages at the destination. On September 1 the Finnmaster arrived at Resolute Bay, location 74.41 N and 94.52 W. The ship's own crew carried out the discharging in three days, the return cargo being 1,680 tons of oil rig parts, pipes, and housing units destined for Houston. Two years previously those things had been taken to Resolute Bay by 94 flights of Hercules transport aircraft.

It was not until August 1983 that the Finnish colours were again to fly in the Northwest Passage. As first to arrive in Greenland, the Scanscot Freighters had chartered the ms Finntimber of Thomesto to fetch a 20,000-ton cargo of zinc concentrate from Little Cornwallis Island. The coordinates of this remote island are 75.23 N and 96.56 W, and it is only 90 kilometers south of the magnetic North Pole. The sailing season at Little Cornwallis Island is brief indeed, as it does not begin until the end of August and lasts a little over one month. That is the time for shipping out the zinc ore that has been mined and dressed during the year. The Finntimber left New York on August 19, 1983 and reached Little Cornwallis Island on August 30 but at arrival could not be moored to the quay immediately. A Canadian tanker bringing an oil cargo for the mine had damaged its bow when berthing and was now being patched up at the quay with cement for the return voyage. On September 1 the cargo was on board and the island of permafrost lay behind as the Finntimber dodged the icebergs and once again made a return trip along the Northwest Passage to Finland and Ykspihlaja.

While the Finntimber had been in the Northwest Passage on the way to Little Cornwallis Island, an unprecedented four-month time-charter party was signed between the Government of India and Finnlines. Under it, another Thomesto vessel, ms Finnpolaris, the newest of the 14,900 dwt Juliana ships, was to proceed for the next Antarctic summer to serve as transport vessel and mother ship of an Indian expedition to Dronning Maud Land, at the edge of the Antarctic ice-cap.

The preparations for an expedition as special as this one were considerable. Accommodations for 81 Indian scientists had to be built on board the vessel. The expedition came aboard at Goa, from where the voyage proceeded south on November 3. There was another call, at Port Louis in Mauritius, for final bunkering and provisioning, but on December 14 the stem was turned towards the great unknown. The historic mooring at the edge of the Antarctic ice took place on December 27, 1983 with curious Adelien penguins watching the event. Because of the frequently recurring bad weather, it was always necessary to be able to take off quickly.

ms FINNPOLARIS and Adelien penguins in Dronning Maud Land, Antarctica
Photo by Kalevi Sundqvist

It was in cruising conditions of this kind that the Finnpolaris reached its southernmost point of the trip, 70.03 S and 12.44 E.

The next winter the Finnpolaris, chartered by India, again made a similar voyage to Dronning Maud Land.

In summer 1986, Finnlines signed a charter-party with Italy on a new voyage to the Antarctic. The departure from Genoa for New Zealand took place on October 22. The Finnpolaris embarked the scientists and last provisions at Lyttelton from where the vessel continued on December 5 in the direction of the Ross Sea on the side of Antarctica opposite to Dronning Maud Land. On December 17 the vessel tied up on the edge of the one-year-old one-meter-thick ice at Terra Nova Bay. Here, the scenery is different; a barren stony strip of shore lies uncovered, and the ice-cap does not start until a few hundred meters further in. Still, the familiar Adelien penguins welcomed the visitors here too. The position was southerly indeed, for the coordinates were 74.43 S and 164.10 E.

Once again, for a fourth time, the Finnpolaris proceeded to the Antarctic in the fall of 1987, as a new charter had been made with the Italians for a voyage to the Ross Sea.

Flagging out

The Finnish seafarers' organisations have greatly improved the level of earnings and working conditions of their members. The latest great clash with the shipowners occurred in spring 1980 when, as the result of a long strike involving the entire Finnish merchant fleet world-wide, the wages of the seafarers were raised by 20 per cent. Finland was becoming a hyper-expensive country. In 1984 the Finnish Shipowners Association made a study which showed that Finland had the highest manning costs of vessels in Western Europe, up to seven per cent higher than those in Sweden.

ms CAPELLA was flagged out to Sweden in December 1985
Photo by Matti Pietikäinen

ms FINNOCEANIS under the Cayman flag in 1986
Photo by Matti Pietikäinen

In addition to a high level of wages and generous social benefits, Finland's merchant fleet was encumbered by over-manning relative to similar vessels of competing countries such as Sweden. While foreign ships had a crew of 15–16 persons, corresponding Finnish ships had a crew of 23–24. Moreover, due to the 1/1 at work/free rotation system, there were two persons for each post on board. Thus the Finnish shipowner had to pay the wages and social benefits of an extra 16 expensive personnel.

The Bank of Finland was able to prevent flagging out while it was in control of the entitlement of companies to establish foreign subsidiaries and make investments abroad. It was only in 1984 that the Bank of Finland allowed the first outflagging, giving its consent to the transfer of four small reefer ships to Cyprus. In 1985 as many as 16 Finnish vessels were flagged out to more affordable registers. The cross-traders Finnbeaver, Finnfalcon, Finnfury, Finntimber, Finnwhale, and Puhos, under Finnlines management, got George Town in the Cayman Islands as their home port. A Finnish master and chief engineer were generally left on these vessels but the rest of the crew were mainly Filipinos. Furthermore, Thomesto sold the cargo ferry Capella, which was under Finnlines management, to its Swedish subsidiary, replacing the 40-member Finnish crew with 30 Swedes including the rotation crew.

There was a slight improvement with the Unions when Finnlines reached a settlement in spring 1986 on the outflagging of vessels in regular Finnish traffic and their manning with Finnish crews on the basis of an internationalisation agreement. This meant in practice that the crew would be hired for at least six months and that their earnings would be tax-free in Finland. The arrangement did not, however, allow the outflagging of vessels in Baltic Sea or North Sea traffic. Under the internationalisation agreement, Finnlines in 1986 transferred the Finnarctis, Finnoceanis, Finnpolaris, and Finntrader of Thomesto, the Lapponia of Effoa, the Lotila of the United Paper Mills, and the Pokkinen and Varjakka of Veitsiluoto to the Cayman register. The next year Finnlines was assigned to flag out the rest of the Effoa cargo vessels under the internationalisation agreement. So the Bahamas flag was hoisted on the Ariel, Fennia, Pallas, Patria, Pollux, Taurus, and Tellus; and Finnlines also outflagged the Clio, Finneagle, Finnrover, Koiteli, and Tuira to the Bahamas.

The Finnish merchant fleet had collapsed from its 1981 record of 2.5 million GRT to a mere 0.8 million GRT by 1987. From the beginning of 1992, a Register of Merchant Vessels in International Trade resembling a parallel register was set up in Finland. Cargo vessels up to 25 years old, operated in international trade and entered in the Finnish Register of Ships could be entered in this register, except for vessels involved in the interest subsidy arrangements for small tonnage. A stipulation was that the costs of manning these vessels were to be brought to an international level, i.e. they were to be reduced by 10 per cent by lowering pay, altering the terms of work, or reducing the size of crew. The government promised it would pay back annually to the owner of the vessel an amount equal to the advance tax withheld from seamen's income from work at sea and employer's payroll duties. One effect of the law was that the manning costs of cargo vessels in European traffic could be brought to a reasonable level, i.e. to fall up to 30 per cent from what they had been.

Formation of the New Finnlines Ltd

Formation of the Finnlines Group started at the beginning of 1989, when Effoa – Finland Steamship Co. Ltd. decided to separate off its cargo services and the relevant company holdings. At its Annual General Meeting in April 1989, Effoa resolved to offer shareholders shares in Finncarriers Oy Ab, which was then a fully-owned subsidiary of Effoa, as an alternative to the customary dividend. The Group relationship between Finncarriers and Effoa was thereby severed.

In spring 1989 the name of Finncarriers Oy Ab was changed to Finnlines Group Oy Ab, which at the same time became the transportation group's new parent company. The shares in Finncarriers accepted in lieu of the Effoa 1988 dividend thus became shares in the Finnlines Group Oy Ab. At the same time it was decided to merge Oy Finnlines Ltd with Finnlines Group Oy Ab. In compensation for the merger, shareholders in the company being absorbed would receive shares in the recipient company.

On April 30, 1989, in accordance with the demerger principle, Finnlines Group Oy Ab established a subsidiary, Finncarriers Oy Ab, which took over the operations of the old Finncarriers from the parent company.

At the beginning of June, the old Finnlines established the subsidiary FG-Shipping Oy Ab, following the same demerger principles as with Finncarriers Oy Ab. FG-Shipping Oy Ab, which embarked on operations on July 1, 1989, took over the old Finnlines' business.

At the end of the financial year, when the old Finnlines was merged with Finnlines Group Oy Ab, FG-Shipping Oy Ab became a subsidiary of Finnlines Group Oy Ab.

The board of directors of the Helsinki Stock Exchange approved the application of Finnlines Group Oy Ab for listing, and the shares of the company were first quoted on the stock exchange on July 2, 1990.

The meeting of shareholders of the Finnlines Group decided in April 1991 to shorten the Finnish name of the company to Finnlines Oy and its name in English to Finnlines Ltd, (Finnlines Ab in Swedish, and Finnlines AG in German).

Roro and Railway Ferry Traffic to Sweden

In autumn 1988 some of the shipowners of Finnlines decided to start a lorry and train ferry service between Finland and Sweden the following year. For this purpose an operating company called Oy Finnlink Ab was set up; and, for the future traffic, Finnlines sold its Finnfellow, and Thomesto's subsidiary And. Smith Rederi its Finnmaid, to the part-owner companies formed by the parties involved in Finnlink. Right at the beginning of January 1989, the Finnmaid went into lorry traffic from Uusikaupunki to Hargshamn on the Swedish side. The Finnfellow was converted into a rail ferry and entered operations in September 1989. When SeaWind Line, of the Effoa Group, at the same time started a railway ferry service between Turku and Stockholm and the approaching depression reduced the cargo volume, Finnlink had started operations under less favourable circumstances.

But the situation gradually improved and in 1996 it was decided to charter ms Finnsailor for the Finnlink traffic between Helsinki

ms FINNFELLOW at Hargshamn
Photo by Matti Pietikäinen

ms FINNSAILOR in Helsinki
Photo by Matti Pietikäinen

and Norrköping. Before that, she was converted to a combi-roro vessel with accommodations for over 100 passengers. However, it was decided at the beginning of the following year to concentrate all three vessels on the route between Naantali and Kapellskär, whereupon the Finnfellow was reconverted into an ordinary roro ferry. Meanwhile, Finnlines had become the sole owner of Finnlink.

Concentration on the Baltic, U.K. and Continent Roro Services

Early in 1989 Oy Lars Krogius Ab of the Speditor group which had quickly emerged in the transport business commenced a cargo ferry service in competition with Finncarriers with two chartered roro vessels running between Southern Finland and Kiel. At the same time Oy Bore Line Ab decided to revert to Baltic traffic and opened a roro line of its own on the same route as Krogius. Excess capacity occurred in the traffic on Germany, depressing the freight rates. Eventually in February 1990, Finncarriers signed a long-term transport agreement with Speditor Oy under which the trailer transports of the Speditor group were transferred to Finncarriers as from April.

After the severe competition for Baltic cargoes, Finnlines made an agreement on November 14, 1991 with Oy Rettig Ab about the purchase of Oy Bore Line Ab. When the ownership arrangements went into effect on January 1, 1992, Rettig became a shareholder in Finnlines with a 10 per cent holding. From the beginning of 1992 the business operations of Bore Line were mainly combined with Finncarriers, while Finnlines time-chartered six vessels that had been operated by Bore Line. Bore's Scandinavian business became a new business sector for Finncarriers.

ms BORE SEA with Finnlines funnel mark in April 1994
Photo by Matti Pietikäinen

ms FINNPARTNER
Photo by Kaius Hedenström

The New Finnlines Makes a Big Investment in the Baltic Trade

In June 1990, at the very start of the depression, Finnlines Ltd invested boldly by ordering three new "super-jumbo" roro vessels of 3,200 lane meters each from Poland. In October, an option for a fourth vessel was exercised, while one of the vessels ordered earlier was turned over to Poseidon, a joint sailing partner. The order was soon amended, however, because it seemed reasonable to increase the passenger capacity of the vessels to above 100, making them combi-roros. By the time the vessels Finnhansa, Finnpartner, Transeuropa, and Finntrader were eventually completed in 1994–1995, the depression in the forest industry was over and the increase in carrying capacity occurred at just the right time. As the vessels were to be loaded and discharged as quickly as the old, smaller vessels, changes were made to the construction of the vessels and the ramp arrangements in the ports. The traffic between Helsinki and Lübeck is now maintained with these four ships with daily departures in both directions.

Finncarriers' Traffic in 1997

Finncarriers Oy Ab, a subsidiary fully owned by Finnlines, operates liner services in four traffic areas. In the Baltic Sea service, between Helsinki and Lübeck, Finncarriers has the three combi-roro vessels, the Finnhansa, Finnpartner, and Finntrader owned by Finnlines as well as the Transeuropa of the German joint sailing partner Poseidon. The Antares, Finnmerchant, Oihonna, and Railship I are also sailing in the service between Finland and Germany as well as Poseidon vessels and chartered ships. Railship moreover runs two railway ferries between Hanko and

Travemünde. Furthermore, the Polfin Line runs chartered roro tonnage to Gdynia and Stettin. The Scandinavian traffic is likewise run with chartered roro tonnage from Helsinki and Kotka to Copenhagen, Aarhus, Helsingborg, and Gothenburg. In the North Sea services, the cargo ferry Finnmaster alone sails in the company of vessels owned by the United Baltic Corporation and Poseidon, and of chartered vessels. On the Biscay line there are the Astrea and Finnpine as well as the chartered ms Polaris. Traffic is also maintained with chartered small tonnage from Lake Saimaa and the Gulf of Bothnia to the Continent of Europe and to Britain.

Finncarriers roro vessels discharging and loading in Helsinki
Photo by Kaius Hedenström

The Fleet Will Grow

In November 1997 Finnlines entered into an agreement with Stinnes AG stipulating, among other things, that Finnlines will acquire the total stock of shares of Poseidon Schiffahrt AG. Due to that agreement, the Finnlines fleet will in the beginning of 1998 grow by the vessels Transeuropa, Translubeca, Transfinlandia, Transbaltica, Transrussia, Railship I, Railship II, and Railship III.

Ships Managed by Baltic Chartering /Finnlines /FG-Shipping

No.	Name of vessel	Years managed
1	WILLE	1947–1960
2	KALLE	1947–1957
3	EERO	1947–1953
4	TORNATOR	1947–1954
5	PANKAKOSKI	1947–1953
6	HAMINA	1947–1954
7	ENSO	1950–1959
8	NESTE	1951–1953
9	FINNTRADER (I)	1951–1970
10	FINNSAILOR (I)	1953–1968
11	FINNPULP	1953–1968
12	FINNMERCHANT (I)	1953–1969
13	TUPAVUORI	1954–1958
14	PAMILO /FINNMASTER (I)	1954–1964
15	FINNMAID (I)	1954–1964
16	FINNKRAFT (I)	1956–1973
17	NUNNALAHTI	1957–1964
18	FINNBOARD	1958–1969
19	OUTOKUMPU	1958–1985
20	AIRISMAA	1958–1964
21	FINNWOOD (I)	1959–1969
22	FINNSTAR (I)	1959–1973
23	FINNBIRCH	1959–1973
24	FINNPINE (I)	1959–1967
25	SIMPELE	1960–1973
26	JURMO	1960–1964
27	KAIPOLA (I) /VARJAKKA (I)	1961–1974
28	FINNALPINO (I)	1961–1971
29	FINNEAGLE (I) /TROLLEHOLM /FINNEAGLE	1962–1978
30	FINNCLIPPER (I)	1962–1978
31	HANSA EXPRESS /FINNDANA	1962–1967
32	VAASA	1962–1963
33	TERVI	1963–1964
34	FINNFOREST (I)	1963–1978
35	FINNSEAL	1964–1975
36	LOTILA (I) /FINNTUBE	1964–1975
37	REKOLA /FINNSTRIP	1964–1975
38	FINNENSO /FINNBOSTON	1964–1973
39	FINNBROD /FINNMILL /CONCORDIA MILL	1965–1971
40	FINNFIGHTER (I)	1965–1975
41	FINNHAWK (I) /MALTESHOLM /FINNHAWK	1965–1979
42	FINNARROW (I) /VASAHOLM /FINNARROW	1965–1979
43	FINNMAID (II)	1965–1979
44	FINN-ENSO	1965–1979
45	FINNLARK	1966–1977
46	FINNHANSA (I)	1966–1978
47	FINNPARTNER (I)	1966–1968
48	TYYSTERNIEMI	1967–1983
49	KOTKANIEMI	1968–1986
50	FINNMINI	1969–1971
51	FINNCARRIER	1969–1975
52	MÄLKIÄ	1970–1973
53	SOSKUA	1970–1974
54	PÄLLI	1970–1974
55	ISLA FINLANDIA	1970–1972
56	ANNIKA /FINNREEL	1971–1977
57	LAURI-RAGNAR /FINNRUNNER	1971–1972
58	LOVISA /FINNROSE (I)	1971–1974
59	NINA /FINNROVER (I)	1971–1973
60	TAINA /FINNRIVER	1971–1973
61	VELI	1971–1971
62	FINN-AMER /CONCORDIA AMER /FINN-AMER	1971–1981
63	KAIPOLA (II) /FINNOAK (I)	1971–1987
64	FINNBUILDER /CONCORDIA BUILDER /FINNBUILDER	1971–1981
65	FINNSAILOR (II) /CONCORDIA SAILOR /FINNSAILOR	1972–1981
66	FINNPINE (II)	1972–1986
67	VALKEAKOSKI /FINNKRAFT (II) /CLIO	1972–1989
68	FINNMASTER (II) /CORONA	1972–1986
69	HANS GUTZEIT /CAPELLA /FINNMAID (III)	1972–
70	FINNWOOD (II) /CARELIA	1972–1983
71	TUIRA /FINNOAK (II)	1972–1993
72	FINNTRADER (II) /CASTOR	1972–1985
73	KOITELI /FINNELM	1972–1990
74	FINNPARTNER (II) /OLAU FINN	1973–1982
75	FINNALPINO (II)	1973–1983
76	FINNFELLOW	1973–
77	FINNTIMBER	1975–1987
78	FINLANDIA /FINNSTAR (II)	1975–1981
79	RAUTARUUKKI (I)	1976–1985
80	KUURTANES	1976–1981
81	FINNJET	1977–1989
82	LOTILA (II)	1977–1995
83	WALKI /FINNOCEANIS	1978–1988
84	FINNBEAVER	1978–1988
85	FINNFURY	1978–1988
86	KAIPOLA (III) /FINNFIGHTER (II)	1978–
87	WALKI PAPER	1979–1979
88	FINNFOREST (II) /CANOPUS	1979–1992
89	VARJAKKA (II)	1979–1996
90	PUHOS	1980–1993
91	POKKINEN	1980–1996
92	FINNARCTIS	1980–1991
93	KEMIRA	1981–
94	FINNPOLARIS	1981–1991
95	FINNHAWK (II)	1981–1989
96	FINNROSÉ (II)	1981–1989
97	FINNMERCHANT (II)	1982–
98	FOSSEAGLE /FINNEAGLE (II)	1983–1987
99	FINNFALCON	1984–1988
100	FINNWHALE	1985–1988
101	PARA-CHARLIE	1985–1993
102	PARA-ALFA	1985–1992
103	PARA-BRAVO /PARA-DUO	1985–1995
104	PARA-DELTA	1985–1993
105	JALINA /FINNROVER (II)	1985–1988

106	FINNTRADER (III)	1986–1990
107	RAUTARUUKKI (II)	1986–
108	KALLA	1986–
109	TASKU	1986–
110	LAPPONIA	1986–1990
111	TELLUS	1987–1988
112	FENNIA /FINNMASTER (III)	1987–
113	FINN /STEEL	1987–
114	BALTIC /BOTNIA	1987–
115	BOARD	1987–
116	BULK	1987–
117	TAURUS	1987–1988
118	POLLUX	1987–1988
119	PALLAS	1987–1988
120	PATRIA	1987–1988
121	ARIEL	1987–1988
122	FINNSAILOR (III)	1987–
123	FINNFOREST (III) /ANTARES	1988–
124	FINNWOOD (III) /LANKA ABHAYA /FINNWOOD	1989–
125	TALLINK	1989–1992
126	ARCTURUS	1990–1991
127	OIHONNA	1990–
128	ENVIK	1990–1993
129	FARONA /TRANSESTONIA	1990–1992
130	ASTREA	1991–
131	PARA-UNO	1992–1995
132	MEGA	1993–
133	MOTTI	1993–
134	RAILSHIP I	1994–
135	FINNPINE (III)	1994–
136	FINNHANSA (II)	1994–
137	FINNPARTNER (III)	1995–
138	FINNTRADER (IV)	1995–
139	FINNARROW (II)	1997–
140	NB AESA 78	1998–
141	NB AESA 79	1998–

Owners of the Ships Managed by Baltic Chartering /Finnlines /FG-Shipping

Merivienti Oy 1947–1970

WILLE	1947–1960
KALLE	1947–1957
EERO	1947–1953
TORNATOR	1947–1954
PANKAKOSKI	1947–1953
HAMINA	1947–1954
FINNTRADER (I)	1951–1966
FINNPULP	1953–1968
FINNMAID (I)	1956–1964
FINNKRAFT (I)	1956–1970
FINNSTAR (I)	1959–1970
FINNALPINO (I)	1961–1970
HANSA EXPRESS /FINNDANA	1962–1967
FINNMAID (II)	1965–1970
FINNHANSA (I)	1966–1970
FINNCARRIER	1969–1970

Enso-Gutzeit Oy 1950–1986

ENSO	1950–1959
FINNSAILOR (I)	1953–1968
FINNMERCHANT (I)	1953–1969
PAMILO /FINNMASTER (I)	1954–1964
FINNBOARD	1958–1969
FINNWOOD (I)	1959–1969
FINNBIRCH	1959–1973
FINNPINE (I)	1959–1967
FINNEAGLE (I) /TROLLEHOLM	1962–1978
FINNCLIPPER	1962–1978
FINNFOREST (I)	1963–1978
FINNSEAL	1964–1975
FINNENSO	1964–1964
FINNFIGHTER (I)	1965–1975
FINNHAWK (I) /MALTESHOLM	1965–1979
FINNARROW (I) /VASAHOLM	1965–1979
FINN-ENSO	1965–1979
FINNLARK	1966–1977
FINNMAID (II)	1971–1971
FINNHANSA (I)	1971–1978
FINNCARRIER	1971–1975
FINNKRAFT (I)	1971–1973
FINNSTAR (I)	1971–1973
FINNALPINO (I)	1971–1971
FINNPINE (II)	1971–1972
FINNSAILOR (II)	1972–1972
FINNMASTER (II)	1975–1979
FINLANDIA /FINNSTAR (II)	1975–1981
FINNREEL	1975–1977
FINNJET	1977–1986
FINNHAWK (II)	1982–1985
FINNROSE (II)	1982–1985

Neste Oy 1951–1989

NESTE	1951–1953
TUPAVUORI	1954–1958
NUNNALAHTI	1957–1964
AIRISMAA	1958–1964
JURMO	1960–1964
TERVI	1963–1964
FINNPINE (II)	1982–1986
FINNALPINO (II)	1982–1983
FINNFELLOW	1982–1986
FINNFIGHTER (II)	1982–1988
FINNMERCHANT (II)	1982–1988
FINNSAILOR (III)	1987–1989

Outokumpu Oy 1958–1985

OUTOKUMPU	1958–1985

Yhtyneet Paperitehtaat Oy (United Paper Mills Ltd), Lotila Shipping Ltd 1960–1989

SIMPELE	1960–1973
KAIPOLA (I)	1961–1969
LOTILA (I)	1964–1974
REKOLA	1964–1974
KAIPOLA (II)	1971–1975
VALKEAKOSKI	1972–1977
LOTILA (II)	1977–1989
WALKI	1978–1980
KAIPOLA (III)	1978–1979
WALKI PAPER	1979–1979

Rederi Ab Vasa-Umeå 1962–1963

VAASA	1962–1963

Amer-Tupakka Oy –> Amer-Yhtymä Oy, Amer-Sea Oy 1964–1995

FINNBOSTON	1964–1973
FINNPARTNER (I)	1966–1968
FINN-AMER /CONCORDIA AMER	1971–1981
LOTILA (II)	1993–1995

Vaasan Höyrymylly Oy – Vasa Ångkvarns Ab 1965–1971

FINNBROD /FINNMILL /CONCORDIA FINN	1965–1971

Rakennustoimisto Jussi Ketola, Ky Jussi Ketola & Co., Beaver Shipping Ltd, Fury Shipping Ltd, Falcon Shipping Ltd, Whale Shipping Ltd 1966–1988

FINNTRADER (I)	1966–1970
FINNBUILDER /CONCORDIA BUILDER	1971–1981
FINNBEAVER	1978–1988
FINNFURY	1978–1988
FINNFALCON	1984–1988
FINNWHALE	1985–1988

Rikkihappo Oy –> Kemira Oy, Kemira Chemicals Oy 1967–

TYYSTERNIEMI	1967–1983
KOTKANIEMI	1968–1986
KEMIRA	1981–

Thomesto Oy, And. Smith Rederi AB, Timber Shipping Ltd, Eagle Shipping Ltd, Rover Shipping Ltd 1969–1990

FINNMINI	1969–1971
FINNPARTNER (II) /OLAU FINN	1973–1982
FINNTIMBER	1975–1987
FINNOCEANIS	1980–1988
FINNARCTIS	1980–1989
FINNPOLARIS	1981–1989
CAPELLA /CAPELLA AV STOCKHOLM	1982–1988
FINNTRADER (III)	1986–1990
FINNEAGLE (II)	1987–1987
FINNROVER (II)	1987–1988
FINNFOREST (II)	1988–1988

Oulu Oy –> Veitsiluoto Oy, Oulu Shipping Ltd, Lumi Shipping Oy 1969–

VARJAKKA (I)	1969–1974
FINNMAID (II)	1971–1979
TUIRA	1972–1989
KOITELI	1972–1989
VARJAKKA (II)	1979–1996
POKKINEN	1980–1996
MEGA	1993–
MOTTI	1993–

Saimaan Kanavalaivat Oy 1970–1974

MÄLKIÄ	1970–1973
PÄLLI	1970–1974
SOSKUA	1970–1974

Jouko Korpivaara 1970–1972

ISLA FINLANDIA	1970–1972

Oy Enso-Chartering Ab 1971–1975

ANNIKA /FINNREEL	1971–1975
LAURI-RAGNAR /FINNRUNNER	1971–1972
LOVISA /FINNROSE (I)	1971–1974
NINA /FINNROVER (I)	1971–1973
TAINA /FINNRIVER	1971–1973
VELI	1971–1971
FINNMASTER (II)	1972–1975

Merivienti Oy (new) 1972–1982

FINNSAILOR (II)	1972–1981
FINNPINE (II)	1972–1982
FINNKRAFT (II)	1977–1982
HANS GUTZEIT	1972–1982
FINNWOOD (II)	1972–1982
FINNTRADER (II)	1972–1982
FINNALPINO (II)	1973–1982
FINNFELLOW	1973–1982
FINNHAWK (I)	1979–1979
FINNARROW	1979–1979
FINN-ENSO	1979–1979
FINNFIGHTER (II)	1979–1982
FINNFOREST (II)	1979–1982
FINNMASTER (II)	1979–1982
FINNHAWK (II)	1981–1982
FINNROSE (II)	1981–1982
FINNMERCHANT (II)	1982–1982

Oy Etnarör Ab 1974–1975

FINNTUBE	1974–1975
FINNSTRIP	1974–1975

Oy Torlines Ab, Oak Shipping Ltd 1975–1993

FINNTUBE	1975–1975
FINNSTRIP	1975–1975
FINNOAK (I)	1975–1987
CLIO	1983–1989
FINNOAK (II)	1989–1993
FINNELM	1989–1990

Rautaruukki Oy, Oy JIT-Trans Ltd 1976–

RAUTARUUKKI (I)	1976–1985
RAUTARUUKKI (II)	1986–
KALLA	1986–
TASKU	1986–
FINN /STEEL	1988–
BALTIC /BOTNIA	1988–
BOARD	1988–
BULK	1988–

Alavuden Puunjalostustehdas Oy 1976–1981

KUURTANES	1976–1981

Oy Navire Ab 1979–1979

FINNFOREST (II)	1979–1979

Palkkiyhtymä Oy, Puhos Shipping Ltd 1980–

PUHOS	1980–1993
FINNFIGHTER (II)	1988–
FINNWOOD (III) /LANKA ABHAYA	1989–1997
TALLINK	1989–1992
FARONA	1990–1990

Effoa – Finland Steamship Co. Ltd, Oy Suomi Line /Finland Line Ab, EFF-Shipping Ltd 1982–1990

CLIO	1982–1983
CORONA	1982–1986
CAPELLA	1982–1984
CARELIA	1982–1983
CASTOR	1982–1985
CANOPUS	1982–1986
LAPPONIA	1986–1990
TELLUS	1987–1988
FENNIA	1987–1989
TAURUS	1987–1988
POLLUX	1987–1988
PALLAS	1987–1988
PATRIA	1987–1988
ARIEL	1987–1988

Kansallis-Osake-Pankki, Kansallisrahoitus Oy 1983–1987

FOSSEAGLE /FINNEAGLE (II)	1983–1987
JALINA /FINNROVER (II)	1985–1987

Paratug Companies 1985–1995

PARA-CHARLIE	1985–1993
PARA-ALFA	1985–1992
PARA-BRAVO /PARA-DUO	1985–1995
PARA-DELTA	1985–1993
PARA-UNO	1992–1995

Oy Finnlines Ltd –> Finnlines Ltd 1986–

FINNFELLOW	1986–1988
	1997–
FINNMASTER (III)	1992–
FINNMERCHANT (II)	1994–
FINNSAILOR (III)	1994–
FINNPINE (III)	1994–
FINNHANSA (II)	1994–
FINNPARTNER (III)	1995–
FINNTRADER (IV)	1995–
FINNMAID (III)	1997–
FINNARROW (II)	1997–

Finncarriers Oy Ab, FCRS-Shipping Ltd, Fennia-Shipping Ltd 1986–

CANOPUS	1986–1992
FINNARCTIS	1989–1991
FINNPOLARIS	1989–1991
LOTILA (II)	1989–1993
ANTARES	1988–
FENNIA	1989–1992
ARCTURUS	1990–1991
OIHONNA	1990–
ASTREA	1991–

Finnpusku Partners 1987–1988

FINN	1987–1988
BALTIC	1987–1988
BOARD	1987–1988
BULK	1987–1988

Finnlink Partners 1988–1997

FINNMAID (III)	1988–1997
FINNFELLOW	1988–1997

Finnmerchant-Finnsailor Partners 1988–1994

FINNMERCHANT (II)	1988–1994
FINNSAILOR (III)	1989–1994

Oy Partek Ab –> Partek Sementti Oy –> Finnsementti Oy 1990–1993

ENVIK	1990–1993

Shipping Joint Venture "Tallink" 1990–1992

TRANSESTONIA	1990–1992

Railship Oy Ab 1994–

RAILSHIP I	1994–

Sponsors of the Vessels

Mrs. Sylvi Kekkonen, President Urho Kekkonen's wife, was sponsor of ms Finnhansa (I) on December 1, 1964.

Mrs. Marjatta Jouhki, the wife of Finnlines Ltd's Chairman, Mr. L. J. Jouhki, was sponsor of ms Finnhansa (II), here with Mr. Antti Lagerroos, President and CEO of Finnlines Ltd, and Captain Sune Jakobsson at the naming ceremonies on September 19, 1994.

Name of sponsor	1st F-name of vessel and name when christened	Naming date
– Abildgaard	Veli ex Silja Dan	15.11.1950
Lisa Ahlbäck	Vaasa	29.9.1962
Lene Ahlström	Finnbeaver ex Matai	19.10.1974
Kirsti Airikkala	Finntrader (III)	26.4.1985
Aune Alakari	Finnmaid (I)	17.3.1956
Hellä Alanko	Finnhawk (I)	2.10.1964
Marianne Andresen	Finnmaster (II)	28.7.1972
Kielo Aura	Finnfighter (I)	27.10.1964

P. Blankholm	Taina ex Manja Dan	21.5.1959	Eleanor Lindholm	Farona ex Arona	23.2.1972
Greta-Stina Brandt	Lotila (I)	25.5.1964	Lola Luostarinen	Finnforest (I)	26.3.1963
Harriet Bruun	Finnbrod	3.7.1964	Annikki Mattila	Finnjet	28.4.1977
Liisa Bryk	Outokumpu	24.1.1958	Aune Mauranen	Puhos	26.2.1977
Anne-Marie Christenson	Pälli ex Royal Paper	19.8.1957	Eila Merikanto	Varjakka (II)	10.3.1978
Princess Christina	Finnpartner (II) ex Saga	18.10.1965	Ira Munch Jensen	Isla Finlandia ex Esso	
Camilla Dettman	Fennia ex Sirius	5.4.1973		Finlandia	15.10.1949
Marie Ebbesen	Finnwood (I) ex Ebbella	2.7.1956	E. van der Murk-Duimel	Lauri-Ragnar ex	
Anna Ehrnrooth	Pollux	10.12.1977		Vaasa Provider	16.11.1963
ditto	Arcturus	11.6.1982	Annikki Mäkinen	Walki	22.11.1976
Louise Ehrnrooth	Finlandia	25.8.1966	Iris Nielsen	Finnpine (III) ex Solano	29.3.1984
Elvi Erho	Airismaa	29.3.1958	Mary Nielsen	Finnmini ex Pinocchio	28.4.1965
Jane Erkko	Taurus	1.7.1983	Marianne Nilsson	Finnarrow (II) ex Gotland	19.4.1996
Helena Forsblom	Para-Uno	25.5.1992	Aira Nordström	Annika	25.2.1965
Mariuccia Gilberti	Finnalpino (II)	12.12.1972	Nina Nordström	Finnbirch ex Martti-Ragnar	9.4.1953
Margareta Grönhagen	Finnwood (II)	19.4.1972	Anna Nurmela	Finneagle (I)	3.2.1962
Aune Haavisto	Rautaruukki (I)	12.3.1976	Greta Oker-Blom	Finnstar (I) ex	
Kristiina Hakkarainen	Valkeakoski	8.3.1972		Raimo-Ragnar	16.6.1955
Pirkko Halle	Finnenso	12.6.1964	Armi Oksanen	Kaipola (I)	29.9.1960
ditto	Finn-Enso	7.9.1965	Arja Pajula	Mega – Motti	1.9.1993
Helka Hannunkari	Pokkinen	15.9.1978	Kirsti Paloluoma	Kuurtanes	10.9.1976
Aune Heikkilä	Finn-Amer	19.12.1970	Elsa Pelkonen	Koiteli	4.10.1972
Elisabeth Holma	Finnfellow	2.1.1973	Liisa Pessi	Kemira	30.8.1980
Leena Honkasalo	Finnarctis	27.11.1980	Eleanor Piironen	Hansa Express	2.2.1962
Laila Hovi	Tyysterniemi	12.4.1967	Ejna Poukka	Mega ex Teuvo	9.1.1975
Susan Hussey	Walki Paper	13.10.1977	Irma Pöyhönen	Lotila (II)	28.7.1976
Ingegerd Hägglöf	Tallink ex Svea Regina	26.5.1972	Toini Raade	Nunnalahti	28.6.1957
Marjatta Härmälä	Astrea	14.1.1991	Leila Rautalahti	Oihonna	27.4.1984
ditto	Finnpartner (III)	22.3.1995	Marjatta Roos	Finnmerchant (II)	10.12.1982
Patricia Jacobs	Finnalpino (I) ex Besseggen	6.2.1958	ditto	Finn	28.4.1987
Rakel Jalkanen	Finnforest (II) ex Rolita	30.9.1977	Aino Saari	Pamilo	20.6.1953
Kata Jouhki	Finntimber	20.6.1974	Hertta Schultz	Finnlark	21.9.1965
Marjatta Jouhki	Finnpolaris	25.9.1981	Brita Segercrantz	Ariel	17.9.1970
ditto	Finnforest (III) > Antares	6.9.1989	Gertrud Sellman	Soskua ex Royal Wood	20.10.1956
ditto	Finnhansa (II)	19.9.1994	Gunvor Sjöström	Para-Bravo	27.4.1984
Siiri Järvinen	Finnclipper	15.3.1962	Hilppa Sjöström	Para-Charlie	29.6.1984
Elina Keino	Finnpine (II)	29.11.1971	Greta Skogster-Lehtinen	Finntrader (I)	3.6.1950
ditto	Jalina ex Antares	26.5.1972	ditto	Finnkraft (I)	31.7.1956
Sylvi Kekkonen	Finnpulp	22.1.1953	Eeva-Liisa Sormanto	Finntrader (II)	15.1.1970
ditto	Tervi	1.8.1962	Annie Steen	Finnpine (I) ex Nyx	5.10.1957
ditto	Finnhansa (I)	1.12.1964	Elma Sukselainen	Finnmaid (II)	19.3.1965
ditto	Finnpartner (I)	15.12.1965	Doris Sundström	Finnsailor (III)	12.5.1987
Liisa Ketola	Finnbuilder	5.6.1971	Louise Swanljung	Patria	15.4.1978
Vappu Ketola	Finnwhale	1985	E. Sørensen	Lovisa ex Rimja Dan	10.11.1959
Carola Kiviluoto	Para-Alfa	1.12.1983	Linda Tanner	Finnseal	24.3.1964
ditto	Para-Delta	22.3.1985	Bertta Tiainen	Kaipola (II)	19.4.1971
Pirjo-Riitta Kivimäki	Rautaruukki (II)	31.10.1986	Vappu Tuomioja	Finnmerchant (I)	13.3.1953
Eira Kolho	Finnsailor (I)	11.12.1952	Annikki Tähtinen	Tuira	10.8.1972
Eine Koski	Pallas	26.11.1970	Armi Valleala	Finnsailor (II)	24.9.1971
Elisabeth Krogh	Jurmo ex Nyhammer	15.12.1953	Elina Varis	Finnboard	12.3.1958
Alice Källsson	Mälkiä ex Sunnanhav	26.1.1962	Annikki Vartiainen	Tupavuori	29.9.1953
Elisa Lagerroos	Finntrader (IV)	1.12.1995	Eeva Virkkunen	Finnarrow	11.12.1964
Meri Lahermaa	Tellus	5.4.1984	Meri Walden	Rekola	19.8.1964
Liisa Lanu	Finnrose (II)	24.6.1980	Tellervo Walden	Simpele	3.5.1960
Arnevi Lassila	Kaipola (III)	3.5.1977	Alice Wartemann	Finncarrier	26.3.1969
Karin Lehto	Envik	2.12.1983	– Wegener	Tornator ex Nordlys	19.4.1916
Margit Leskinen	Kotkaniemi	26.6.1968	Daniela Westphal	Railship I	10.2.1975
Ebba Lindahl	Finnfury ex Forano	28.3.1975	Eva-May Åberg	Lapponia ex Astrea	3.9.1977
Aura Lindblom	Hans Gutzeit	27.4.1972	Brita Örö	Nina	26.4.1963

Fleet List Notes

The vessels are arranged in chronological order. For newbuildings the date of delivery is decisive, and for second hand vessels it is the Bill of Sale date. If two or more ships were purchased or delivered on the same day, they are arranged according to their age, the older vessel having the highest priority.

Arabic number before the name
Place in chronological order according to the above rule, concerning vessels managed by Baltic Chartering, Finnlines or FG-Shipping.

Roman number after the name in brackets
Identification number for vessels with same name.

Years after the name
Period when managed by Baltic Chartering, Finnlines or FG-Shipping.

Call sign
Call signs mentioned are those being used when managed by Baltic Chartering, Finnlines or FG-Shipping.

Type, tonnages, dimensions and engine
Last/latest particulars and figures in the management of Baltic Chartering, Finnlines or FG-Shipping. Earlier and/or later particulars and figures are mentioned in the text, if for instance lengthened or converted.

Dimensions
Length overall x breadth x draught fully loaded in metres.

Date on the left in connection of a sale
Date, if known, when the Bill of Sale has been signed. (day.month.year)

Finnish place names
Bilingual places in Finland are mentioned both in Finnish and Swedish with the Finnish name first and after a stroke the Swedish name, viz.:
Hamina /Fredrikshamn
Hanko /Hangö
Helsinki /Helsingfors
Kaskinen /Kaskö
Kokkola /Gamlakarleby
Lappohja /Lappvik
Loviisa /Lovisa
Naantali /Nådendal
Nauvo /Nagu
Oulu /Uleåborg
Parainen /Pargas
Pietarsaari /Jakobstad
Pori /Björneborg
Porvoo /Borgå
Raahe /Brahestad
Rauma /Raumo
Tammisaari /Ekenäs
Turku /Åbo
Uusikaupunki /Nystad
Vaasa /Vasa

However, Swedish place names are mentioned only once per vessel.

Manager(s) and managing owners
Manager(s) and parent company are mentioned after the owners' name in parentheses, followed by the home port.
Managing owners are listed in parentheses with c/o, as (c/o …)

Home ports and building places
Home ports are spelt as they appear(ed) on the vessel, e.g. Göteborg. Building places are spelt as the shipyard has done, e.g. København.
    Routes in the text are, however, written in English, e.g. Gothenburg – Copenhagen.

Services and lines
The first service or line of every ship is told in many cases, but further moves only occasionally.

Abbreviations of "Company Limited" and the Finnish and Swedish equivalents, i.e. "Osakeyhtiö" and "Aktiebolaget"
Finnish company names are abbreviated as per Finnish Ship Register books, viz.:
Oy and **Ab**

Contemporary abbreviations are used in
– British and American company names as per Lloyd's Register, viz.:
    Co. Ld. before 1954 and
    Co. Ltd. from 1955 on.
– in Swedish company names as per Sveriges Skeppslista, viz.:
    ab. or **Ab.** to 1975 as abbreviated individually for each company in Sveriges Skeppslista and
    AB from 1976 on.

Double/triple names of Finnish companies are divided from each other by a dash as for instance
    Suomen Höyrylaiva Oy – Finska Ångfartygs Ab
    and parallel names by strokes as Finnlines Oy / Finnlines Ab / Finnlines Ltd / Finnlines AG
    Translations in English are in brackets as
    Laivanisännistöyhtiö Finnmaid (Part Owners Finnmaid)

The vessel histories are updated up to December 1997.
    Although every effort has been made by cross checking several independent sources of information to ensure correctness and accuracy in the fleet list, the details are believed to be true, but not guaranteed. If any reader can find something to be amended or corrected, I welcome such comments to my home address: Uurtajantie 16, FIN-00430 Helsinki.

Matti Pietikäinen

Abbreviations Used in the Fleet List

AGM	Annual General Meeting	m	metres
BHP	Brake Horsepowers	MoA	Memorandum of Agreement
BoS	Bill of Sale	NE	Northeast
cy.	cylinders	NRT	Net Register Tons
dwt	deadweight tons	NT	Net Tonnage as per the 1969 Convention
EGM	Extraordinary General Meeting	NW	Northwest
4 DA	four-stroke double-acting	SE	Southeast
4 SA	four-stroke single-acting	SHP	Shaft Horsepowers
GRT	Gross Register Tons	SW	Southwest
GT	Gross Tonnage as per the 1969 Convention	TEU	Twentyfoot Equivalent Units (Container)
IHP	Indicated Horsepowers	2 DA	two-stroke double-acting
kW	kiloWatts	2 SA	two-stroke single-acting
		USEC	United States East Coast
		WW II	Second World War

Fleet List

1. WILLE

1947–1960

General Cargo Steamer, Singledecker
Call: OFIQ Ice class: II
2,200 GRT, 1,169 NRT, 3,347 dwt
88.67 x 12.35 x 5.98 m
Triple Steam Engine 3 cy.
by the Shipbuilders
1,120 IHP   10 knots

ss WILLE was built as HELMWOOD to carry coal from the Tyne to London
Photo from A. Duncan

ss WILLE still bearing M for Merivienti as her funnel mark
Photo from A. Duncan

25.9.1923: Launched by Vickers, Ld., Barrow (#603), and named HELMWOOD.
Yard No. erroneously stated as #613 in Lloyd's Register.

10.1923: Completed and delivered to Wm. France, Fenwick & Co. Ld., London. Tanktops in the after holds raised to the shafting tunnel-top level in order to eliminate damages to the tunnel caused by discharging grabs. However, the vessel was found to be extremely tender when fully loaded with coal and in order to improve the stability the tanktop was removed from No. 3 hold. – Employed in carrying coal from the Tyne to London.

2.1947: Sold to Hai Ying Steamship Co. Ld., Shanghai, and renamed HAI PUNG. Provisional Chinese National Certificate issued on Mar. 17, 1947. Made one trip under Chinese flag from Falmouth to Naples and back to the Tyne.

ss AURA ex WILLE awaiting her final fate in January 1964 at Gothenburg
Photo by Krister Bång

6.5.1947:	Acquired by Merivienti Oy, (c/o Oy Baltic Chartering Ab), Helsinki /Helsingfors (1012), and renamed WILLE.
1.4.1954:	Managers were wound up and management was taken over by Oy Finnlines Ltd.
26.8.1960:	Sold to Airiston Laiva Oy, (Meritoimi Oy), Turku / Åbo (1389), and renamed AURA when delivered on Sep. 28.
20.4.1963:	Owners went bankrupt and Aura was on Apr. 25 laid up at Turku.
12.7.1963:	Sold at an auction to Compañia Naviera Dorita S.A., Panama, (c/o Torsten Carlbom & Co. AB, Stockholm) without change of name. BoS 10.9.1963.
1964:	Sold for demolition to Skrot & Avfallprodukter, Göteborg, where arrived on Jan. 6. However, resold to Walter Ritscher for scrapping in Hamburg and arrived there on Jan. 22.

2. KALLE 1947–1957

General Cargo Steamer, Singledecker
Call: OFIS
2,472 GRT, 1,250 NRT, 4,150 dwt
79.80 x 13.25 x 7.38 m
Triple Steam Engine 3 cy.
by the Shipbuilders
1,550 IHP   9 knots

30.12.1918:	Launched by Great Lakes Engineering Works, Ashtabula, Ohio (#502). Built as per U.S. Shipping Board standard design #1060, contract #1274.
29.3.1919:	Completed and delivered as COWBOY to United States Shipping Board (Emergency Fleet Corporation), Cleveland, Ohio.
1920:	Owners listed as United States Shipping Board, Cleveland, Ohio.
1921:	Home port changed to Boston, Mass.
3.7.1922:	Sold to Matson Navigation Co. Inc., San Francisco, Cal., and renamed MAKENA. Employed in picking up sugar from Port Allen on Kauai, Hana on Maui and Mahukona, Kawaihae and Kukuihaele on Hawaii Island.
1940:	Sold to Compagnie Générale d'Armements Maritimes, Le Havre, and to be renamed HONFLEUR. Sailed on June 3 from Los Angeles via Baltimore to New York with arrival on July 7. However, due to the capitulation of France, the sale was cancelled and the vessel was laid up in New York.

ss KALLE was completed as COWBOY for U.S. Shipping Board
Photo by Richard Hildebrand, collection of Eric Johnson

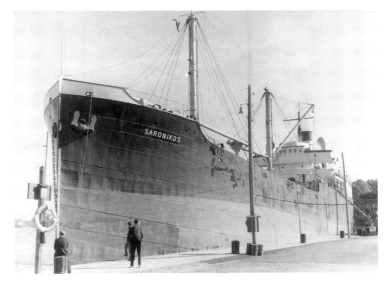

The Greek ss SARONIKOS ex KALLE before leaving Helsinki in September 1957
Photo by Matti Pietikäinen

30.12.1940:	Sold to Makena Steamship Co. Ld., Panama, (Goulandris Bros., Piraeus), (c/o Lombardi & Icaza, Panama & General Steam Nav. Co. Ld. of Greece, New York). Sailed on Feb. 24, 1941 from New York for Halifax.
11.1946:	Sold to Compañia Charco Azul de Navegacion S.A., (Reginald Lucraft), Panama, and renamed NADA.
10.7.1947:	Acquired by Merivienti Oy, (c/o Oy Baltic Chartering Ab), Helsinki /Helsingfors (1029), and renamed KALLE. Employed in carrying iron ore from Sweden to Turku /Åbo and in winter-time coal from England and Poland to Denmark, later also pulp from Finland to England.
1.4.1954:	Managers were wound up and management transferred to Oy Finnlines Ltd.
23.8.1957:	Sold to Compania de Vapores Santa Elena S.A., (Constantine V. Colocotronis), Piraeus, and renamed SARONIKOS when delivered on Sep. 2.
1960:	Sold to Greek shipbreakers and scrapping began on March 3 in Sava shipyard at Neon Ikonion, St. George's Bay, Keratsini.

ss KALLE
Photo by Esa Hänninen

3. EERO   1947–1953

General Cargo Steamer, Singledecker
Call: OFKJ
2,090 GRT, 1,145 NRT, 3,500 dwt
79.55 x 13.22 x 6.15 m
Triple Steam Engine 3 cy.
by Canadian Allis-Chalmers Ld., Toronto
1,560 IHP   8.5 knots

ss EERO
Photo by F. W. Hawks

10.1919:	Completed by British American Shipbuilding Co., Welland, Ont. (#3), as WAR RACOON for The Shipping Controller, London. Managed by Tyzack & Branfoot, London.
1919:	Sold to Société Maritime & Commerciale du Pacifique, Marseilles, and renamed SHOURAGALLUS.
1924:	Sold to Compagnie Nationale de Navigation, Bordeaux, and renamed PRAIRIAL.
1929:	Sold to Société Générale de Transactions Industrielles, Rouen, and renamed SARA.
1931:	Sold to Compagnie Franco-Africaine de Navigation, "Francafrica", Casablanca, and renamed KAMSA.
1933:	Home port changed to Rouen, when Société Anonyme de Gérance & d'Armement (S.A.G.A.) took a controlling interest in the company.
1936:	Sold to Antonios G. Pappadakis, Piraeus (c/o American Ship Brokerage Corp., New York), and renamed ELISE.
1940:	Detained at Dakar in June during the capitulation of France. Sailed end August under French control with an armed guard on board via Casablanca to Port Lyautey (Kenitra), Morocco.
2.12.1940:	Detained at Port Lyautey by French authorities.
5.11.1941:	Seized at Port Lyautey by French (Vichy) Govt. Renamed TROPIQUE and managed by Compagnie

Nantaise des Chargeurs de l'Ouest, Nantes. Sailed in January 1942 to Casablanca and from there in July via St. Louis to Marseilles, where laid up.

27.8.1942: French (Vichy) Govt. was forced by Germans to sign "Accord de Nevers", in which all Greek ships once seized by France had to be returned to their owners and at the same moment they were seized by Germans.

11.1942: Taken over by German Govt. and put into management of Mittelmeer Reederei G.m.b.H., Hamburg.

2.1943: Transferred to Italy and renamed FIRENZE. Sailed in July from Marseilles to Maddalena, Sardinia, where lying on Oct. 1, when Allied troops arrived there.

4.1944: Returned in Malta to Antonios G. Pappadakis and name reverted to ELISE.

25.8.1947: Acquired by Merivienti Oy, (c/o Oy Baltic Chartering Ab), Helsinki /Helsingfors (1032), and renamed EERO.

2.6.1953: Sold to Laivayhtiö Roine, (Matti Heusala), (c/o Merirahtaus Oy – Seachartering Ltd.), Helsinki, and renamed ROINE.

20.2.1956: Sold to Varustamo Matti Heusala & co. Shipowners, Helsinki, without change of name.

10.1.1957: Sold to Mount Olympos Shipping Corp., Monrovia, (F. Theorides, Durban), (c/o Rallis Shipping Co. Ltd., London), and renamed MOUNT DELPHI.

1958: Struck rock and sprang leak in the engine room one mile south of Sail Rock, off Mormugao on June 2, while on passage from Moulmein to Karachi with timber and rice. Beached at Grand Island. Declared a constructive total loss.

4. TORNATOR 1947–1954

General Cargo Steamer, two decks – Tweendecker
Call: OFMX
3,768 GRT, 2,209 NRT, 6,800 dwt
115.02 x 15.60 x 7.21 m
Triple Steam Engine 3 cy.
by the Shipbuilders
1,860 IHP   9.5 knots

ss TORNATOR was purchased from Denmark as KARLA DAN
Photo from Søren Thorsøe

19.4.1916: Launched by A/S Burmeister & Wains Maskin- og Skibsbyggeri, Kjøbenhavn (#305), and named NORDLYS by Mrs. Wegener, née Brown.

22.6.1916: Completed and delivered to A/S Dampskibsselskabet Norden, (P. Brown, Jr. & Co.), Kjøbenhavn.

1940: During the German occupation of Denmark on Apr. 9 she was at sea and was intercepted by Royal Navy Forces and taken to Kirkwall on Apr. 16.

7.6.1940: Taken over by British Ministry of Shipping (later Ministry of War Transport), London, and placed under management of W.A. Massey & Sons Ld., Hull.

ss TORNATOR with new F funnel mark
Photo by Skyfotos

3.11.1945:	Returned to A/S Dampskibsselskabet Norden.	1.4.1954:	Managers were wound up and management was taken over by Oy Finnlines Ltd.
24.4.1946:	Sold to Rederiet Ocean A/S, (J. Lauritzen), Esbjerg, and renamed KARLA DAN.	21.9.1954:	Sold to Société Anonyme Cinda, Liége, for demolition in Antwerp, where arrived on Sep. 28.
12.9.1947:	Acquired by Merivienti Oy, (c/o Oy Baltic Chartering Ab), Helsinki /Helsingfors (1036), and renamed TORNATOR.	6.5.1955:	Towed on to Boom for completion of scrapping.
5.2.1948:	After drydocking at Rauma /Raumo inaugurated Finnlines liner service from Finland to USEC.		

5. PANKAKOSKI 1947–1953

General Cargo Steamer, two decks – Tweendecker
Call: OFLZ
4,138 GRT, 2,682 NRT, 5,426 dwt
113.18 x 14.04 x 7.14 m
Quadruple Steam Engine 4 cy.
by the Shipbuilders, Detroit, Mich.
1,870 IHP   10 knots

24.6.1909:	Launched by Detroit Shipbuilding Company, Wyandotte, Mich. (#179).	1916:	Forced by Anti-trust legislation, railroad companies had to get out of steamship business and therefore 5 companies, incl. Pennsylvania Railroad, formed together Great Lakes Transit Corporation, registered at Buffalo, N.Y., by a merger of their Lakes transit subsidiaries.
1909:	Completed as Package Freight Steamer CONEMAUGH for Erie & Western Transportation Co. (Anchor Line), (Pennsylvania Railroad), Philadelphia, Del.		

ss PANKAKOSKI was rebuilt during WW II from an old laker W.W. ATTERBURY
Photo by Wm. J. Taylor, collection of Jay N. Bascom

1920:	Renamed W.W. ATTERBURY by Great Lakes Transit Corporation.
1942:	Acquired by U.S. Maritime Commission / U.S. War Shipping Administration, New Orleans, La., and delivered on July 26 at Chicago, Ill. – Pole masts, funnel, bridge on the fo'c'sle and poopdeck structures were stripped off before floating out of the Lakes through Chicago Sanitary and Ship Canal and down the Mississippi.
5.1943:	Completed after conversion by Todd-Johnson Drydocks, Algiers, La. The conversion involved hull reinforcement, removal of coal bunkers and alteration of boilers to oil firing, installation of evaporators, removal of internal cargo elevators, welding up sideport openings in the hull, reconstruction of decks and hatchways and fitting of cargo gear, new funnel and bridge amidships. Bareboat-chartered to War Dept. (U.S. Army Transportation Corps.) and delivered on May 3. Entered service on May 22 and employed in military transports in the Pacific.
1945:	Arrived on Nov. 11 at San Francisco and redelivered to U.S. War Shipping Adminstration. Laid up in Suisan Bay, Cal.
1947:	Sold to Overlakes Freight Corporation, (Troy M. Browning), Wilmington, Del., and delivered on Sep. 30.
28.10.1947:	Acquired by Merivienti Oy, (c/o Oy Baltic Chartering Ab), Helsinki /Helsingfors (1037), and renamed PANKAKOSKI, when delivered on Nov. 6. Sailed on Nov. 11 from San Francisco for Finland.
21.2.1948:	After drydocking at Rauma /Raumo entered Finnlines liner service from Finland to USEC.
26.11.1953:	Sold to Lunghua Dock & Engineering Works Ld. for scrapping in Hong Kong, where arrived on Dec. 13 for demolition.

ss W.W. ATTERBURY was in 1943–45 an armed military transport in the Pacific
Photo from World Ship Photo Library

ss PANKAKOSKI
Photo from A. Duncan

6. HAMINA   1947–1954

General Cargo Steamer, two decks – Tweendecker
Call: OFLY
4,068 GRT, 2,759 NRT, 5,426 dwt
113.05 x 14.04 x 7.14 m
Quadruple Steam Engine 4 cy.
by the Shipbuilders
1,850 IHP   10 knots

*ss HAMINA was rebuilt during in 1942–43 from an old laker H.A. SCANDRETT
Photo by Wm. J. Taylor, collection of Jay N. Bascom*

2.10.1909:	Launched by Great Lakes Engineering Works, St. Clair, Mich. (#70).
1909:	Completed as Package Freight Steamer NORTH STAR for Mutual Transit Company, (Great Northern/North Pacific Railroad), Buffalo, N.Y.
1916:	Forced by Anti-trust legislation, railroad companies had to get out of steamship business and therefore 5 companies, incl. Great Northern/North Pacific Railroad, formed together Great Lakes Transit Corporation, registered at Buffalo, N.Y., by a merger of their Lakes transit subsidiaries.
1928:	Renamed H.A. SCANDRETT by Great Lakes Transit Corporation.
1942:	Acquired by U.S. Maritime Commission / U.S. War Shipping Administration, Mobile, Ala., and delivered on July 21 at Chicago, Ill. – Pole masts, funnel, bridge on the fo'c'sle and poopdeck structures were stripped off before floating out of the Lakes through Chicago Sanitary and Ship Canal and down the Mississippi.
3.1943:	Completed after conversion by Alabama Dry Dock & Shipbuilding Co., Mobile, Ala. The conversion involved hull reinforcement, removal of coal bunkers and alteration of boilers to oil firing, installation of evaporators, removal of internal cargo elevators, welding up sideport openings in the hull, reconstruction of decks and hatchways and fitting of cargo gear, new funnel and bridge amidships. Bareboat-chartered to War Dept. (U.S. Army Transportation Corps.) and delivered on Feb. 18 at Mobile, Ala. Entered service on Mar. 4 and employed in military transports in the Pacific.
1945:	Arrived on Oct. 12 at San Francisco and redelivered to U.S. War Shipping Adminstration. Laid up in Suisan Bay, Cal.
1947:	Sold to Overlakes Freight Corporation, (Troy M. Browning), Wilmington, Del., and delivered on Oct. 3.
28.10.1947:	Acquired by Merivienti Oy, (c/o Oy Baltic Chartering Ab), Helsinki /Helsingfors (1040) and renamed HAMINA. Sailed on Nov. 19 from San Francisco for Finland.

ss HAMINA in the Cape Cod Canal in August 1950
Photo from Eric Johnson

The tank top of ss HAMINA as a floating bunkering station at Flushing in May 1982
Photo by Matti Pietikäinen

20.3.1948:	After drydocking at Turku /Åbo entered Finnlines liner service from Finland to USEC.
1.4.1954:	Managers were wound up and management transferred to Oy Finnlines Ltd.
30.9.1954:	Sold to Leon Engelen, Boom, for scrapping in Antwerp, where arrived on Oct. 3 for demolition.
1955:	Double bottom section with a length of 104 metres sold to Steenkolen-Handelsvereeniging N.V. (SHV), Vlissingen, for further use as a floating bunkering station in Flushing (Vlissingen) Outer Harbour. Still called HAMINA.
1967:	Partly sunk on Mar. 23 after collision with German ms Hainig. Salvage operations started on Mar. 31 and raised on Apr. 2 by six floating cranes. Repaired and returned to same duty.
1982:	Towed on May 24 from Flushing Outer Harbour via locks to Inner Harbour to be demolished by the local breakers "Nimeta".

7. ENSO

1950–1959

General Cargo Steamer, Singledecker
Call: OFPZ Ice class: I C
1,803 GRT, 966 NRT, 3,050 dwt
85.60 x 12.85 x 5.79 m
Triple Steam Engine 3 cy.
by the Shipbuilders
1,085 IHP   9.5 knots

ss ENSO was built as the German ERNST BROCKELMANN
Photo from A. Duncan

ss ENSO
Photo by Skyfotos

ss HAKUNI ex ENSO
Photo by Bertil Zandelin

8.10.1927:	Launched by A.G. Neptun, Rostock (#412), and named ERNST BROCKELMANN.
9.11.1927:	Completed and delivered to Erich Ahrens, Rostock.
5.1945:	Taken as a prize at Flensburg by Allied forces.
3.7.1945:	Allocated to Great Britain and operated by Ministry of War Transport as EMPIRE CONCESSION. Managed for MoWT by Burnett Steamship Co. Ld., London.

3.1946:	Operators' name changed after WW II to Ministry of Transport.	5.2.1966:	Sold to Isla del Rey Shipping Co., Panama, (Alejandro D. Mendez Moreno, Madrid), and renamed ISLA DEL REY.
1947:	Sold to Blandy Bros. & Co. (London) Ld., London, and renamed BRAZEN HEAD.	1966:	Drifting icebound on Feb. 13 at Avagrundet southwest of Fårösund Lighthouse, north of Gotland due to engine trouble, while on voyage from Uusikaupunki / Nystad to Slite. Towed on Feb. 15 to Slite by salvage vessels Triton and Herakles. Had sustained propeller, rudder and shell damage. Surveyed on Mar. 15 in Gdynia and classification surveyor allowed to sail until May 15 without final repairs. Sailed on Mar. 17 for Palma de Mallorca with arrival on Apr. 20. After discharge laid up at Carthagena on May 2 and offered for sale.
5.4.1950:	Acquired by Enso-Gutzeit Oy, Kotka (538), (c/o Oy Baltic Chartering Ab, Helsinki /Helsingfors), and renamed ENSO.		
1.4.1954:	Managers were wound up and management was taken over by Oy Finnlines Ltd.		
3.4.1959:	Sold to Raumanmeri Oy, (A. Fagerström), Rauma / Raumo (596), and renamed HAKUNI when delivered on Apr. 11.		
		1966:	Sold to Spanish shipbreakers and arrived on June 3 at Alicante for demolition.

8. NESTE   1951–1953

Steam Tanker, one deck
Call: OFNY
6,208 GRT, 3,143 NRT, 8,800 dwt
130.00 x 16.39 x 7.88 m
Triple Steam Engine 3 cy.
by the Shipbuilders
2,680 IHP   10 knots

st NESTE
Photo by Skyfotos

5.1921:	Completed by Bethlehem Shipbuilding Corp., Ld., Sparrow's Point, Md. (#4208) as HENRY DEUTSCH DE LA MEURTHE for Lux Navigation Co. Ld., (Davies & Newman Ld.), London.	1932:	Home port changed to Farsund.
		1.1937:	Purchased by Martin Mosvold, Farsund.
1922:	Sold to Lutetian Navigation Co. Ld., (Davies & Newman Ld.), London.	4.1940:	Operation taken over by Nortraship until 1945.
		1947:	Sold to A/S Mosvold Shipping Co., (Martin Mosvold), Farsund.
1.1930:	Sold to A/S Mosvolds Rederi IV, (Martin Mosvold), Kristiansand, and renamed TORBORG.		

The Polish st WSPOLPRACA ex NESTE
Photo by Skyfotos

2.7.1948:	Acquired by Neste Oy, (c/o Henry Nielsen Oy/Ab), Helsinki /Helsingfors (1054), and renamed NESTE.
12.3.1951:	Management handed over to Oy Baltic Chartering Ab, Helsinki.
7.11.1953:	Sold through Centrala Morska Importowo – Exportowa "Centromor" P.P., Gdansk, to Polskie Linie Oceaniczne (Polish Ocean Lines), Gdynia, and renamed WSPOLPRACA.
1956:	Sold having sustained engine damage to Eisen und Metall K.G. Lehr & Co. for scrapping at Bremerhaven, where arrived on Dec. 6.

9. FINNTRADER (I)   1951–1970

General Cargo Motorship, two decks – Open Shelterdecker
Passengers: 12 berths
Call: OFQP Ice class: I C
4,022 GRT, 2,097 NRT, 6,435 dwt
126.04 x 16.60 x 7.00 m
Diesel Engine 2 SA 9 cy. Sulzer 9SD65
by Sulzer Bros. Ld., Winterthur, engine made 1940
3,678 kW / 5,000 BHP   15 knots

3.6.1950:	Launched by N.V. Scheepswerf "De Hoop", Lobith (#210), and named FINNTRADER by Mrs. Greta Skogster-Lehtinen.
18.7.1950:	Towed down the River Rhine to Ijsselmonde, near Rotterdam for machinery installation and final fitting-out.
30.1.1951:	Completed by Scheepsinstallatiebedrijf "Nederland", Ijsselmonde, and delivered to Merivienti Oy, (c/o Oy Baltic Chartering Ab), Helsinki /Helsingfors (1084). Employed on Finnlines liner service from Finland to USEC.
1.4.1954:	Managers were wound up and management was taken over by Oy Finnlines Ltd.
2.11.1966:	Acquired by Rakennustoimisto, Jussi Ketola, Helsinki. Delivered without change of name on Nov. 8. Managers remained Oy Finnlines Ltd.
8.1969:	Transferred to Finnlines Mediterranean service.
25.9.1970:	Sold to Ambassador Shipping Corp., Monrovia, (c/o Overland Trust Bank, Maritime Dept., Lugano) and renamed TRITON AMBASSADOR when delivered on Oct. 6.

ms FINNTRADER during machinery installation at Ijsselmonde in 1950
Photo by F.H. van Fijk

ms FINNTRADER
Photo by Skyfotos

ms FINNTRADER as TRITON AMBASSADOR in the 1970s
Photo by Michael Cassar

11.1973: Sold to Almarante Navigation Corp., Panama, (c/o Sovereign Marine Lines Inc., New York), and renamed SOVEREIGN SAPPHIRE.

4.1975: Renamed PYGMALION JUPITER by Almarante Nav. Corp.

6.1976: Sold to Panam City Navigation Corp., Panama, and renamed EQUUS.

1978: Sold to República de Cuba, (Empresa de Navegacion Caribe), Habana, and renamed PUERTO DE VITA.

1987: Owners amended to Empresa de Navegacion Caribe, Habana.

1988: Sold for demolition to Soc. Industrial de Productos Siderurgica S.A. (S.I.P.S.A.), who began work on Mar. 25 at Mamonal, Colombia.

10. FINNSAILOR (I)   1953–1968

General Cargo Motorship, two decks – Open Shelterdecker
Passengers: 12 berths
Call: OFSS Ice class: I C
4,048 GRT, 2,066 NRT, 6,604 dwt
126.10 x 16.60 x 7.10 m
Diesel Engine 2 SA 8 cy. Sulzer 8SD72
by Sulzer Bros. Ltd., Winterthur
4,119 kW / 5,600 BHP   15 knots

ms FINNSAILOR
Photo by Bertil Zandelin

ms FINNSAILOR as the Peruvian TUMI in Venezuela
Photo from K. Brzoza

11.12.52:	Launched by N.V. Scheepswerf en Machinefabriek "De Merwede" v/h van Vliet & Co., Hardinxveld (#526), and named FINNSAILOR by Mrs. Eira Kolho.
18.4.1953:	Completed and delivered to Enso-Gutzeit Oy, Kotka (540), (c/o Oy Baltic Chartering Ab, Helsinki / Helsingfors). Employed on Finnlines liner service from Finland to USEC.
1.4.1954:	Managers were wound up and management was taken over by Oy Finnlines Ltd.
9.8.1968:	Sold to Ab Vasa Shipping Oy, (Nils Berg), Vaasa / Vasa (221), and renamed GRACIA when delivered on Aug. 22.
11.7.1972:	Sold to Naviera Neptuno S.A., Callao, Peru, and renamed TUMI.
1983:	After being adrift off Yucatan due to machinery problems, reported on Dec. 13 as being in tow of ms Smit Salvor, during a voyage from Matarani, Peru, for Fort Pierce, Fla. with zinc concentrates. Arrived in tow at New Orleans on Dec. 15 for inspection.
1984:	Having been found not worth repairing, sold to Goldwils Inc. for demolition at Brownsville, Tex., where arrived in tow by ms Taurus on Jan. 26. Demolition started on Mar. 1 with expected end on May 31.

11. FINNPULP   1953–1968

General Cargo Motorship, two decks – Open Shelterdecker
Call: OFSR Ice class: I C
4,049 GRT, 2,067 NRT, 6,604 dwt
126.10 x 16.60 x 7.10 m
Diesel Engine 2 SA 8 cy. Sulzer 8SD72
by Sulzer Bros. Ltd., Winterthur
4,119 kW / 5,600 BHP   15 knots

22.1.1953:	Launched by Werf Jan Smit & Czn., Alblasserdam (#550), and named FINNPULP by Mrs. Sylvi Kekkonen.
22.4.1953:	Completed and delivered to Merivienti Oy, (Enso-Gutzeit Oy), (c/o Oy Baltic Chartering Ab), Helsinki /Helsingfors (1124). Employed on Finnlines liner service from Finland to USEC.
1.4.1954:	Managers were wound up and management was taken over by Oy Finnlines Ltd.

ms FINNPULP
Photo by Skyfotos

ms FINNPULP as the Greek GINA
Photo by Michael Cassar

ms SCAPLAKE ex FINNPULP in 1989 at Aliaga breakers
Photo by Selim San, collection of K. Brzoza

23.4.1968:	Sold to G.Z. Lanaras, (c/o Grecomar Shipping Agency Ltd.), Piraeus, and renamed GINA.	1986:	Managers changed to Vernicos Maritime Co. S.A., Piraeus.
1971:	Sold to Pyxis Special Shipping Co. Ltd., Piraeus (c/o Circe Shipping Enterprises Co. Ltd., Athens), and renamed SCAPLAKE.	1989:	Reported as sold to Greek shipbreakers and arrived at Piraeus on March 14 from Chalkis, where she had been laid up since May 26, 1979. However, sold to Leyal Gemi Sokum Ticaret A.S. and arrived in tow at Aliaga, Turkey, on May 18 for demolition.
1982:	Managers changed to Alpha Managing & Financing Inc., Athens.		

12. FINNMERCHANT (I) 1953–1969

General Cargo Motorship, two decks – Open Shelterdecker
Call: OFTA   Ice class: I C
5,391 GRT, 2,778 NRT, 8,590 dwt
141.80 x 17.83 x 7.68 m
Diesel Engine 2 SA 9 cy. MAN
by Maschinenfabrik Augsburg-Nürnberg A.G., Augsburg
4,476 kW / 6,000 BHP   15.5 knots

ms FINNMERCHANT as built
Photo by Farabee's Studio

ms FINNMERCHANT in her later livery
Photo from Matti Pietikäinen

13.3.1953:	Launched by Amsterdamsche Droogdok Mij. N.V., Amsterdam (#91), and named FINNMERCHANT by Mrs. Vappu Tuomioja.
4.8.1953:	Completed and delivered to Enso-Gutzeit Oy, Kotka (542), (c/o Oy Baltic Chartering Ab, Helsinki / Helsingfors).
1.4.1954:	Managers were wound up and management was taken over by Oy Finnlines Ltd.
20.6.1956:	Entered Finnlines liner service from Finland to USEC.
11.7.1969:	Sold to Capo Testa S.p.A. di Navigazione, (Pasquale Maglione), Cagliari, and renamed ANGELINA MAGLIONE when delivered on July 12.
1971:	Sold to Giovanni di Maio, Torre del Greco, and renamed MARIA DI MAIO.
1972:	Renamed CONCORDIA MARIA by Giovanni di Maio for duration of charter to Concordia Line, (Chr. Haaland), Haugesund.
1972:	Name reverted to MARIA DI MAIO after redelivery from charter.
1973:	Sold to Oromar S.A., Panama, (c/o Giovanni di Maio, Torre del Greco), and renamed MARIA D.
1974:	While lying moored at St. Nazaire in ballast condition to carry out repairs prior to being sold, a fire broke out on Dec. 21 at 0400, caused by a short-circuit, spread rapidly in the crew's quarters and ravaged all the superstructure.

ms CONCORDIA MARIA ex FINNMER-CHANT in 1972 at Las Palmas
Photo by Matti Pietikäinen

1975:	Found beyond an economical repair and sold to Eckhardt & Co. G.m.b.H. Left St. Nazaire on Mar. 10 in tow for Hamburg to be broken up.	1976:	Sold to Nikolas Shipping Co. S.A., (c/o A.N. Athanassiades), Piraeus, and renamed NIKOLAS II.
1975:	However, sold further to Marmonaria Nav. S.A., Piraeus. Repaired and returned to service in November under new name RESOLUTE SPIRIT.	1977:	Sold to Alexia Navigation Co. Ltd., Limassol, (c/o A.N. Athanassiades, Piraeus), and renamed ALEK.
		1982:	Sold to Pakistan shipbreakers and left Mogadishu on June 20 for Karachi. Arrived on July 15 at Gadani Beach, where broken up.

13. TUPAVUORI   1954–1958

Motor Tanker, one deck
Call: OFTU Ice class: I C
10,214 GRT, 5,580 NRT, 15,225 dwt
159.20 x 19.85 x 8.78 m
Diesel Engine 2 SA 9 cy. MAN K9Z 70/120
by Maschinenfabrik Augsburg-Nürnberg A.G., Augsburg
4,100 kW / 5,540 BHP   14 knots

29.9.1953: Launched by N.V. C.van der Giessen & Zonen's Scheepswerven, Krimpen a/d Ijssel (#766), and named TUPAVUORI by Mrs. Annikki Vartiainen.

12.1.1954: Completed and delivered to Neste Oy, (c/o Oy Baltic Chartering Ab), Helsinki /Helsingfors (1132).

1.4.1954: Managers were wound up and management was taken over by Oy Finnlines Ltd.

1958: Capsized and sank in 10 minutes after an explosion in her centre tank No. 6 on Oct. 5 at 1940, while lying empty and cleaning her tanks at Tupavuori oil terminal in Naantali /Nådendal. Settled on starboard side with less than half of her hull above the water, with extensive damages in her starboard and centre tanks. Three persons on board lost their lives. Salvage contract signed on Oct. 17 with Finska Bergnings Ab Neptun, (Finnish Neptun Salvage Co. Ltd.). Hired Swedish lifting pontoons Frigg and Oden arrived on Oct. 25 and salvage work started on Oct. 28. Very big underwater welding work needed in order to tighten the vessel for lifting. Righted in November, but refloating suspended to the following spring due to winter. Lying submerged with only fo'c'sle, bridge and top of funnel above the ice. Declared a constructive total loss on Dec. 31 and taken over by Vakuutus Oy Pohjola, (Pohjola Insurance Co. Ltd.), Helsinki.

1959: Refloating started on July 1 by Neptun Salvage Co. Ltd. with help of lifting pontoons. Lifted on even keel on July 15 and refloated on July 22, but declared beyond economical repair and handed over on July 23 as a salvage reward to Neptun Salvage Co. Ltd. Towed on Aug. 4 to Crichton-Vulcan shipyard in Turku for further tightening. Sold on Sep. 23 to Teijon Tehtaat Oy for demolition at Mathildedal, where arrived in tow on Oct. 10. The engine was, however, removed and reported as sold for further use.

mt TUPAVUORI
Photo by Hede Foto

14. PAMILO
FINNMASTER (I)

1954–1956
1956–1964

General Cargo Steamer, two decks – Open Shelterdecker
Call: OFTJ Ice class: I A
2,227 GRT, 975 NRT, 3,513 dwt
96.85 x 13.90 x 5.90 m
Compound Steam Engine 4 cy. Christiansen & Meyer
by Amsterdamsche Droogdok Maats. N.V., Amsterdam
1,720 IHP   11 knots

ss PAMILO
Photo from World Ship Photo Library

ss FINNMASTER
Photo by Holger Nyström

20.6.1953:	Launched by N.V. Arnhemsche Scheepsbouw Maats., Arnhem (#358), and named PAMILO by Mrs. Aino Saari.
6.2.1954:	Completed and delivered in Rotterdam to Enso-Gutzeit Oy, Kotka (543), (c/o Oy Baltic Chartering Ab, Helsinki /Helsingfors).
1.4.1954:	Managers were wound up and management was taken over by Oy Finnlines Ltd.
3.1955:	Inaugurated regular Finnlines liner service from Hull and London to Finland.
23.3.1956:	Renamed FINNMASTER by Enso-Gutzeit Oy according to Finnlines' nomenclature.

The Taiwanese ss CENTRAL MASTER leaving Helsinki for ever in January 1968
Photo by Matti Pietikäinen

27.5.1964: Acquired by Oy Thombrokers Ab, (Leo Jouhki), Helsinki (1326), and renamed MASTER when delivered on Aug. 6.

2.1.1968: Sold to Central Marine Corp., Keelung, Taiwan, and renamed CENTRAL MASTER when delivered on Jan. 20 in Helsinki.

1971: Caught fire due to fuel leak in the boiler room on Aug. 15 at Kaohsiung while discharging scrap iron from Nagoya and burnt for 4 hours. Boiler and engine room, accommodations and bridge burnt and wetted by sea water.

1972: Declared a constructive total loss and sold to Taiwan shipbreakers for demolition. Broken up in February 1972.

15. FINNMAID (I)   1956–1964

General Cargo Steamer, two decks – Open Shelterdecker
Call: OFWR Ice class: I A
2,288 GRT, 1,037 NRT, 3,500 dwt
102.57 x 14.32 x 5.82 m
Compound Steam Engine 4 cy.
by Christiansen & Meyer, Hamburg
1,770 IHP   12 knots

ss FINNMAID
Photo by Skyfotos

ss MAID of Oy Thombrokers Ab, ex FINN-MAID
Photo by Tomas Johannesson

17.3.1956:	Launched by N.V. Scheepswerf en Machinefabriek "De Biesbosch", Dordrecht (#352), and named FINNMAID by Mrs. Aune Alakari.
24.7.1956:	Completed and delivered in Rotterdam to Merivienti Oy, (Enso-Gutzeit Oy), Helsinki /Helsingfors (1183). Managed by Oy Finnlines Ltd. Employed on Finnlines liner service from England to Finland.
12.10.1963:	Acquired by Oy Thombrokers Ab, (Leo Jouhki), Helsinki, and renamed MAID when delivered on Jan. 7.
2.10.1968:	Sold to Transworld Maritime Co. Inc., Panama, (Transmare Societa di Navigazione, Genova), and delivered on Nov. 19 without change of name. Put into Transmare liner service from Genoa and Marseille to West Africa, mainly Dakar, Conakry and Abidjan.
1.1972:	Renamed GAMBIA by Transworld Maritime Co. Inc., in order to fit better to her liner route.
2.1974:	Sold to Maldives Shipping Ltd., Male, and renamed MALDIVE MERCHANT.
1977:	Sold to Pakistan shipbreakers and arrived on Sep. 10 at Karachi, from where left prior to Nov. 30 for demolition at Gadani Beach.

16. FINNKRAFT (I) 1956–1973

General Cargo Motorship, two decks – Open Shelterdecker
Call: OFXB Ice class: I A
1,990 GRT, 1,032 NRT, 3,567 dwt
97.85 x 14.20 x 5.82 m

Diesel Engine 2 SA 7 cy. MAN G7Z 52/90
by Kieler Howaldtswerke A.G., Kiel
1,716 kW / 2,300 BHP   13 knots

31.7.1956:	Launched by Rauma-Repola Oy, Rauman telakka, Rauma /Raumo (#86), and named FINNKRAFT by Mrs. Greta Skogster-Lehtinen.
21.12.1956:	Completed and delivered to Merivienti Oy, (Enso-Gutzeit Oy), (c/o Oy Finnlines Ltd), Helsinki / Helsingfors (1194). Employed on Finnlines liner service from England to Finland.
31.12.1970:	Owners amalgamated with the parent company Enso-Gutzeit Oy as per EGM resolution on Apr. 17. Merger registered on Aug. 3, 1971.
3.8.1971:	Home port changed to Kotka (578).
22.3.1973:	Sold to Antiparos Shipping Co. Ltd., Famagusta, (c/o Dalex Shipping Co. S.A., [G. Dalacouras], Piraeus), and renamed RED SKY.
1975:	Home port changed to Limassol.
1976:	Management taken over by Karlog Shipping Co. S.A. (Epaminondas G. Logethetis), Piraeus.
6.1977:	Sold to Parthenon Shipping Enterprises S.A., (Karlog Shipping Co. S.A.), Piraeus, and renamed PARTHENON.

ms FINNKRAFT
Photo by Skyfotos

The Greek ms PARTHENON ex FINNKRAFT
Photo by FotoFlite

1982: Sold to North Lebanez Co., (Dr. Sahl Adbul-Salam Dennaoui), Tripoli, Lebanon, (c/o Al Kamal Shipping & Trading Co. Ltd., Piraeus), and renamed NADA D.

1986: Arrived at Beirut on Oct. 22 from Mersin with water in her holds.

1987: Sold to shipbreakers at Tripoli, Lebanon. Reported on Feb. 10 to be at Tripoli in course of demolition.

17. NUNNALAHTI 1957–1964

Motor Tanker, one deck
Call: OFXS Ice class: I C
11,841 GRT, 6,676 NRT, 18,287 dwt
165.15 x 21.53 x 9.13 m
Diesel Engine 2 SA 9 cy. Werkspoor
by N.V. Werkspoor, Amsterdam
5,285 kW / 7,185 BHP   14.5 knots

mt NUNNALAHTI
Photo by Bertil Zandelin

NUNNALAHTI on her last voyage in tow from Naantali to Aliaga for demolition
Photo from K. Brzoza

28.6.1957:	Launched by N.V. C.van der Giessen & Zonen's Scheepswerven, Krimpen a/d Ijssel (#782), and named NUNNALAHTI by Mrs. Toini Raade.
18.10.1957:	Completed and delivered to Neste Oy, (c/o Oy Finnlines Ltd), Helsinki /Helsingfors (1210).
1.4.1964:	Management taken over by Neste Oy, Helsinki.
19.10.1964:	Home port changed to Naantali /Nådendal (27).
23.12.1976:	Sold to Valtion Viljavarasto (Finnish State Grainery), Helsinki.

22.8.1977:	Towed from Turku to Naantali for use as a grain storage vessel in Naantali.
24.11.1977:	Registered as grain storage lighter/ barge without engines and deleted from Finnish ship register.
1987:	Sold to Eckhardt & Co., Hamburg, and resold to Oge Gemi Sokum Ticaret A.S. for demolition at Aliaga, Turkey. Left Naantali in tow of ms Koral on Dec. 23.

Broke from tow on Feb. 8, 1988 while 7 miles south of Les Hanois Lighthouse, Guernsey, in position 49.20 N, 03.11 W. French tug Abeille Languedoc managed to get line on board with help of helicopter and took the barge in tow for Cherbourg. Towage continued from Cherbourg on Feb. 23 by icebreaker Perkun and arrived finally on March 15 at Aliaga for scrapping.

18. FINNBOARD 1958–1969

General Cargo Motorship, two decks – Open/Closed Shelterdecker
Call: OFYM Ice class: I C
4,082/6,403 GRT, 2,145/3,623 NRT, 7,475/9,230 dwt
130.90 x 17.22 x 7.24/8.22 m
Diesel Engine 2 SA 6 cy. MAN K6Z 70/120
by Kockums Mek. Verkstads AB, Malmö
3,678 kW / 5,000 BHP   15 knots

	Order placed with Ab. Oskarshamns Varv, Oskarshamn, by Part Owners (Partrederi) with Rederi ab. Virginia, (Mauritz Thore), Jonstorp, Ab. Aug. Leffler & Son, Göteborg, and Rederi ab. Jan, Göteborg, as partners.
22.8.1957:	Keel laid at Ab. Oskarshamn Varv.
3.1.1958:	Newbuilding contract purchased by Enso-Gutzeit Oy, Kotka, with take over of vessel immediately after delivery in June from Shipbuilders.
12.3.1958:	Launched by Ab. Oskarshamns Varv, Oskarshamn (#356), and named FINNBOARD by Mrs. Elina Varis.

ms FINNBOARD
Photo by Skyfotos

ms FINNBOARD was sold to Wagria Reederei in 1969 but chartered back to Finnlines
Photo by Matti Pietikäinen

ms MAN CHEONG of Panama ex FINNBOARD at Singapore
Photo from Krister Bång

26.6.1958: Completed and delivered to Rederi ab. Virginia, Jonstorp, Ab. Aug. Leffler & Son, Göteborg, and Rederi ab. Jan, Göteborg. Handed as per MoA the same day over to Enso-Gutzeit Oy, Kotka (544), (c/o Oy Finnlines Ltd, Helsinki /Helsingfors). Employed on Finnlines liner service from Finland to USEC.

30.5.1969: Sold to Wagria Reederei G.m.b.H. & Co. K.G., (c/o Sartori & Berger), Rendsburg, and chartered back for 18 months without change of name to Oy Finnlines Ltd.

1970: Renamed NESSHÖRN by Wagria Reederei G.m.b.H. & Co. K.G. after redelivery on Apr. 29 from charter.

1972: Transferred to Panama flag by Wagria Reederei G.m.b.H. & Co. K.G. Name now spelled without dots on Ö as NESSHORN.

11.1972: Sold to Tricontinental Transport Corp., (Simbouras Bros.), Piraeus, (c/o Syros Shipping Co. [L.M. Valmas & Son] Ltd., Epsom, U.K.), and renamed KAPTANIKOS.

1979: Sold to Bodium Shipping Inc., Panama, and renamed MAN CHEONG.

1980: Sold to Granard Line, Panama, (c/o Hesco Shipmanagement Ltd., Hong Kong).

1981: Renamed SEATRA by Granard Shipping Agencies (S) Pte. Ltd., Panama. Managers changed to Mondale Maritime & Enterprises (S) Pte. Ltd., Singapore.

1983: Sold to Indian shipbreakers and arrived on her last voyage at Madras Roads on Mar. 10.

19. **OUTOKUMPU** 1958–1985

Motor Ore Carrier, Singledecker
Call: OFYJ Ice class: I A
3,781 GRT, 1,798 NRT, 5,075 dwt
110.17 x 15.76 x 6.40 m
Diesel Engine 2 SA 8 cy. B & W 750 VTF 110
by A/S Burmeister & Wain's Maskin- og Skibsbyggeri, København
2,162 kW / 2,900 BHP   13 knots

ms OUTOKUMPU
Photo from FG-Shipping Oy Ab

24.1.1958: Launched by Valmet Oy, Pansion Telakka, Turku / Åbo (#232), and named OUTOKUMPU by Mrs. Liisa Bryk.

25.7.1958: Completed and delivered to Outokumpu Oy, (c/o Oy Finnlines Ltd), Helsinki /Helsingfors (1215). Employed by her owners carrying their supplies and products to and from Finland.

1985: Arrived on Oct. 11 from Rotterdam in ballast at Naantali and delivered on Oct. 16 to Nater Ltd. Oy for demolition.

20. AIRISMAA 1958–1964

Motor Tanker, one deck
Call: OFYS Ice class: I A
1,680 GRT, 1,041 NRT, 3,060 dwt
83.55 x 11.39 x 5.24 m
Diesel Engine 4 SA 8 cy. Werkspoor
by N.V. Werkspoor, Amsterdam
1,268 kW / 1,700 BHP   12 knots

mt AIRISMAA
Photo by Matti Pietikäinen

mt MARK VII ex AIRISMAA in January 1977
after delivery to her Greek buyers
Photo by Sea-Foto

29.3.1958: Launched by N.V. Arnhemsche Scheepsbouw Maats., Arnhem (#385), and named AIRISMAA by Mrs. Elvi Erho.

12.8.1958: Completed and delivered to Neste Oy, (c/o Oy Finnlines Ltd), Helsinki /Helsingfors (1216).

1.4.1964: Management taken over by Neste Oy, Helsinki.

26.10.1964: Home port changed to Naantali /Nådendal (29).

17.1.1977: Sold to Eviaki Maritime S.A., (Evangelos Kourbetsoglu), (c/o Avlis Shipping Ltd), Piraeus, and renamed MARK VII.

1978: Owners listed as Eviaki Shipping S.A., (c/o Avlis Shipping Ltd), Piraeus.

1985: Sold to Faliriki Shipping Co., Piraeus, and renamed NELLI. Name painted on the bows as NELLY.

1993: Sold to Karmel V Shipping Co., (Aegean Petroleum International Trading Inc.), Piraeus, and renamed AEGEAN V.

1996: Remeasured in accordance with the 1969 Convention as follows: 1,764 GT, – NT, 2,216 dwt.

21. FINNWOOD (I) 1959–1969

General Cargo Motorship, two decks – Open/Closed Shelterdecker
Call: OFZO   Ice class: I C
1,184/1,883 GRT, 537/1,028 NRT, 2,210/3,117 dwt
83.97 x 12.19 x 4.95/6.09 m
Diesel Engine 4 SA 8 cy. MAN G8V 40/60
by Maschinenfabrik Augsburg-Nürnberg A.G., Augsburg
1,236 kW / 1,680 BHP   12.5 knots

ms FINNWOOD was purchased from
Norway as ORIZABA
Photo by P-E. Johnsen

ms FINNWOOD
Photo by Skyfotos

2.7.1956: Launched by Ottensener Eisenwerk A.G., Hamburg-Altona (#499), and named EBBELLA by Mrs. Marie Ebbesen.

26.9.1956: Completed and delivered as ORIZABA to Skips A/S Sjøbro, (Niels Ebbesen), (c/o Ebbesens Rederi A/S), Oslo.

16.2.1959: Acquired by Enso-Gutzeit Oy, Kotka (546), (c/o Oy Finnlines Ltd, Helsinki /Helsingfors), and renamed FINNWOOD, when delivered on Mar. 3. Employed on Finnlines liner service from England to Finland.

26.6.1969: Sold to Gösta Lindström, Uno Söderström, Bror Lindholm and Bengt Karlsson, Porvoo /Borgå (551), acting on behalf of a company under formation and chartered back to Oy Finnlines Ltd until end 1969.

12.9.1969: Owners registered as Oy Gäddrag Rederi Ab, (Gösta Lindström), Porvoo.

16.12.1969: Renamed REX after redelivery from charter.

29.5.1973:	Sold to Locat-Locazioni Atrezzature S.p.A, Torino, and handed over to Marittima del Nord S.p.A., Genova. Renamed MAR DEL NORD when delivered on June 1.	1982:	Returned to Michele Looz, Napoli.
1976:	Sold to Michele Looz, Napoli.	!1982:	Transferred to Mi.Lo.Mar. S.r.l., Napoli, and renamed SRI LANKA.
1981:	Sold to Giuseppe Chiaschetti & Angelino e Filippo Mortolo, Napoli. Registered as open shelterdecker with following tonnage: 998 GRT, 523 NRT, 2,157 dwt.	1983:	Seriously damaged by an engine room fire, which broke out on July 9, when she was near Vieste during a voyage from Bari to Venice. Arrived later in tow outside the port of Manfredonia, where anchored for surveys. Left Manfredonia on Nov. 8 in tow for Ortona to be scrapped by Cantiere Romiti. Demolition started on July 3, 1984.

22. FINNSTAR (I)   1959–1973

General Cargo Motorship, two decks – Open Shelterdecker
Call: OFVS Ice class: I C
2,914 GRT, 1,383 NRT, 4,915 dwt
112.93 x 15.31 x 6.43 m
Diesel Engine 2 SA 6 cy. Sulzer
by Sulzer Bros. Ltd., Winterthur
2,207 kW / 3,000 BHP   13.5 knots

ms FINNSTAR was built as RAIMO-RAGNAR
Photo by F. W. Hawks

16.6.1955:	Launched by N.V. Scheepswerf en Machinefabriek "De Biesbosch", Dordrecht (#351), and named RAIMO-RAGNAR by Mrs. Greta Oker-Blom.	26.6.1959:	Acquired by Merivienti Oy, (Enso-Gutzeit Oy), (c/o Oy Finnlines Ltd), Helsinki /Helsingfors (1227), and renamed FINNSTAR. Entered Finnlines liner service from Finland to USEC.
24.10.1955:	Completed and delivered to Lovisa Rederi Ab, (Ab R. Nordström & Co. Oy), Loviisa /Lovisa (489).	6.1962:	Transferred to Finnlines Mediterranean service.

ms FINNSTAR
Photo by Skyfotos

ms MALDIVE STAR ex FINNSTAR
Photo by Airfoto

31.12.1970: Owners amalgamated with the parent company Enso-Gutzeit Oy as per EGM resolution on Apr. 17. Merger registered on Aug. 3, 1971.

10.8.1971: Home port changed to Kotka (580).

6.4.1973: Sold to Maldives Shipping Ltd., Male, and renamed MALDIVE STAR when deliverd on Apr. 13.

1984: Sold to Pakistan shipbreakers and arrived on Feb. 5 at Gadani Beach for demolition.

23. FINNBIRCH   1959–1973

General Cargo Motorship, two decks – Open Shelterdecker
Call: OFSZ Ice class: I C
2,731 GRT, 1,344 NRT, 4,910 dwt
112.50 x 14.60 x 6.65 m
Diesel Engine 2 SA 8 cy. MAN
by Maschinenfabrik Augsburg-Nürnberg A.G., Augsburg
2,207 kW / 3,000 BHP   13.5 knots

ms FINNBIRCH was completed as MARTTI-RAGNAR
Photo by Holger Nyström

ms FINNBIRCH
Photo from Matti Pietikäinen

9.4.1953: Launched by N.V. Scheepswerf en Machinefabriek "De Biesbosch", Dordrecht (#341), and named MARTTI-RAGNAR by Mrs. Nina Nordström.

25.7.1953: Completed and delivered to Lovisa Rederi Ab, (Ab R. Nordström & Co. Oy), Loviisa /Lovisa (479).

19.8.1959: Acquired by Enso-Gutzeit Oy, Kotka (548), (c/o Oy Finnlines Ltd, Helsinki /Helsingfors), and renamed FINNBIRCH. Entered Finnlines liner service from Finland to USEC.

8.1962: Transferred to Finnlines Mediterranean service.

The Greek ms PANOREA ex FINNBIRCH
Photo by Airfoto

16.4.1973: Sold to Dimitra Compania Naviera S.A., (c/o Kollintzas Marine Co. S.A.), Piraeus, and renamed PANOREA.

5.1976: Sold to Guernica Shipping Inc., (A.J. Politis), (c/o Tamita Shipping Co. Ltd.), Piraeus, and renamed JOHN P.

1979: Arrived in tow at Manfredonia on Sep. 21 with leaks, having left Rijeka on Sep. 17 for Jeddah, and laid up there, later under arrest.

1986: Sold to Fer Mar S.N.C. for demolition at Ravenna, where work started in February.

24. FINNPINE (I)   1959–1967

General Cargo Motorship, two decks – Open/Closed Shelterdecker
Call: OGAU Ice class: I C
1,317/1,999 GRT, 615/1,268 NRT, 2,290/3,050 dwt
78.59 x 12.53 x 4.96/5.90 m
Diesel Engine 4 SA 8 cy. MAN G8V 40/60
by Maschinenfabrik Augsburg-Nürnberg A.G., Augsburg
1,194 kW / 1,600 BHP   12.5 knots

ms FINNPINE
Photo by Skyfotos

ms DOMINION TRADER ex FINNPINE
Photo by Michael Cassar

5.10.1957:	Launched by Paul Lindenau Schiffswerft & Maschinenfabrik, Kiel-Friedrichsort (#107), and named NYX by Mrs. Annie Steen.	31.8.1967:	Sold to Dominion Shipping Co. Ltd., (c/o Bank of Nova Scotia Trust Co. [Cayman] Ltd.), George Town, Grand Cayman, and renamed DOMINION TRADER when delivered on Sep. 6.
9.1.1958:	Completed and delivered to A/S Nyegaard & Co. (90/100) og Aksel Molvigs Rederi A/S (10/100), (Sverre Blix), Oslo.	1975:	Sold to Sealink Co. Ltd., (Thomaides Bros.), (c/o Eurointerlink Ltd.), Limassol, without change of name.
24.10.1959:	Acquired by Enso-Gutzeit Oy, Kotka (549), (c/o Oy Finnlines Ltd, Helsinki /Helsingfors), and renamed FINNPINE, when delivered the same day. Employed on Finnlines liner service from England to Finland.	1978:	Fire broke out in her engine room on Nov. 16, while lying at anchor in Sidon roads loaded with 2,370 tons sugar and steel for Tartous. Engine room and accommodation, boat deck and wheelhouse totally gutted by fire. Drove aground in Sidon by strong winds on Dec. 1 and broke in two.

25. SIMPELE 1960–1973

General Cargo Motorship, two decks – Open Shelterdecker
Call: OGBU Ice class: I A
1,994 GRT, 1,018 NRT, 3,650 dwt
96.88 x 14.20 x 5.83 m
Diesel Engine 4 SA 6 cy. MAN K6Z 57/80-A
by Maschinenfabrik Augsburg-Nürnberg A.G., Augsburg
1,942 kW / 2,640 BHP   13 knots

3.5.1960:	Launched by Rauma-Repola Oy, Rauman Telakka, Rauma /Raumo (#107), and named SIMPELE by Mrs. Tellervo Walden.	26.2.1973:	Sold to Ab Vasa Shipping Oy, (Sixten Erickson), Vaasa /Vasa (238), and renamed LISA.
22.9.1960:	Completed and delivered to Yhtyneet Paperitehtaat Oy (United Paper Mills Ltd.), Rauma /Raumo (601), (c/o Oy Finnlines Ltd, Helsinki /Helsingfors). Employed mainly on Finnlines Continent service.	14.2.1974:	Sold to Oy Vasa Ocean Carriers Ab, (Jan Wasenius), Vaasa.

ms SIMPELE
Photo by Skyfotos

ms LISA ex SIMPELE at Rauma
Photo by K. Brzoza

ms AI SHAN ex SIMPELE
Photo by Michael Cassar

17.7.1975:	Sold to Luen Yick Shipping Co., Macao, (Yick Fung Shipping & Enterprises Co. Ltd., Hong Kong, as registered owners). Renamed AI SHAN and registered in Mogadishu, Somalia.
1976:	Transferred to Panama flag by Yick Fung Shipping & Enterprises Co. Ltd.
1980:	Taken over by China Ocean Shipping Co. (COSCO), Guangzhou / Canton, and renamed LING JIANG.
1986:	Transferred to Zhejiang Ocean Shipping Company (COSCO ZHEJIANG), Ningbo.
10.1994:	Transferred to Zhejiang Haimen Shipping Service Co., Ningbo, and renamed ZHE HAI 319.
12.1997:	*The above latest change of owners and name not yet listed in Lloyd's Register.*

26. JURMO
1960–1964

Motor Tanker, one deck
Call: OGCY Ice class: II
11,401 GRT, 6,519 NRT, 16,137 dwt
165.21 x 20.88 x 8.86 m
Diesel Engine 2 DA 8 cy. MAN D8Z 60/110
by Maschinenfabrik Augsburg-Nürnberg A.G., Augsburg
4,847 kW / 6,500 BHP   13.5 knots

mt NYHAMMER was renamed JURMO in 1960 by Neste Oy
Photo by P-E. Johnsen

mt JURMO
Photo by Skyfotos

15.12.1953:	Launched by Nordseewerke Emden G.m.b.H., Emden (#255), for D/S A/S Alaska, (Christian Haaland), Haugesund, and named NYHAMMER by Mrs. Elisabeth Krogh.	1.4.1964:	Management taken over by Neste Oy, Helsinki.
		19.10.1964:	Home port changed to Naantali /Nådendal (28).
31.3.1954:	Completed and delivered to Skibs A/S Hilda Knudsen, (Christian Haaland), Haugesund.	18.7.1968:	Sold to Ensign Shipping Co. S.A., Piraeus, (Harry Hadjipateras Bros. Ltd., London), and renamed KATINGO H.
6.6.1959:	Entered lay-up at Haugesund.	1973:	Sold to Aegean Shipping Corp., Monrovia, and renamed REGINA.
9.11.1960:	Acquired by Neste Oy, (c/o Oy Finnlines Ltd), Helsinki /Helsingfors (1257), and renamed JURMO. Delivered on Nov. 9 at Haugesund, from where towed by ms Herkules to Hamburg for repairs. Delivered from shipyard on Dec. 19.	1974:	Sold to Spanish shipbreakers and arrived at Carthagena on Sep. 18 for demolition.

27. KAIPOLA (I)   1961–1969
VARJAKKA (I)   1969–1974

General Cargo Motorship, two decks – Open Shelterdecker
Call: OGBV Ice class: I A
2,203 GRT, 1,099 NRT, 3,570 dwt
97.86 x 14.20 x 5.83 m
Diesel Engine 4 SA 6 cy. MAN K6Z 57/80-A
by Maschinenfabrik Augsburg-Nürnberg A.G., Augsburg
1,942 kW / 2,640 BHP   13 knots

ms KAIPOLA
Photo by Skyfotos

ms VARJAKKA
Photo by Matti Pietikäinen

29.9.1960:	Launched by Rauma-Repola Oy, Rauman Telakka, Rauma /Raumo (#108), and named KAIPOLA by Mrs. Armi Oksanen.
25.1.1961:	Completed and delivered to Yhtyneet Paperitehtaat Oy (United Paper Mills Ltd.), Rauma /Raumo (602), (c/o Oy Finnlines Ltd, Helsinki /Helsingfors). Inaugurated on her first voyage Finnlines service to Biscay and thereafter Finnlines Mediterranean service.
23.9.1969:	Sold to Oulu Oy, Oulu /Uleåborg (514), and renamed VARJAKKA. Managers remained Oy Finnlines Ltd.
1969:	Remeasured as above. Her original tonnages were: 1,988 GRT, 1,017 NRT, 3,570 dwt
9.4.1974:	Sold to Partrederi Lux, (Gösta Lindström), Porvoo /Borgå (568), and renamed SVANÖ. *(In Supplements of the Finnish Merchant Marine -register book 1974 the owners stated as Rederibolaget Lux).*
5.11.1974:	Sold to Oy Gäddrag Rederi Ab, (Gösta Lindström), Porvoo.
18.6.1975:	Sold to Luen Yick Shipping Co., Macao, (Yick Fung Shipping & Enterprises Co. Ltd., Hong Kong, as registered owners). Renamed PO SEA and registered in Mogadishu, Somalia.
1976:	Transferred to Panama flag by Yick Fung Shipping & Enterprises Co. Ltd.
1980:	Taken over by China Ocean Shipping Co. (COSCO), and renamed AO JIANG.
1986:	Transferred to Zhejiang Ocean Shipping Company (COSCO ZHEJIANG), Wenzhou.
3.1994:	Transferred to Zhejiang Jinfan Shipping Co. and renamed JIN YUE.
12.1997:	*The above latest change of owners and name not yet listed in Lloyd's Register.*

28. FINNALPINO (I) 1961–1971

General Cargo Motorship, two decks – Open/Closed Shelterdecker
Call: OGER Ice class: I C
2,883/4,595 GRT, 1,295/2,379 NRT, 4,600/5,800 dwt
114.31 x 15.42 x 6.20/7.05 m
Diesel Engine 2 SA 7 cy. Stork
by Gebr. Stork & Co. N.V., Hengelo
2,686 kW / 3,600 BHP   15 knots

6.2.1958:	Launched by A/S Stord Verft, Lervik Stord (#39), and named BESSEGGEN by Mrs. Patricia Jacobs.
5.6.1958:	Completed and delivered to Rederiet Besseggen A/S, (Chr. Østberg), Oslo.

ms FINNALPINO
Photo by Esa Hänninen

The Greek ms DANAOS ex FINNALPINO
Photo by Michael Cassar

1.6.1961: Acquired by Merivienti Oy, (Enso-Gutzeit Oy), (c/o Oy Finnlines Ltd) Helsinki /Helsingfors (1272), and renamed FINNALPINO when delivered on June 16. Employed on Finnlines Mediterranean service.

31.12.1970: Owners amalgamated with the parent company Enso-Gutzeit Oy as per EGM resolution on Apr. 17. Merger registered on Aug. 3, 1971.

3.8.1971: Home port changed to Kotka (579).

14.12.1971: Sold to Frasanav S.p.A. di Navigazione, Palermo, and renamed CITTA DI FIRENZE.

6.1974: Sold to Danaos Shipping Co., (Christos D. Kessaniotis), (c/o Tramp Shipping Agencies S.A.), Piraeus, and renamed DANAOS.

1978: Sustained serious hull damage on Dec. 3 when in collision with ms Satsuma 17 miles north of Cherbourg during a voyage from Liverpool to Gdynia in ballast. Towed to Cherbourg later the same day. Found beyond an economical repair and sold for scrapping to D. Miguel Martins y Hijos at Vigo, where arrived in tow on Jan. 4, 1979. Demolition began at Guixar-Vigo on June 20, 1979.

29. FINNEAGLE (I)   1962–1971
TROLLEHOLM   1971–1976
FINNEAGLE (I)   1976–1978

General Cargo /Container Motorship, two decks – Open/Closed Shelterdecker
Call: OGGA Ice class: I B
6,449/8,816 GRT, 3,399/4,861 NRT, 8,014/11,200 dwt
150.38 x 18.74 x 7.05/8.52 m
Diesel Engine 2 SA 6 cy. B&W 662 VT2 BF-140
by Fried. Krupp Masch., Abt. Dieselmotoren, Essen
4,781 kW / 6,500 BHP   16 knots

ms FINNEAGLE
Photo by Skyfotos

3.2.1962: Launched by Rheinstahl Nordseewerke G.m.b.H., Emden (#338), and named FINNEAGLE by Mrs. Anna Nurmela.

3.5.1962: Completed and delivered as general cargo vessel to Enso-Gutzeit Oy, Kotka (553), (c/o Oy Finnlines Ltd, Helsinki /Helsingfors). Employed on Finnlines liner service from Finland to USEC.

6.1968: Delivered after lengthening by a cargo section of 14.7 metres and conversion to a semi-container vessel at the Builders. Her original particulars as general cargo vessel were:
5,097/7,651 GRT, 2,353/3,965 NRT, 7,180/9,178 dwt
135.68 x 18.74 x 7.29/8.32 m

21.9.1971: Renamed TROLLEHOLM when time-chartered to Ab. Svenska Atlant Linien, Göteborg, and operated by Atlantic Gulf Service Ab., Göteborg.

ms TROLLEHOLM
Photo by Matti Pietikäinen

16.12.1976:	Reverted to her original name FINNEAGLE and was operated by Atlantic Cargo Services AB, Göteborg.	
5.9.1978:	Sold to Everett-Orient Line Inc., Monrovia, (c/o Everett Steamship Corp. S.A., Tokyo), and renamed ROSSEVERETT.	

Registered as open shelterdecker with following tonnage:
6,187 GRT, 3,442 NRT, 8,014 dwt

1987: Sold to Chinese shipbreakers and left Kobe on Apr. 25 for China to be broken up.

30. FINNCLIPPER 1962–1978

General Cargo /Container Motorship, two decks – Open/Closed Shelterdecker
Call: OGGB   Ice class: I B
6,449/8,816 GRT, 3,399/4,861 NRT, 8,014/11,200 dwt
150.38 x 18.74 x 7.05/8.52 m
Diesel Engine 2 SA 6 cy. B&W 662 VT2 BF-140
by Fried. Krupp Masch., Abt. Dieselmotoren, Essen
4,781 kW / 6,500 BHP   16 knots

ms FINNCLIPPER in Finnlines colours
Photo by Skyfotos

ms FINNCLIPPER with AGS funnel mark
Photo by Aeromarine

15.3.1962:	Launched by Rheinstahl Nordseewerke G.m.b.H., Emden (#339), and named FINNCLIPPER by Mrs. Siiri Järvinen.
18.6.1962:	Completed and delivered as general cargo vessel to Enso-Gutzeit Oy, Kotka (554), (c/o Oy Finnlines Ltd, Helsinki /Helsingfors). Employed on Finnlines liner service from Finland to USEC.
26.7.1968:	Delivered after lengthening by a cargo section of 14.7 metres and conversion to a semi-container vessel at the Builders. Her original particulars as general cargo vessel were: 5,097/7,651 GRT, 2,353/3,965 NRT, 7,180/9,178 dwt 135.68 x 18.74 x 7.29/8.32 m
9.1971:	Time-chartered to Atlantic Gulf Service Ab., Göteborg.
12.1976:	Reverted to her original colours and was operated by Atlantic Cargo Services AB, Göteborg.
5.9.1978:	Sold to Everett-Orient Line Inc., Monrovia, (c/o Everett Steamship Corp. S.A., Tokyo), and renamed LEONOREVERETT.
1978:	Registered as open shelterdecker with following tonnage: 6,187 GRT, 3,442 NRT, 8,014 dwt
1986:	Sold to Taiwan shipbreakers and arrived at Kaohsiung on July 7 for demolition.

31. HANSA EXPRESS 1962–1966
FINNDANA 1966–1967

Passenger /RoRo Cargo Motor Ferry, three decks – Open Shelterdecker, bow and stern doors
Passengers: 178 berths
Call: OGFZ Ice class: I A
2,977 GRT, 1,096 NRT, 835 dwt
96.00 x 15.85 x 4.47 m
2 Diesel Engines 2 SA each 6 cy. NOHAB M66TS
by Nydqvist & Holm AB, Trollhättan
2 x 2,118 kW / 2 x 2,880 BHP
Total 4,236 kW / 5,760 BHP 16 knots Twin screw

ms HANSA EXPRESS as built
Photo from Matti Pietikäinen

ms HANSA EXPRESS after lengthening
Photo from Matti Pietikäinen

3.1960:	Order placed with Hanseatische Werft G.m.b.H., Hamburg, by Rederi Ab Vikinglinjen, Mariehamn, for Parainen /Pargas – Kapellskär service, but the contract was later cancelled.	18.1.1962:	Memorandum of Agreement signed between Hanseatische Werft G.m.b.H., Hamburg, and Merivienti Oy, Helsinki /Helsingfors, for delivery on June 15, 1962.
15.9.1961:	Keel laid on speculation by Hanseatische Werft G.m.b.H., Hamburg.	2.2.1962:	Launched by Hanseatische Werft G.m.b.H., Hamburg-Harburg (#20), and named HANSA EXPRESS by Mrs. Eleanor Piironen.

ms FINNDANA
Photo by Matti Pietikäinen

ms GRYF ex HANSA EXPRESS in Gdansk
Photo from Matti Pietikäinen

ms EOLOS ex HANSA EXPRESS in 1990 at
Kerkyra (Corfu)
Photo by Raimo A. Wirrankoski

18.7.1962: Completed and delivered to Merivienti Oy, (Enso-Gutzeit Oy), Helsinki (1293), (c/o Oy Finnlines Ltd).

24.7.1962: Inaugurated a new passenger/roro cargo liner service from Hanko /Hangö via Visby/Slite to Travemünde.

4.1963:	Delivered after lengthening by a section of 7.8 metres during January–April at Kieler Howaldtswerke A.G., Kiel. Her original particulars were: 133 berths, 40 pullman chairs, 419 deck pass. 2,268 GRT, 695 NRT, 660 dwt 88.20 x 15.85 x 4.40 m Returned on Apr. 16 to Hanko – Travemünde service, from May 12 via Slite, and moved on Sep. 1 to Helsinki – Kalmar – Travemünde line.	1.1.1970:	Transferred to Polskie Linie Oceaniczne (Polish Ocean Lines), Gdynia.
		1973:	Entered Gdansk – Helsinki service. First departure from Helsinki on June 16.
		2.4.1976:	Transferred to Polska Zegluga Baltycka (Polish Baltic Shipping Co.), Kolobrzeg.
1.9.1964:	Swedish port of call changed to Karlskrona.	1981:	Sold to Fragmar Shipping Corp., Piraeus, (c/o Fr. Fragoudakis S.A. [FRAGLINE], Athens), and renamed EOLOS. Employed on Patras – Igoumenitsa – Corfu – Brindisi ferry service.
1.1.1965:	New Swedish port of call, Nynäshamn, added to the route.		
25.2.1966:	Renamed FINNDANA by Merivienti Oy, while drydocked in Kiel and moved on Apr. 1 to Helsinki – Copenhagen service.	1994:	Remeasured in accordance with the 1969 Convention as follows: 4,275 GT, 1.828 NT, 585 dwt
1.10.1966:	Chartered to TT-Linie G.m.b.H. for Trelleborg – Travemünde service.	1995:	Sold to International Lines, (A.K. Ventouris Shipping Co.), Piraeus, and renamed AGIOS VASSILIOS. Sailing on Igoumenitsa – Brindisi line.
15.6.1967:	Sold through Centrala Morska Importowo – Exportowa "Centromor" P.P., Gdansk, to Polska Zegluga Morska (Polish Steamship Co.), Szczecin, and renamed GRYF. Inaugurated on June 21 the first Polish ferry service, between Swinoujscie and Ystad.	1996:	Sold to Watermark Navigation Inc., Panama. Managers remained A.K. Ventouris Shipping Co., Piraeus.

32. VAASA 1962–1963

General Cargo Motorship, two decks – Open/Closed Shelterdecker
Call: OGGC Ice class: I B Car door and lift on port side
499/1,099 GRT, 283/763 NRT, 1,105/1,917 dwt
74.47 x 10 82 x 3.67/5.02 m
Diesel Engine 4 SA 8 cy. MWM TBRH348AU
by Motoren-Werke Mannheim A.G., Mannheim
956 kW / 1,300 BHP   12 knots

ms VAASA
Photo by P-E. Johnsen

The Portuguese ms LAGOA ex VAASA
Photo from Matti Pietikäinen

29.9.1962: Launched by Falkenbergs Varv Ab., Falkenberg (#134), and named VAASA by Mrs. Lisa Ahlbeck.

15.12.1962: Completed and delivered to Rederi Ab Vasa-Umeå, (F. Evert Nyman), Vaasa /Vasa (210). Managed by Oy Finnlines Ltd, Helsinki /Helsingfors. Entered Finnlines liner service from England to Finland. *(In the Finnish Merchant Marine -register books 1963–1964 the owners stated bilingually as Rederi Ab Wasa-Umeå – Varustamo Oy Vaasa-Uumaja).*

5.1963: Management taken over by Rederi Ab Vasa-Umeå.

Sailed during high seasons in July 1963 and 1964 along with ss Örnen daily between Vaasa and Örnsköldsvik carrying cars and their passengers.

18.9.1964: Sold to A/S Ganger Rolf, A/S Bonheur, A/S Borgå, A/S Jelølinjen & Den Norske Middelhavslinje A/S, (Fred. Olsen & Co.), Oslo, and renamed BURE.

26.11.1971: Sold to Empresa Insulana de Navegação S.a.r.L., Lisboa, and renamed LAGOA.

1973: Reported erroneously by Lloyd's Register as sold to Jose Luis Blanco Aquero, San Esteban de Pravia, and renamed Somar for the delivery voyage to breakers at Gandia. – She was, however, mixed up with ss Lagoa 2,415/50 of Cia. de Nav. Carregadores Açoreanos, which actually was sold for demolition. – Re-entered in Lloyd's Register in 1977 as Lagoa.

1974: Owners amalgamated with Companhia Colonial de Navegação S.a.r.L., Lisboa, and Companhia de Navegação Carregadores Açoreanos, Ponta Delgada, forming after merger a new company called C.T.M. – Companhia Portuguesa de Transportes Marítimos, E.P., Lisboa.

5.1985: Owners went into liquidation and Lagoa was acquired by Vianalis Ltda., (c/o Empresa de Transportes Marítimos Ltda.), Lisboa.

2.1991: Sold to Solmar S.A., São Tomé, São Tomé & Principe, and renamed MAGO.
Name reported painted as MAGOS on the ship.

1996: Sold to TOMEMAR – Sociedade Industria, Pesca, Turismo & Agricultura, São Tomé.

12.1997: New GT and NT in accordance with the 1969 Convention not yet reported to Lloyd's Register.

33. TERVI   1963–1964

Motor Tanker, one deck
Call: OGGR Ice class: I A
11,121 GRT, 4,165 NRT, 15,697 dwt
163.87 x 20.03 x 8.98 m
Diesel Engine 2 SA 8 cy. Götaverken 630/1300
by Ab. Götaverken, Göteborg
4,891 kW / 6,650 BHP   14.5 knots

mt TERVI
Photo from Krister Bång

mt JUSSARA ex TERVI
Photo by FotoFlite

1.8.1962:	Launched by Rauma-Repola Oy, Rauman telakka, Rauma /Raumo (#139), and named TERVI by Mrs. Sylvi Kekkonen.
2.4.1963:	Completed and delivered to Neste Oy, Naantali / Nådendal (24), (c/o Oy Finnlines Ltd, Helsinki / Helsingfors).
1.4.1964:	Management taken over by Neste Oy, Helsinki.
29.11.1984:	Sold to Ridgeway Maritime Inc., Panama, (c/o Polembros Maritime Co. Ltd., [Spiridon Polemis], Piraeus), and renamed JUSSARA.
1984:	Remeasured as 9,143 GRT, 5,093 NRT, 16,320 dwt
1986:	Transferred to Jussara Shipping Co., (c/o Polembros Maritime Co. Ltd.), Piraeus.
1988:	Home port changed to Andros.
1994:	Sold to Andros Maritime Co. Ltd., Valletta, (c/o Miramar Enterprises, Havana, Cuba).
1994:	Remeasured in accordance with the 1969 Convention as follows: 10,841 GT, 6,264 NT, 16,320 dwt

34. FINNFOREST (I) 1963–1978

General Cargo /Container Motorship, two decks – Open/Closed Shelterdecker
Call: OGIL Ice class: I B
6,602/8,981 GRT, 3,528/5,078 NRT, 8,190/11,510 dwt
152.32 x 18.74 x 7.11/8.58 m
Diesel Engine 2 SA 6 cy. B&W 662 VT2 BF-140
by Fried. Krupp Masch., Abt. Dieselmotoren, Essen
4,781 kW / 6,500 BHP   16 knots

ms FINNFOREST
Photo by Skyfotos

ms BRADEVERETT ex FINNFOREST
Photo from Donald Mac Fie

26.3.1963: Launched by Rheinstahl Nordseewerke G.m.b.H., Emden (#345), and named FINNFOREST by Mrs. Lola Luostarinen.

28.6.1963: Completed and delivered as general cargo vessel to Enso-Gutzeit Oy, Kotka (555), (c/o Oy Finnlines Ltd, Helsinki /Helsingfors). Employed on Finnlines liner service from Finland to USEC.

23.8.1968: Delivered after lengthening by a cargo section of 12.6 metres and conversion to a semi-container vessel at the Builders. Her original particulars as general cargo vessel were:
5,735/7,947 GRT, 2,572/4,195 NRT, 7,610/9,674 dwt
139.72 x 18.74 x 7.29/8.34 m

1973: Time-chartered to Atlantic Gulf Service Ab., Göteborg.

12.1976: Reverted to her original colours and was operated by Atlantic Cargo Services AB, Göteborg.

6.9.1978: Sold to Everett-Orient Line Inc., Monrovia, (c/o Everett Steamship Corp. S.A., Tokyo), and renamed BRADEVERETT.

1979: Registered as open shelterdecker with following tonnage:
6,306 GRT, 3,575 NRT, 8,269 dwt

1988: Sold to Taiwan shipbreakers and arrived at Kaohsiung on May 24 for demolition.

35. FINNSEAL

1964–1975

General Cargo Motorship, two decks – Open/Closed Shelterdecker
Call: OGKH Ice class: I A
1,735/2,738 GRT, 795/1,399 NRT, 2,530/3,727 dwt
91.55 x 14.03 x 5.42/6.67 m
Diesel Engine 2 SA 6 cy. Sulzer 6TD56
by the Shipbuilders
1,765 kW / 2,400 BHP   13.5 knots

ms FINNSEAL
Photo by Skyfotos

24.3.1964: Launched by Wärtsilä-yhtymä Oy – Wärtsilä-koncernen Ab, Crichton-Vulcan, Turku /Åbo (#1118), and named FINNSEAL by Mrs. Linda Tanner.

10.7.1964: Completed and delivered to Enso-Gutzeit Oy, Kotka (557), (c/o Oy Finnlines Ltd, Helsinki /Helsingfors). Employed on Finnlines liner service from Finland to England.

24.6.1975: Sold to Luen Yick Shipping Co., Macao, (Yick Fung Shipping & Enterprises Co. Ltd., Hong Kong, as registered owners). Renamed KUN SHAN and registered in Mogadishu, Somalia.

9.1976: Transferred to Panama flag by Yick Fung Shipping & Enterprises Co. Ltd.

ms FINNSEAL
Photo by Matti Pietikäinen

1985: Sold to Ceram Shipping Inc., Panama, (Yick Fung Shipping & Enterprises Co. Ltd., Hong Kong).

1986: Sold to Shekou Shipping & Transportation Co. Ltd., Shekou, China, and renamed HUANG LONG.

1992: Transferred to Guangdong Shantou Water Transport General Co., Shantou, China, and renamed AN DA.

1994: Remeasured in accordance with the 1969 Convention as follows:
2,674 GT, 1,146 NT, 3,785 dwt

36. LOTILA (I)   1964–1974
FINNTUBE   1974–1975

General Cargo Motorship, two decks – Open/Closed Shelterdecker
Call: OGKI Ice class: I A
1,739/2,740 GRT, 787/1,390 NRT, 2,530/3,725 dwt
91.55 x 14.03 x 5.42/6.67 m
Diesel Engine 2 SA 6 cy. Sulzer 6TD56
by the Shipbuilders
1,765 kW / 2,400 BHP   13.5 knots

25.5.1964: Launched by Wärtsilä-yhtymä Oy – Wärtsilä-koncernen Ab, Crichton-Vulcan, Turku /Åbo (#1119), and named LOTILA by Mrs. Greta-Stina Brandt.

2.10.1964: Completed and delivered to Yhtyneet Paperitehtaat Oy, (United Paper Mills Ltd.), Rauma /Raumo (607), (c/o Oy Finnlines Ltd, Helsinki /Helsingfors).

15.1.1974: Sold to Oy Etnarör Ab, Lappohja /Lappvik, (Hanko / Hangö 231), and renamed FINNTUBE. Managers remained Oy Finnlines Ltd.

15.2.1975: Sold to Oy Torlines Ab, (Tor Johansson), Tammisaari /Ekenäs (114). Still managed by Oy Finnlines Ltd without change of name.

26.6.1975: Sold to Luen Yick Shipping Co., Macao, (Yick Fung Shipping & Enterprises Co. Ltd., Hong Kong, as registered owners). Renamed PING SHAN and registered in Mogadishu, Somalia.

9.1976: Transferred to Panama flag by Yick Fung Shipping & Enterprises Co. Ltd.

ms LOTILA
Photo by Skyfotos

ms FINNTUBE
Photo by Foto-Martin

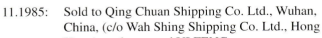

The Chinese ms YI FENG ex LOTILA in Hong Kong
Photo from K. Brzoza

11.1985: Sold to Qing Chuan Shipping Co. Ltd., Wuhan, China, (c/o Wah Shing Shipping Co. Ltd., Hong Kong), and renamed YI FENG.

10.1990: Sold to Federal Shipping Ltd., Panama, (c/o Al Vakil Enterprises, Dubai), and renamed LILY.

1991: Transferred by Federal Shipping Ltd. to St. Vincent flag with Kingstown as home port.

1993: Managers changed to Orange Shipping.

1993: Sold for scrapping to Rahul Ship Breaking Co. in Bombay, where arrived on Dec. 8. Demolition began on Jan. 27, 1994.

37. REKOLA / FINNSTRIP

1964–1974
1974–1975

General Cargo Motorship, two decks – Open/Closed Shelterdecker
Call: OGKJ Ice class: I A
1,686/2,731 GRT, 752/1,397 NRT, 2,571/3,725 dwt
91.55 x 14.03 x 5.42/6.67 m
Diesel Engine 2 SA 6 cy. Sulzer 6TD56
by the Shipbuilders
1,765 kW / 2,400 BHP   13.5 knots

ms REKOLA
Photo from FG-Shipping Oy Ab

ms FINNSTRIP
Photo from Matti Pietikäinen

19.8.1964:	Launched by Wärtsilä-yhtymä Oy – Wärtsilä-koncernen Ab, Crichton-Vulcan, Turku /Åbo (#1120), and named REKOLA by Mrs. Meri Walden.
27.11.1964:	Completed and delivered to Yhtyneet Paperitehtaat Oy, (United Paper Mills Ltd.), Rauma /Raumo (609), (c/o Oy Finnlines Ltd, Helsinki /Helsingfors).
15.1.1974:	Sold to Oy Etnarör Ab, Lappohja /Lappvik, (Hanko /Hangö 232), and renamed FINNSTRIP. Managers remained Oy Finnlines Ltd.
15.2.1975:	Sold to Oy Torlines Ab, (Tor Johansson), Tammisaari /Ekenäs (115). Still managed by Oy Finnlines Ltd without change of name.

10.7.1975:	Sold to Luen Yick Shipping Co., Macao, (Yick Fung Shipping & Enterprises Co. Ltd., Hong Kong, as registered owners). Renamed DU SHAN and registered in Mogadishu, Somalia.		1977:	Transferred to Panama flag by Yick Fung Shipping & Enterprises Co. Ltd.
			1985:	Sold to Fu Mow & Co. Ltd. for demolition in Junk Bay, Hong Kong. Work commenced in August.

38. FINNENSO   1964–1964
FINNBOSTON   1964–1973

General Cargo /Container Motorship, two decks – Open/Closed Shelterdecker
Call: OGKM Ice class: I B
6,391/9,047 GRT, 3,505/5,442 NRT, 8,732/10,895 dwt, 168 TEU
151.54 x 18.94 x 7.81/8.61 m
Diesel Engine 2 SA 6 cy. Sulzer 6RND68
by the Shipbuilders
5,296 kW / 7,200 BHP   16 knots

ms FINNBOSTON in Antwerp
Photo from Matti Pietiläinen

12.6.1964:	Launched by Wärtsilä-yhtymä Oy – Wärtsilä-koncernen Ab, Crichton-Vulcan, Turku /Åbo (#1122), to order of Enso-Gutzeit Oy, Kotka, and named FINNENSO by Mrs. Pirkko Halle.			Her original particulars as general cargo vessel were: 5,543/7,914 GRT, 2,789/4,272 NRT, 7,733/9,473 dwt 137.66 x 18.94 x 7.47/8.37 m
25.8.1964:	Sold while fitting out to Amer-Tupakka Oy, Helsinki /Helsingfors, and renamed FINNBOSTON.		1972:	In collision on May 24 with German ms Doris H two miles off Kylmäpihlaja pilot station near Rauma / Raumo. Doris H sank, but her crew was saved.
12.12.1964:	Completed and delivered as general cargo vessel to Amer-Tupakka Oy, (c/o Oy Finnlines Ltd), Helsinki (1333). Employed on Finnlines liner service to USEC.		12.7.1973:	Sold to China Navigation Co. Ltd., (John Swire & Sons Ltd.), London, and renamed ASIAN EXPORTER while operated by Asia Australia Express.
1969:	Arrived on Jan. 22 at Valmet Oy, Helsingin Telakka, Helsinki, for lengthening by a cargo section of 13.88 metres and delivered on Mar. 23 after conversion to a semi-container vessel.		4.1975:	Renamed POYANG by China Navigation Co. Ltd., London.
			1977:	Home port changed to Hong Kong.

ms ASIAN EXPORTER ex FINNBOSTON
Photo from Matti Pietikäinen

ms POYANG ex FINNBOSTON
Photo from Matti Pietikäinen

9.1981: Sold to China Ocean Shipping Co., Qingdao / Tsingtao, and renamed HUE LU.

1983: Renamed FENG NING by China Ocean Shipping Co. (COSCO), Qingdao /Tsingtao.

1983: Registered as closed shelterdecker with following tonnage:
8,705 GRT, 5,413 NRT, 10,936 dwt

1986: Transferred to Hebei Province Subcorporation China Ocean Shipping Co. (COSCO HEBEI), Qingdao / Tsingtao.

1990: Home port restyled as Qinhuangdao.

1994: Remeasured in accordance with the 1969 Convention as follows:
9,237 GT, 5,941 NT, 10,936 dwt

1995: Sold to Eckardt Marine G.m.b.H., Hamburg, and transferred to St. Vincent flag. The name shortened as FENG for last voyage from Singapore on Feb. 11 to Alang, India. Sold to Lucky Steel Industries, Bhavnager, and anchored off Alang on Feb. 19 and beached there on Mar. 2 for demolition.

39. **FINNBROD**	1965–1967
FINNMILL	1967–1968
CONCORDIA FINN	1968–1968
FINNMILL	1968–1970
CONCORDIA FINN	1970–1971

General Cargo Motorship, two decks – Open/Closed Shelterdecker
Call: OGKP   Ice class: I B
3,028/4,822 GRT, 1,424/2,514 NRT, 4,637/6,112 dwt
118.00 x 16.30 x 6.12/7.11 m
Diesel Engine 2 SA 6 cy. B&W 650-VT2 BF-110
by A/S Burmeister & Wain's Maskin- og Skibsbyggeri, København
3,089 kW / 4,200 BHP   16 knots

ms FINNBROD
Photo by Esa Hänninen

ms FINNMILL
Photo from FG-Shipping Oy Ab

ms CONCORDIA FINN
Photo by P-E. Johnsen

3.7.1964:	Launched by Valmet Oy, Helsingin Telakka, Helsinki /Helsingfors (#225), and named FINNBROD by Mrs. Harriet Bruun.
30.12.1964:	Taken over while still fitting out by Vaasan Höyrymylly Oy – Vasa Ångkvarns Ab, Vaasa /Vasa (217), (c/o Oy Finnlines Ltd, Helsinki).
13.1.1965:	Completed by Valmet Oy, Helsingin Telakka, Helsinki, and entered Finnlines Mediterranean service.
18.7.1967:	Renamed FINNMILL by Vaasan Höyrymylly Oy and new name painted on Aug. 4.
25.6.1968:	Renamed CONCORDIA FINN by Vaasan Höyrymylly Oy for duration of charter to Concordia Line, (Chr. Haaland), Haugesund.
6.9.1968:	Name reverted to FINNMILL after redelivery from charter.
18.6.1970:	Renamed again CONCORDIA FINN, when chartered to Concordia Line.
5.8.1971:	Sold to Frasanav S.p.A. di Navigazione, Palermo, and renamed CITTA DI VIAREGGIO.
5.1974:	Sold to Inversiones Navieras Imparca C.A., Puerto Cabello (Caracas), and renamed TAMANACO.
1979:	Sold to Tacamar Panamena S.A., Panama, (Tacarigua Marina C.A., Caracas), and renamed TACAMAR VII.
1980:	Transferred to Canaima S.A., Panama, (Tacarigua Marina C.A., Caracas).
1984:	Sold to Colombian shipbreakers and arrived at Cartagena on July 3 for demolition.

40. FINNFIGHTER (I)   1965–1975

General Cargo Motorship, two decks – Open/Closed Shelterdecker
Call: OGKL Ice class: I A
1,682/2,727 GRT, 752/1,398 NRT, 2,530/3,725 dwt
91.55 x 14.03 x 5.42/6.67 m
Diesel Engine 2 SA 6 cy. Sulzer 6TD56
by the Shipbuilders
1,765 kW / 2,400 BHP   13.5 knots

27.10.1964:	Launched by Wärtsilä-yhtymä Oy – Wärtsilä-koncernen Ab, Crichton-Vulcan, Turku /Åbo (#1121), and named FINNFIGHTER by Mrs. Kielo Aura.
6.2.1965:	Completed and delivered to Enso-Gutzeit Oy, Kotka (559), (c/o Oy Finnlines Ltd, Helsinki /Helsingfors). Employed on Finnlines liner service from Finland to England.

ms FINNFIGHTER
Photo by Skyfotos

ms LUN SHAN ex FINNFIGHTER
Photo from Donald Mac Fie

24.6.1975: Sold to Luen Yick Shipping Co., Macao, (Yick Fung Shipping & Enterprises Co. Ltd., Hong Kong, as registered owners). Renamed LUN SHAN and registered in Mogadishu, Somalia.

1977: Transferred to Panama flag by Yick Fung Shipping & Enterprises Co. Ltd.

1981: Sold to Evermore Bloom Shipping S.A., Panama, (Yick Fung Shipping & Enterprises Co. Ltd., Hong Kong).

2.1986: Sold to Ying Kou Marine Transport Co., Ying Kou, China, and renamed WAN FU.

1990: Transferred to St. Vincent flag with Kingstown as home port by Ying Kou Marine Shipping Co.

1994: Remeasured in accordance with the 1969 Convention as follows: 2,563 GT, 1,283 NT, 3,725 dwt

1995: Sold to Eversail Shipping (St. Vincent) Ltd., Kingstown, St. Vincent & the Grenadines.

41. FINNHAWK (I)   1965–1971
MALTESHOLM   1971–1976
FINNHAWK (I)   1976–1979

General Cargo /Container Motorship, two decks – Open/Closed Shelterdecker
Call: OGKN Ice class: I B

6,387/9,043 GRT, 3,502/5,441 NRT, 8,732/10,895 dwt, 168 TEU
151.36 x 18.94 x 7.81/8.61 m

Diesel Engine 2 SA 6 cy. Sulzer 6RND68
by the Shipbuilders
5,296 kW / 7,200 BHP   16 knots

ms FINNHAWK after lengthening
Photo by Skyfotos

2.10.1964:	Launched by Wärtsilä-yhtymä Oy – Wärtsilä-koncernen Ab, Crichton-Vulcan, Turku /Åbo (#1123), and named FINNHAWK by Mrs. Hellä Alanko.	26.3.1965:	Completed and delivered as general cargo vessel to Enso-Gutzeit Oy, Kotka (561), (c/o Oy Finnlines Ltd, Helsinki /Helsingfors). Employed on Finnlines liner service to USEC.

ms FINNHAWK as MALTESHOLM
Photo by Skyfotos

1969:	Arrived on Feb. 10 at Oy Wärtsilä Ab, Turku Shipyard, Turku, for lengthening by a cargo section of 13.70 metres, and delivered on Mar. 30 after conversion to a semi-container vessel. Her original particulars as general cargo vessel were: 5,543/7,914 GRT, 2,789/4,272 NRT, 7,733/9,473 dwt 137.66 x 18.94 x 7.47/8.37 m
21.9.1971:	Renamed MALTESHOLM when time-chartered to Ab. Svenska Atlant Linien, Göteborg, and operated by Atlantic Gulf Service Ab., Göteborg.
16.12.1976:	Reverted to her original name FINNHAWK and was operated by Atlantic Cargo Services AB, Göteborg.
12.1978:	Moved to Finnlines-Sisco liner service to the Middle East.
1.6.1979:	Sold to Merivienti Oy, (Enso-Gutzeit Oy), Kotka.
3.9.1979:	Sold to Everett-Orient Line Inc., Monrovia, (c/o Everett Steamship Corp. S.A., Tokyo), and renamed FERNANDOEVERETT.
1980:	Registered as open shelterdecker with following tonnage: 6,255 GRT, 3,614 NRT, 8,555 dwt
1990:	Sold for demolition to Rupsha Ship Breakers, Sitalpur, Bangladesh, and arrived at Chittagong Roads on Dec. 20. Scrapping started at Sitalpur on Jan. 3, 1991.

42. FINNARROW (I)   1965–1971
VASAHOLM   1971–1976
FINNARROW (I)   1976–1979

General Cargo /Container Motorship, two decks – Open/Closed Shelterdecker
Call: OGKO Ice class: I B

6,381/9,050 GRT, 3,407/5,338 NRT, 8,732/10,895 dwt, 168 TEU
151.54 x 18.94 x 7.81/8.61 m

Diesel Engine 2 SA 6 cy. Sulzer 6RND68
by the Shipbuilders
4,781 kW / 6,500 BHP   16 knots

ms FINNARROW as a semi-container vessel
Photo from FG-Shipping Oy Ab

11.12.1964: Launched by Wärtsilä-yhtymä Oy – Wärtsilä-koncernen Ab, Crichton-Vulcan, Turku /Åbo (#1124), and named FINNARROW by Mrs. Eeva Virkkunen.

28.5.1965: Completed and delivered as general cargo vessel to Enso-Gutzeit Oy, Kotka (562), (c/o Oy Finnlines Ltd, Helsinki /Helsingfors). Employed on Finnlines liner service to USEC.

1968: Arrived on Dec. 17 at Valmet Oy, Helsingin Telakka, Helsinki, for lengthening by a cargo section of 13.70 metres, and delivered on Mar. 3, 1969 after conversion to a semi-container vessel.
Her original particulars as general cargo vessel were:
5,539/7,909 GRT, 2,792/4,275 NRT, 7,711/9,671 dwt
137.66 x 18.94 x 7.63/8.47 m

ms FINNARROW as VASAHOLM
Photo from Tomas Johannesson

21.9.1971:	Renamed VASAHOLM when chartered to Ab. Svenska Atlant Linien, Göteborg, and operated by Atlantic Gulf Service Ab., Göteborg.
16.12.1976:	Reverted to her original name FINNARROW and was operated by Atlantic Cargo Services AB, Göteborg.
9.1978:	Moved to Finnlines-Sisco liner service to the Middle East.
1.6.1979:	Sold to Merivienti Oy, (Enso-Gutzeit Oy), Kotka.
28.8.1979:	Sold to Janco Handelsmaatschappij B.V., Amsterdam, and further to D.B. Shipping & Finance Inc., Panama, and renamed CORDILLERA.
1979:	Sold to Transmares Naviera Chilena Ltda., Panama, (Santiago de Chile).
1981:	Sold to Sociedad Naviera Ultragas Ltda., (c/o Transmares Naviera Internacional S.A.), Valparaiso, (Santiago de Chile).
1983:	Registered as closed shelterdecker with following tonnage: 8,164 GRT, 5,308 NRT, 11,069 dwt
1985:	Transferred back to Transmares Naviera Chilena Ltda., Valparaiso.
1990:	Went aground on May 31 in Paso Shoal, north of Canal Smyth in the Strait of Magellan, in position 52.30 S, 73.40 W during a voyage from Rio de Janeiro to Valparaiso. Forepeak, No. 1 double bottom tank and No. 1 lower hold flooded. Refloated on June 7 and proceeded for temporary repairs to Punta Arenas, where arrived on June 19. Arrived on Aug. 7 at Talcahuano for discharge and inspection, but found to be beyond an economical repair and sold for demolition in India. Loaded for her final voyage at Punta Arenas, and sailed on Sep. 23 for Bombay, and from there on Nov. 8 for scrapping to Alang, where she arrived on Nov. 9.

ms CORDILLERA ex FINNARROW in Santos
Photo by Raimo A. Wirrankoski

43. FINNMAID (II)   1965–1979

General Cargo /Container Motorship, two decks – Open/Closed Shelterdecker
Call: OGQK Ice class: I B

6,386/9,045 GRT, 3,498/5,442 NRT, 9,121/10,918 dwt, 168 TEU
151.36 x 18.94 x 7.81/8.61 m

Diesel Engine 2 SA 6 cy. Sulzer 6RND68
by the Shipbuilders
5,296 kW / 7,200 BHP   16 knots

ms FINNMAID as built
Photo by Skyfotos

19.3.1965:	Launched by Wärtsilä-yhtymä Oy – Wärtsilä-koncernen Ab, Crichton-Vulcan, Turku /Åbo (#1130), and named FINNMAID by Mrs. Elma Sukselainen.	
30.7.1965:	Completed and delivered as general cargo vessel to Merivienti Oy, (Enso-Gutzeit Oy), Helsinki /Helsingfors (1343). Managed by Oy Finnlines Ltd, Helsinki. Employed on Finnlines liner service to USEC.	
1969:	Arrived on Aug. 21 at Oy Wärtsilä Ab, Turku Shipyard, Turku, for lengthening by a cargo section of 13.70 metres, and delivered on Oct. 30 after conversion to a semi-container vessel. Her original particulars as general cargo vessel were: 5,555/7,936 GRT, 2,779/4,269 NRT, 7,711/9,671 dwt 137.66 x 18.94 x 7.46/8.47 m	
31.12.1970:	Owners amalgamated with the parent company Enso-Gutzeit Oy, as per EGM resolution on Apr. 17. Merger registered on Aug. 3, 1971.	
27.7.1971:	Home port changed to Kotka (577).	
27.7.1971:	Sold to Oulu Oy, Oulu /Uleåborg (519), without change of name. Managers remained Oy Finnlines Ltd.	
9.1971:	Time-chartered to Atlantic Gulf Service Ab., Göteborg.	
16.12.1976:	Reverted to her original colours and was operated by Atlantic Cargo Services AB, Göteborg.	

ms FINNMAID after sale to Oulu Oy
Photo from FG-Shipping Oy Ab

ms CONDOR ex FINNMAID in Santos
Photo by Raimo A. Wirrankoski

9.1978:	Moved to Finnlines-Sisco liner service to the Middle East.
25.5.1979:	Sold to Palladia Shipping Corp., (Arcadis Brothers Shipping Corp.), Piraeus, and renamed PALLADIA.
1980:	Sold to Transmares Naviera Chilena Ltda., Valparaiso, (Santiago de Chile), and renamed CONDOR.
1983:	Registered as closed shelterdecker with following tonnage: 8,164 GRT, 5,308 NRT, 8,786 dwt
1990:	Sold for demolition to Amar Shipbreaking Corp., Alang, India, where arrived on Dec. 31.

44. FINN-ENSO   1965–1979

General Cargo /Container Motorship, two decks – Open/Closed Shelterdecker
Call: OGQL Ice class: I B

6,384/9,043 GRT, 3,495/5,436 NRT, 8,600/11,100 dwt, 168 TEU
151.36 x 18.94 x 7.49/8.62 m

Diesel Engine 2 SA 6 cy. Sulzer 6RND68
by the Shipbuilders
5,296 kW / 7,200 BHP   16 knots

ms FINN-ENSO after lengthening
Photo from FG-Shipping Oy Ab

7.9.1965: Launched by Wärtsilä-yhtymä Oy – Wärtsilä-koncernen Ab, Crichton-Vulcan, Turku /Åbo (#1131), and named FINN-ENSO by Mrs. Pirkko Halle.

14.12.1965: Completed and delivered as general cargo vessel to Enso-Gutzeit Oy, Kotka (564), (c/o Oy Finnlines Ltd, Helsinki /Helsingfors). Employed on Finnlines liner service to USEC.

12.5.1969: Arrived on Mar. 24 at Oy Wärtsilä Ab, Turku Shipyard, Turku, for lengthening by a cargo section of 13.70 metres, and delivered on May 12 after conversion to a semi-container vessel.
Her original particulars as general cargo vessel were:
5,553/7,935 GRT, 2,775/4,260 NRT, 7,711/9,671 dwt
137.66 x 18.94 x 7.46/8.46 m

9.1971: Time-chartered to Atlantic Gulf Service Ab., Göteborg.

12.1976: Reverted to her original colours and was operated by Atlantic Cargo Services AB, Göteborg.

9.1978: Inaugurated Finnlines-Sisco liner service to the Middle East.

1.6.1979: Sold to Merivienti Oy, (Enso-Gutzeit Oy), Kotka.

3.9.1979: Sold to Mah Boonkrong Shipping Co. Ltd., Bangkok, (c/o Chin Seng Hong Ltd., Hong Kong), and renamed MAH.

1980: Sold to Transmares Naviera Internacional S.A., Panama, (Santiago de Chile), (c/o Hanseatic Shipping Co. Ltd., Limassol), and renamed CORRAL.

1983: Transferred to Chilean flag with Valparaiso as home port and managers changed to Transmares Naviera Chilena Ltda., Santiago de Chile.

1983: Registered as closed shelterdecker with following tonnage:
8,164 GRT, 5,308 NRT, 11,278 dwt

4.1991: Sold to Ontario Maritime Corp., Panama, (c/o World-Wide Ship Management [World-Ship], Valparaiso), and renamed GOLDEN HILL.

1992: Found by a U.S. Coast Guard cutter as renamed HARBOUR in Windward Passage, about 50 miles south of Guantanamo Bay on Jan. 5, 1992 with her engine room flooding, while on voyage from Valpa-

ms CONDOR ex FINN-ENSO
Photo by Raimo A. Wirrankoski

raiso to Baltimore, having passed through the Panama Canal on Dec. 24, 1991 still bearing the name GOLDEN HILL.
Guardsmen found 4.5 tons of cocaine hidden in a cargo hold under a shipment of zinc oxide. The Coast Guard seized the vessel and towed her on Jan. 6 to the U.S. Navy Base at Guantanamo Bay for dewatering and further investigation. The vessel's 28 Chilean crew members were brought to Miami and jailed on smuggling charges. The vessel arrived on Jan. 18 in tow at Port Everglades to be checked by U.S. Customs and to be unloaded. Thereafter left on Jan. 30 in tow for Tampa with arrival on Feb. 1.

1993: Sold at a U.S. Government auction on July 15 to Mexican shipbreakers and left Tampa on July 27 in tow for Tuxpan, where she arrived on Aug. 2 for demolition.

45. FINNLARK 1966–1977

Motor Chemical Tanker, one deck
Call: OGQV Ice class: I A

689 GRT, 273 NRT, 952 dwt
56.85 x 9.70 x 4.37 m

Diesel Engine 4 SA 6 cy. MWM TRH 348S
by Motoren-Werke Mannheim A.G., Mannheim
662 kW / 900 BHP   11 knots

21.9.1965:	Launched by Valmet Oy, Helsingin Telakka, Helsinki/Helsingfors (#236), and named FINNLARK by Mrs. Hertta Schultz.
30.12.1965:	Taken over while still fitting out by Enso-Gutzeit Oy, Kotka (565), (c/o Oy Finnlines Ltd, Helsinki).
22.1.1966:	Completed by Valmet Oy, Helsingin Telakka, Helsinki.
7.2.1977:	Sold to Nimrod Shipping Ltd, (c/o Sealion Shipping Ltd.), London, and renamed ICE LARK.
1985:	Managers' name re-styled as TNT Sealion Ltd.
12.1987:	Sold to Financial Enterprises of Bahamas Ltd., Nassau, (c/o Sandford Ship Management Ltd., Sandford, IoM), and renamed SANDLARK.

mt FINNLARK
Photo by Skyfotos

mt ICE LARK ex FINNLARK in Hull
Photo from K. Brzoza

12.1992: Sold to Seamartin Tankers Ltd., Douglas, Isle of Man, (c/o Seamartin Shipping Services Ltd., Hull), and renamed SILVERLARK.

1994: Remeasured in accordance with the 1969 Convention as follows:
688 GT, 227 NT, 952 dwt

9.1994: Sold to Balata Ltd., Douglas, (c/o b.v.b.a. D.N.R. Tankvaart en Agenturen, Ossendrecht), and renamed SANDLARK.

46. FINNHANSA (I) 1966–1978

Passenger /RoRo Cargo Motor Ferry, three decks, bow and stern doors
Passengers: 576 berths, total capacity 1,700 pass.
Call: OGKK Ice class: I A

7,820 GRT, 3,867 NRT, 2,510 dwt
134.40 x 19.90 x 5.70 m

2 Diesel Engines 2 SA each 8 cy. Sulzer 8RD56
by Oy Wärtsilä Ab, Turku /Åbo
2 x 5,149 kW / 2 x 7,000 BHP
Total 10,298 kW / 14,000 BHP   20 knots Twin screw

ms FINNHANSA
Photo from Matti Pietikäinen

ms PRINSESSAN
Photo by K. Brzoza

1.12.1964:	Launched by Wärtsilä-yhtymä Oy – Wärtsilä-koncernen Ab, Hietalahden Telakka – Sandvikens Skeppsdocka, Helsinki /Helsingfors (#377), with intended delivery on June 15, 1965. Christened FINNHANSA by Mrs. Sylvi Kekkonen.
18.3.1965:	Extensively gutted by fire while fitting out in Helsinki. Delivery delayed.
28.3.1966:	Completed by Oy Wärtsilä Ab, Helsinki Shipyard, Helsinki, and delivered to Merivienti Oy, (Enso-Gutzeit Oy), Helsinki (1355), (c/o Oy Finnlines Ltd). Entered Helsinki – Slite/Nynäshamn – Karlskrona – Lübeck service.

ms PRINCESA MARISSA ex FINNHANSA at Rhodes
Photo by K. Brzoza

31.12.1970: Owners amalgamated with the parent company Enso-Gutzeit Oy, as per EGM resolution on Apr. 17. Merger registered on Aug. 3, 1971.

1972: Rebuilt by Howaldtswerke – Deutsche Werft A.G. in Kiel during Mar. 1–Apr. 27 increasing her berth capacity from 350 to 576 berths. Her original particulars were: 7,481 GRT, 3,496 NRT

9.1.1978: Sold to Birka Line Ab, Mariehamn (1237), and renamed PRINSESSAN, when delivered the same day. Entered on Jan. 18 Stockholm – Mariehamn cruise service.

1980: Rebuilt by Howaldtswerke – Deutsche Werft A.G. in Hamburg, increasing her passenger capacity to 905 berths with following new tonnages: 9,491 GRT, 4,928 NRT, 2,002 dwt

24.4.1987: Sold to Louis Cruise Line Ltd., (c/o Interorient Navigation Co. Ltd.), Limassol, and renamed PRINCESA MARISSA. Employed on Piraeus – Rhodes – Limassol – Alexandria liner service.

1990: Transferred to Princesa Marissa Co. Ltd., (c/o Interorient Navigation Co. Ltd.), Limassol. Still operated by Louis Cruise Lines on Limassol – Haifa/Port Said – Limassol service.

1993: Managers changed to Seascope Navigation Ltd., Limassol.

1994: Remeasured in accordance with the 1969 Convention as follows: 10,487 GT, 4,600 NT

1994: Managers changed to Louis Shipmanagement Ltd., (Louis Cruise Lines), Limassol.

47. FINNPARTNER (I) 1966–1968

Passenger /RoRo Cargo Motor Ferry, three decks, bow and stern doors
Passengers: 612 berths, total capacity 1,400 pass.
Call: OGRR   Ice class: I A

7,458 GRT, 3,470 NRT, 1,600 dwt
134.50 x 19.90 x 5.70 m

2 Diesel Engines 2 SA each 8 cy. Sulzer 8RD56
by Oy Wärtsilä Ab, Turku /Åbo
2 x 5,149 kW / 2 x 7,000 BHP
Total 10,298 kW / 14,000 BHP   20 knots Twin screw

ms FINNPARTNER
Photo from Matti Pietikäinen

15.12.1965:	Launched by Wärtsilä-yhtymä Oy – Wärtsilä-koncernen Ab, Hietalahden Telakka – Sandvikens Skeppsdocka, Helsinki /Helsingfors (#380), and christened FINNPARTNER by Mrs. Sylvi Kekkonen.	27.12.1968:	Sold to Oy Svea Line (Finland) Ab, Turku /Åbo (1454), (Stockholms Rederi ab. Svea, Stockholm), (c/o Oy Siljavarustamo – Ab Siljarederiet, Turku), and chartered back to Oy Finnlines Ltd.
22.6.1966:	Completed by Oy Wärtsilä Ab, Helsinki Shipyard, Helsinki, and delivered to Amer-Tupakka Oy, Helsinki (1360), (c/o Oy Finnlines Ltd). Entered Helsinki – Slite/Nynäshamn – Karlskrona – Lübeck service.	15.1.1969:	Renamed SVEABORG by Oy Svea Line (Finland) Ab after redelivery from the charter. Thereafter operated by Trave Line on Helsingborg – Copenhagen – Travemünde line.
1968:	Left Helsinki on Oct. 3 with the "Finnfocus" export exhibition on board and sailed up the River Thames to London, where anchored near Tower Bridge for 5 days.	11.1.1972:	Sold to the parent company Stockholms Rederi ab. Svea, (Carl Hall) with Helsingborg as home port. (11248). Operated further on the same service by Trave Line.

ms SVEABORG ex FINNPARTNER
Photo from Matti Pietikäinen

ms STENA BALTICA in May 1982 just renamed IALYSSOS, but still with Stena Line funnel mark
Photo by Krister Bång

ms IALYSSOS ex FINNPARTNER at Kos
Photo by Matti Pietikäinen

3.3.1977:	Renamed PEER GYNT by Stockholms Rederi AB Svea for duration of charter to Aarhus-Oslo Linie G.m.b.H., (J.A. Reinecke), Hamburg, for Aarhus – Oslo service.
9.11.1978:	Sold to Stena Line AB, (Sten A. Olsson), Göteborg, and renamed STENA BALTICA.
11.3.1979:	Delivered after rebuilding and conversion to an accommodation passenger /roro cargo vessel by Werft Nobiskrug, Rendsburg. Fitted with sponsons for increasing her stability. Her new particulars were 8,586 GRT, 5,187 NRT and breadth 22.53 m Passenger capacity was increased from 612 to 800 berths. She was used as an accommodation ship for oil field workers in the North Sea.
8.4.1982:	Sold to Dodekanissiaki Anonimos Naftiliaki Eteria (D.A.N.E.), Rodos, and renamed IALYSSOS, when delivered on May 6. Converted back to a passenger / roro cargo ferry and employed on Rhodes – Piraeus liner service.
1996:	Remeasured in accordance with the 1969 Convention as follows: 10,670 GT, – NT, 1,900 dwt

48. TYYSTERNIEMI 1967–1983

Motor Bulk Carrier /Sulphur Acid Tanker, Singledecker
Call: OGTG Ice class: I A

1,984 GRT, 982 NRT, 2,753 dwt
87.60 x 13.03 x 5.98 m

Diesel Engine 2 SA 6 cy. Werkspoor TEBS-456
by N.V. Werkspoor, Amsterdam
1,765 kW / 2,400 BHP   13.7 knots

ms TYYSTERNIEMI
Photo from FG-Shipping Oy Ab

12.4.1967:	Launched by Ateliers & Chantiers du Havre – Duchesne & Bossiere et Augustin Normand Réunis S.A., Le Havre (#189), and named TYYSTERNIEMI by Mrs. Laila Hovi.
20.9.1967:	Completed and delivered to Rikkihappo Oy, (c/o Oy Finnlines Ltd), Helsinki /Helsingfors (1375).
30.6.1972:	Owners registered as Kemira Oy as per EGM resolution on Dec. 16, 1971.

*ms SUSAN.C ex TYYSTERNIEMI in September 1988 before departure from Helsinki
Photo by Matti Pietikäinen*

6.4.1983:	Sold to Kansallisrahoitus Oy, (Kansallis Finance Ltd.), Helsinki, and leased to Pori Shipping Oy, (Pori /Björneborg), who renamed her STERN.
1983:	Converted to a pure bulk carrier by removing the acid tanks.
1984:	Pori Shipping Oy went into liquidation and Kansallisrahoitus Oy leased STERN on Mar. 13 to Rederi Ab Högship, (c/o Oy Hangö Ship-Owners Ab, Hanko /Hangö).
1.9.1984:	Rederi Ab Högship filed for bankruptcy and STERN was arrested at Oulu /Uleåborg.
25.1.1985:	Sold at auction to Juhani Kontio, Oulu. The sale did not, however, materialize, as the buyer did not pay his bid.
22.2.1985:	Sold at another auction to Chantal Oy, (Asko Pölönen), Helsinki, and the name reverted to TYYSTERNIEMI. (BoS 29.5.1985).
9.1.1986:	Arrived in tow at Helsinki, where laid up.
12.8.1986:	Sold to Oy Stock-Lines Ltd., (Asko Pölönen), Helsinki.
1988:	Reported as sold to Markku Kaipila, but the sale was cancelled on Mar. 31.
10.7.1988:	Sold to Naviera Perla del Sur S.D.E.R.L., San Lorenzo, Honduras, and renamed SUSAN. C. Sailed from Helsinki on Sep. 15.
7.1989:	Sold to Southern Shipping Group, Valletta, (Dublin), and renamed TARA ROSE.
5.1991:	Sold to unknown Honduran flag buyers and renamed FIDAA. Managed by Fayza Shipping Co. Ltd., Limassol.
1992:	Sold to S.M. Spiridon Shipping, Beirut, (c/o Sherimar Management Co. Ltd., Athens), and renamed S.M. SPIRIDON.
12.1997:	Sold to unidentified buyers and renamed MAYSSA JUNIOR. Remained under Lebanese flag.
12.1997:	*New GT and NT in accordance with the 1969 Convention not yet reported to Lloyd's Register.*

49. KOTKANIEMI 1968–1986

Motor Bulk Carrier, Singledecker
Call: OGUY Ice class: I C

12,052 GRT, 7,254 NRT, 18,000 dwt
158.15 x 21.71 x 9.58 m

Diesel Engine 2 SA 6 cy. Sulzer 6RD68
by the Shipbuilders
4,781 kW / 6,500 BHP   14.5 knots

ms KOTKANIEMI
Photo by Studio-Eira

26.6.1968: Launched by Oy Wärtsilä Ab, Turku Shipyard, Turku /Åbo (#1162), and named KOTKANIEMI by Mrs. Margit Leskinen.

30.10.1968: Completed and delivered to Rikkihappo Oy, (c/o Oy Finnlines Ltd), Helsinki /Helsingfors (1388).

30.6.1972: Owners registered as Kemira Oy as per EGM resolution on Dec. 16, 1971.

23.5.1986: Sold to Clyde Seaways S.A., Panama, (Theodoros E. Veniamis), (c/o Golden Union Shipping Co. S.A., Piraeus), and renamed FLAG ADRIENNE.

1987: Transferred to Greek flag with Piraeus as home port.

1994: Remeasured in accordance with the 1969 Convention as follows:
11,855 GT, 7,172 NT, 18,289 dwt

1996: Sold to Adrienne Shipping Inc., (Alvargonzales S.A.), Panama.

ms FLAG ADRIENNE ex KOTKANIEMI
Photo from Krister Bång

50. FINNMINI 1969–1971

Motor Chemical Tanker, one deck
Call: OGQJ Ice class: I B

496 GRT, 178 NRT, 712 dwt
59.98 x 8.52 x 3.45 m

Diesel Engine 2 SA 6 cy. B&W Alpha 406 VO
by Alpha-Diesel A/S, Frederikshavn
309 kW / 420 BHP   10 knots

mt PINOCCHIO, later FINNMINI
Photo by Bertil Zandelin

28.4.1965: Launched by Valmet Oy, Pansion Tehdas, Turku /Åbo (#285), and named PINOCCHIO by Mrs. Mary Nielsen.

26.7.1965: Completed and delivered to Oy Tank-Tonnage Ab, (Henry Nielsen Oy/Ab), Helsinki /Helsingfors (1342).

10.3.1969: Acquired by Oy Thombrokers Ab, (Oy Thomén Metsätoimisto – Thomés Skogsbyrå Ab), Helsinki, and renamed FINNMINI. Managed by Oy Finnlines Ltd, Helsinki.

1969: Owners amalgamation with the parent company, the name of which changed to Thomesto Oy, registered on Oct. 17 as per merger arrangement signed on Jan. 7 and EGM resolution on Aug. 15.

25.2.1971: Sold to Oy Gustav Paulig Ab, (c/o Henry Nielsen Oy/Ab), Helsinki, and renamed MINI.

9.7.1975: Sold to Sagar Lines (India) Pvt. Ltd., Calcutta, and renamed SAGAR TARANI.

1995: Deleted from Indian ship register. Most probably sold to local shipbreakers.

Still listed as Sagar Tarani in Lloyd's Register 1997.

mt FINNMINI
Photo by Skyfotos

mt MINI ex FINNMINI in Helsinki
Photo by Matti Pietikäinen

51. FINNCARRIER 1969–1975

RoRo Cargo/Passenger Motor Ferry, four decks
Two stern doors, two side doors
Passengers: 36 berths
Call: OGVM   Ice class: I A Super

6,209 GRT, 2,257 NRT, 4,736 dwt
137.34 x 24.56 x 5.70 m

2 Vee Diesel engines 4 SA each 12 cy. Pielstick 12PC2V-400
by the Shipbuilders
2 x 4,104 kW / 2 x 5,580 BHP
Total 8,208 kW / 2 x 11,160 BHP   18 knots Twin screw

ms FINNCARRIER approaching Helsinki
Photo by Rolf Mieritz

ms POLARIS ex FINNCARRIER
Photo by Matti Pietikäinen

ms SCANDINAVIA LINK ex FINNCARRIER
Photo by Tomas Johannesson

26.3.1969: Launched by Oy Wärtsilä Ab, Helsinki Shipyard, Helsinki /Helsingfors (#390), and named FINNCARRIER by Mrs. Alice Wartemann.

15.11.1969: Completed and delivered to Merivienti Oy, (Enso-Gutzeit Oy), Helsinki (1406), (c/o Oy Finnlines Ltd, Helsinki). Employed on Finnlines roro service from Helsinki to Travemünde.

31.12.1970: Owners amalgamated with the parent company Enso-Gutzeit Oy as per EGM resolution on Apr. 17. Merger registered on Aug. 3, 1971.

16.6.1975: Acquired by Suomen Höyrylaiva Oy – Finska Ångfartygs Ab, Helsinki, in exchange for ms Finlandia. Chartered back to Oy Finnlines Ltd with delivery the same day until end 1975.

2.1.1976: Renamed POLARIS after redelivery from charter by Suomen Höyrylaiva Oy – Finska Ångfartygs Ab. Chartered to Oy Finncarriers Ab and employed on Helsinki/Kotka – (Copenhagen) – Lübeck roro service.

13.2.1981: Owners' name registered as Effoa – Finska Ångfartygs Ab / Effoa – Suomen Höyrylaiva Oy / Effoa – Finland Steamship Co. Ltd. as per EGM resolutions on Nov. 12 and Dec. 12, 1980.

19.4.1984: Sold to Rederi AB Nordö, (Bernt Berntsson), Malmö, and renamed SCANDINAVIA. (SLBD)

5.1984: Completed after repairs by Cityvarvet, Gothenburg. Fitted with internal ramps and with an extension of superstructure for additional passengers. Total capacity: 120 berths. Entered Helsingborg – Malmö – Travemünde liner service.

ms STENA SEARIDER ex FINNCARRIER in Gothenburg
Photo by Matti Pietikäinen

2.1986:	Majority of shares in Rederi AB Nordö purchased by Rederi AB Sea-Link.	26.7.1991:	Renamed SEARIDER when chartered to Principal Lines Inc., Miami, Fla.
11.3.1986:	Sold to Rederi AB Nordline, Malmö.	15.1.1992:	Name reverted to STENA SEARIDER after redelivery from charterers.
21.10.1986:	Owners' name changed to Rederi AB Nordö-Line.	1992:	Transferred to Stena Searider Line Ltd., Nassau. Same managers remained.
4.1987:	Completed after lengthening by a cargo section of 41 metres, heightening of main deck by 0.80 m and conversion to a passenger/roro cargo rail vehicles ferry at Wärtsilä Meriteollisuus Oy / Wärtsilä Marine Industries Inc., Turku Shipyard, Turku /Åbo (#1502). New particulars: 20,914 GT, 6,274 NT, 14,800 dwt 178.70 x 24.54 x 5.71 m 750 metres rail for 55 waggons Passengers: 150 berths Left shipyard being renamed SCANDINAVIA LINK and employed on Malmö – Travemünde train ferry service.	4.1992:	Renamed NORSE MERSEY when chartered to Norse Irish Ferries for Belfast – Liverpool service.
		25.1.1995:	Sold to AB Stena Line Treasury, (c/o Stena Line Ship Management AB), Göteborg, and name reverted again to STENA SEARIDER. Entered Stena Line service Gothenburg – Kiel.
		29.4.1997:	Sold to Stena Line Ships B.V., Hoek van Holland, while moved to Hoek van Holland – Harwich line. Registered, however, in London.
9.5.1990:	Sold to Fernwood Inc., Nassau, (c/o Northern Marine Management Ltd., Clydebank), and renamed STENA SEARIDER when delivered on May 17.		

52. MÄLKIÄ 1970–1973

General Cargo Motorship, two decks – Open Shelterdecker
Call: OGXI Ice class: I C

499 GRT, 281 NRT, 1,065 dwt
62.35 x 10.02 x 3.81 m

Diesel Engine 2 SA 4 cy. NOHAB Polar 14NS
by Nydqvist & Holm AB, Trollhättan
736 kW / 1,000 BHP   12 knots

ms MÄLKIÄ
Photo from FG-Shipping Oy Ab

ms PAOLETTA ex MÄLKIÄ
Photo from Donald Mac Fie

26.1.1962:	Launched by Ab. Falkenbergs Varv, Falkenberg (#128), and named SUNNANHAV by Mrs. Alice Källsson.
2.6.1962:	Completed and delivered to Partrederiet för ms Sunnanhav, Helge Källsson m.fl., (50% Erik Thun Ab. and 50% Thunrederier Ab.), Lidköping. (10293)
30.12.1965:	Sold to Partrederiet för ms Birgitta, Clary Thordén m.fl., Uddevalla, and renamed BIRGITTA.
25.5.1970:	Acquired by Saimaan Kanavalaivat Oy, (c/o Oy Finnlines Ltd), Helsinki/Helsingfors (1413), and renamed MÄLKIÄ. Chartered to Oy Saimaa Lines Ltd., Helsinki.
5.2.1973:	Sold to Capo Spartivento S.p.A., (Tino Campi), Cagliari, and renamed PAOLETTA.
1978:	Sold to Trimarconavi S.a.s., Napoli, without change of name.
1980:	Registered as open/closed shelterdecker with following tonnages: 498/845 GRT, 253/479 NRT, –/1,559 dwt 62.31 x 10.04 x 3.81/4.71 m
9.1982:	Sold to Selam Shipping Co. Ltd., Limassol (Liverpool), and renamed SYROS.
1983:	Went aground on Dec. 2 at Sarakiniko on Elafonisos Island 6 miles from Neapolis in southeastern Peloponnisos on flat rock, 60 metres from coast when trying to enter Neapolis as port of refuge, after encountering very bad weather during a voyage from Thessaloniki to Dellys, Algeria, with 1,114 tons semolina in bags. Abandoned the following day by her crew. Salvage operations unsuccessful. Declared a constructive total loss.

53. PÄLLI   1970–1974

General Cargo Motorship, two decks – Open Shelterdecker
Call: OGXJ Ice class: I B

499 GRT, 290 NRT, 1,130 dwt
74.40 x 10.83 x 3.68 m

Vee Diesel Engine 4 SA 12 cy. Ruston Paxman 12YLCM
by Davey, Paxman & Co. Ltd., Colchester
954 kW / 1,280 BHP   12.5 knots

ms ROYAL PAPER, later PÄLLI
Photo from Donald Mac Fie

19.8.1957: Launched by Ab. Gävle Varv, Gävle (#97), and named ROYAL PAPER by Mrs. Anne-Marie Christenson.

28.10.1957: Completed and delivered to Ab. Statens Skogsindustrier, (Knut O. Norlin), Stockholm. (9787)

31.10.1968: Sold to Stena Ab., (Sten A. Olsson), Göteborg, and renamed STENA PAPER.

18.6.1970: Acquired by Saimaan Kanavalaivat Oy, (c/o Oy Finnlines Ltd), Helsinki /Helsingfors (1412), and renamed PÄLLI. Chartered to Oy Saimaa Lines Ltd., Helsinki.

24.9.1974: Sold to Horseshoe Bay Shipping Co. Ltd., Panama, (Thomas A. Tsourinakis), (c/o Fairlead Enterprises [Maritime] Ltd., Piraeus), and renamed COSTIS TAF.

1976: In collision on Nov. 20 with the Greek ms Mini Lord in the entrance to Corinth Canal. Mini Lord sank immediately with all hands. Costis Taf was heavily damaged, but still floating. Repaired and resumed trading.

1979: Renamed DOVER by Horseshoe Bay Shipping Co. Ltd., Panama.

1979: Extensively damaged by fire which followed an engine room explosion on June 27 when 15 miles off Canea, Crete, during a voyage from Iraklion to Marseilles with a cargo of skins. Arrived in tow on June 28 at Iraklion. Declared a constructive total loss and sold for demolition.

ms PÄLLI
Photo by Bernt Fogelberg

54. SOSKUA 1970–1974

General Cargo Motorship, two decks – Open Shelterdecker
Call: OGXK Ice class: I B

499 GRT, 289 NRT, 1,136 dwt
74.40 x 10.83 x 3.68 m

Vee Diesel Engine 4 SA 12 cy. Ruston Paxman 12YLCM
by Davey, Paxman & Co. Ltd., Colchester
1,044 kW / 1,400 BHP   12.5 knots

ms ROYAL WOOD, later SOSKUA
Photo by Bertil Zandetin

20.10.1956: Launched by Ab. Gävle Varv, Gävle (#94), and named ROYAL WOOD by Mrs. Gertrud Sellman.

16.1.1957: Completed and delivered to Ab. Statens Skogsindustrier, (Knut O. Norlin), Stockholm. (9725)

22.6.1969: Sold to Stena Ab., (Sten A. Olsson), Göteborg, and renamed STENA WOOD.

18.6.1970: Acquired by Saimaan Kanavalaivat Oy, (c/o Oy Finnlines Ltd), Helsinki /Helsingfors (1414), and renamed SOSKUA. Chartered to Oy Saimaa Lines Ltd., Helsinki.

ms SOSKUA
Photo by H.-J. Reinecke

8.1974:	Sold to Capricorn Bay Shipping Co. Ltd., Panama, (Thomas A. Tsourinakis), (c/o Fairlead Enterprises [Maritime] Ltd., Piraeus), and renamed ALEXIS TAF.	8.1977:	Sold after completed repairs to Seabell Co. Ltd., Limassol, and renamed BRISTOL. Managers remained Fairlead Enterprises (Maritime) Ltd., Piraeus.
1977:	Dragged her anchor and went aground on Feb. 21 whilst undergoing engine repairs between Almeria and Cabo de Gata while on passage from Piraeus to Mauritania. Refloated on Feb. 27 and towed to Gibraltar for inspection, where the whole bottom was found heavily damaged. Declared a constructive total loss.	1978:	Fire broke out in her engine room on Jan. 28 when off Marmara Island in the Sea of Marmara while bound from Novorossisk for Italy with timber. Towed to Saraylar harbour on Marmara Island on Jan. 30, where beached in shallow water. During efforts to extinguish the fire the vessel, however, capsized and foundered with her bottom up alongside the breakwater.
1977:	Purchased back by Capricorn Bay Shipping Co. Ltd., but registered in Limassol, Cyprus, as SFAKIA. Left Gibraltar on May 29 and arrived on June 4 at Piraeus for repairs.	1980:	The wreck was not righted until June 1, following which she was towed to Aliaga, near Izmir, for demolition.

55. ISLA FINLANDIA   1970–1972

Motor Tanker, one deck
Call: OFQA Ice class: I B

939 GRT, 360 NRT, 1,085 dwt
63.54 x 10.02 x 4.40 m

Diesel Engine 4 SA 8 cy. Mirrlees
by Associated British Oil Engines Ltd., Stockport
596 kW / 810 BHP   10.5 knots

mt ISLA FINLANDIA laid up in Helsinki
Photo by Matti Pietikäinen

15.10.1949:	Launched by Wärtsilä-yhtymä Oy – Wärtsilä-koncernen Ab, Crichton-Vulcan, Turku /Åbo (#876), and named ESSO FINLANDIA by Mrs. Ira Munch Jensen. The first all-welded tanker built in Finland.
25.4.1950:	Completed and delivered to Oy Nobel-Standard Ab, Helsinki /Helsingfors (1076).
17.12.1951:	Owners' name registered as Oy Esso Ab as per EGM resolution on June 8.
21.12.1970:	Acquired by Jouko Korpivaara, (c/o Oy Finnlines Ltd), Helsinki, and renamed ISLA FINLANDIA when delivered on Dec. 28.
26.9.1972:	Sold to C.P. Stathatos & Co., Piraeus, and renamed ALKYON.

Name spelt in Lloyd's register as ALKYON, however, painted as ALKION on the bows of the ship. ALKYON was entered in Lloyd's Register without owners until 1976 edition. Thereafter:

1976:	Owners: Piraeus Maritime Co. S.A., Piraeus.
1986:	Sold to local shipbreakers for demolition at Eleusis.

mt ALKION ex ISLA FINLANDIA at Perama
Photo by Matti Pietikäinen

56. ANNIKA   1971–1971
FINNREEL   1971–1977

General Cargo Motorship, two decks – Open/Closed Shelterdecker
Call: OGQG Ice class: I A

1,805/2,956 GRT, 827/1,537 NRT, 2,891/4,097 dwt
96.87 x 14.03 x 5.43/6.57 m

Diesel Engine 2 SA 6 cy. Sulzer 6TD56
by the Shipbuilders
1,765 kW / 2,400 BHP   13.5 knots

ms ANNIKA
Photo from John Clarkson

25.2.1965:	Launched by Wärtsilä-yhtymä Oy – Wärtsilä-koncernen Ab, Crichton-Vulcan, Turku /Åbo (#1129), and named ANNIKA by Mrs. Aira Nordström.
5.6.1965:	Completed and delivered to Lovisa Rederi Ab, (Ab R. Nordström & Co. Oy), Loviisa /Lovisa (520).
5.5.1969:	Owners' amalgamation with the parent company Ab R. Nordström & Co. Oy registered as per EGM resolutions on Sep. 30, 1968.
29.12.1970:	Shares of Ab R. Nordström & Co Oy acquired from Kansallis-Osake-Pankki by Enso-Gutzeit Oy.
1.1.1971:	Management of the vessels of Ab R. Nordström & Co Oy assigned to Oy Finnlines Ltd.
20.4.1971:	Renamed FINNREEL by Ab R. Nordström & Co Oy, Loviisa.
23.4.1971:	Owners' name registered as Oy Enso-Chartering Ab as per EGM resolution on Jan. 22.
3.11.1975:	Owners' amalgamation with the parent company Enso-Gutzeit Oy registered as per AGM resolutions on Apr. 11.
1.1.1976:	Time-chartered to Oy Finncarriers Ab, Helsinki.
25.10.1977:	Sold to Luen Yick Shipping Co., Macao, (Yick Fung Shipping & Enterprises Co. Ltd., Hong Kong, as registered owners). Renamed TIAN SHAN and registered in Panama.
2.1986:	Sold to Ying Kou Marine Transport Co., Ying Kou, China, and renamed XIAN REN.
1986:	When leaving Hong Kong on Mar. 6 for Shanghai, reported to be delivered to Chinese shipbreakers.

ms FINNREEL
Photo from J.K. Byass

Deleted from Lloyd's Register in 1986. The demolition did not, however, materialize and therefore re-entered in Lloyd's Register in 1992 as follows:

1992: Transferred to Ying Kou Marine Shipping Co., Kingstown, St. Vincent and the Grenadines.

1992: Foundered in 66 metres of water off Komatsushima in Kii Suido in position 33.53 N, 124.52 E during stormy weather, presumably on Mar. 24 while on passage from Toyohashi to Kagoshima, where she was due on Mar. 25 during a voyage from Dalian to Shanghai with 2,600 tons iron scrap. Of 29 crew members on board, 17 were found dead, others missing.

57. LAURI-RAGNAR   1971–1971
FINNRUNNER   1971–1972

General Cargo Motorship, two decks – Open/Closed Shelterdecker
Call: OGJH Ice class: I A

1,599/2,496 GRT, 777/1,498 NRT, 2,278/3,470 dwt
90.21 x 13.30 x 5.06/6.33 m

Diesel Engine 2 SA 6 cy. Werkspoor TEBS456
by N.V. Werkspoor, Amsterdam
1,790 kW / 2,400 BHP   13.2 knots

ms VAASA PROVIDER, later FINNRUNNER
Photo from Matti Pietikäinen

18.12.1962: Launched by N.V. Terneuzensche Scheepsbouw Maats., Terneuzen (#85), without naming ceremonies.

16.11.1963: Christened VAASA PROVIDER by Mrs. E. van der Murk-Duimel in Rotterdam and delivered to Vaasan Laiva Oy, (Alf Korhonen), Helsinki /Helsingfors (1313).

1.11.1966: Sold to M. Rauanheimo Oy, Kokkola /Gamlakarleby (76), (Ab R. Nordström & Co Oy, Loviisa /Lovisa), and renamed LAURI-RAGNAR.

1.12.1970: Sold to the parent company Ab R. Nordström & Co Oy, Loviisa (532).

29.12.1970: Shares of Ab R. Nordström & Co Oy acquired from Kansallis-Osake-Pankki by Enso-Gutzeit Oy.

*ms FINNRUNNER at Sunila, Kotka
Photo by Bengt Sjöström*

1.1.1971:	Management of the vessels of Ab R. Nordström & Co Oy assigned to Oy Finnlines Ltd.
20.4.1971:	Renamed FINNRUNNER by Ab R. Nordström & Co Oy, Loviisa.
23.4.1971:	Owners' name registered as Oy Enso-Chartering Ab as per EGM resolution on Jan. 22.
10.4.1972:	Sold to Les Armateurs du St. Laurent Inc., (Desgagnes Groupe), Quebec, and renamed MAURICE DESGAGNES.
1980:	Foundered on Mar. 12 about 75 miles SSE of Halifax N.S. in position 43.50 N, 62.10 W after her cargo had shifted and taking on a severe list in galeforce weather, while on voyage from New Orleans to Sept Iles with 3,080 tons of railway sleepers. All 21 crew members were safely picked up by a military helicopter shortly before their vessel went down.

58. LOVISA   1971–1971
FINNROSE (I)   1971–1974

General Cargo Motorship, Singledecker
Call: OGUI   Ice class: I A

3,641 GRT, 2,203 NRT, 4,275 dwt
99.37 x 14.53 x 7.01 m

Diesel Engine 2 SA 5 cy. B&W 550-VTBF-110
by Fried. Krupp Dieselmotoren G.m.b.H., Essen
2,424 kW / 3,250 BHP   13.4 knots

ms FINNROSE
Photo by Skyfotos

10.11.1959: Launched by Fr. Lürssen Werft, Bremen-Vegesack (#13301), and named RIMJA DAN by Mrs. E. Sørensen.

18.3.1960: Completed and delivered to Rederiet Ocean A/S, (J. Lauritzen), Esbjerg.

26.1.1968: Acquired by Lovisa Ångfartygs Ab, (Ab R. Nordström & Co Oy), Loviisa /Lovisa (526), and renamed LOVISA when delivered on Jan. 30.

5.5.1969: Owners' amalgamation with the parent company Ab R. Nordström & Co. Oy registered as per EGM resolutions on Sep. 30, 1968.

1969: Arrived on Aug. 9 at Aalborg Værft for conversion from a closed shelterdecker to a singledecker. Her 2 masts and 8 derricks were replaced by 3 cranes, and 4 old hatchcovers by 3 new bigger ones. Delivered on Oct. 16 after completed rebuilding. Tonnages before conversion were: 3,407 GRT, 1,971 NRT, 4,275 dwt

29.12.1970: Shares of Ab R. Nordström & Co Oy acquired from Kansallis-Osake-Pankki by Enso-Gutzeit Oy.

1.1.1971: Management of the vessels of Ab R. Nordström & Co Oy assigned to Oy Finnlines Ltd.

20.4.1971: Renamed FINNROSE by Ab R. Nordström & Co Oy, Loviisa.

23.4.1971: Owners' name registered as Oy Enso-Chartering Ab as per EGM resolution on Jan. 22.

24.9.1974: Sold to Compañia de Navegacion Maylie S.A., Panama, (c/o Sandro Ferraro, Napoli), and renamed CARMENCITA when delivered on Nov. 19.

*ms GELINDA ex FINNROSE at Trieste two weeks before foundering in April 1983
Photo by Nereo Castelli*

1979: Sold to Castalia Compañia de Navegacion S.A., Panama, (c/o Pan Nautic S.A., Lugano), and renamed GELINDA.

1983: Struck bottom and grounded on Feb. 14 in Corinth Canal when on passage from Gallipoli to Jeddah. Repaired at Trieste and sailed on Apr. 12 for Marina di Carrara. – Having left Marina di Carrara on Apr. 22 foundered on Apr. 25 about 20 miles SE of Minorca in position 39.12 N, 04.42 E after developing leaks. Crew rescued from lifeboats by the French destroyer Georges Leygues.

59. NINA   1971–1971
FINNROVER (I)   1971–1973

General Cargo Motorship, two decks – Open /Closed Shelterdecker
Call: OGIO Ice class: I A

1,593/2,635 GRT, 721/1,373 NRT, 2,567/3,842 dwt
93.79 x 13.79 x 5.07/6.36 m

Diesel Engine 2 SA 6 cy. Sulzer 6TAD48
by Maschinenfabrik Buckau R. Wolf A.G., Kiel
1,692 kW / 2,300 BHP   14 knots

26.4.1963: Launched by A/S Langesunds Mekaniske Verksted, Langesund (#49), and named NINA by Mrs. Brita Örö.

7.9.1963: Completed and delivered to Lovisa Ångfartygs Ab, (Ab R. Nordström & Co Oy), Loviisa /Lovisa (514).

5.5.1969: Owners' amalgamation with the parent company Ab R. Nordström & Co. Oy registered as per EGM resolutions on Sep. 30, 1968.

29.12.1970: Shares of Ab R. Nordström & Co Oy acquired from Kansallis-Osake-Pankki by Enso-Gutzeit Oy.

ms FINNROVER
Photo by A. Duncan

1.1.1971:	Management of the vessels of Ab R. Nordström & Co Oy assigned to Oy Finnlines Ltd.
20.4.1971:	Renamed FINNROVER by Ab R. Nordström & Co Oy, Loviisa.
23.4.1971:	Owners' name registered as Oy Enso-Chartering Ab as per EGM resolution on Jan. 22.
8.11.1973:	Sold to Marseille-Fret S.A., Marseilles, and renamed TAMARIS.
1979:	Sold to Santa Margarita Compañia Naviera S.A., Panama, (c/o A. Attalia Shipping & Trading Co., Piraeus), and renamed NANOULA.
1981:	Transferred to Greek flag with Piraeus as home port.
3.1983:	Sold to Overseas Shipping and Trading Co., Alexandria, and renamed NEW DALIA.
3.1991:	Sold to Silver Star Lines, Alexandria, and renamed UNITED I.
1993:	Arrived on Aug. 1 in tow at Carthagena, Spain, from Tangier due to engine room leakage, while on voyage from Antwerp on July 21 to Alexandria. After discharge on Oct. 14 arrested by the towing company and moved on Oct. 28 to Escombreras Bay, where anchored. Berthed on Jan. 7, 1994 due to strong wind.
1994:	Sold by court auction on Apr. 20 to Hierros Hontoria in Segovia. Scrapped thereafter inside Escombreras dock.

ms NANOULA ex FINNROVER
Photo by FotoFlite

60. TAINA
FINNRIVER

1971–1971
1971–1973

General Cargo Motorship, two decks – Closed Shelterdecker
Call: OGUU Ice class: I A

3,407 GRT, 1,971 NRT, 4,275 dwt
99.37 x 14.53 x 7.01 m

Diesel Engine 2 SA 5 cy. B&W 550-VTBF-110
by Fried. Krupp Dieselmotoren G.m.b.H., Essen
2,424 kW / 3,250 BHP 13 knots

ms FINNRIVER in July 1973 at Tolkis without name, but already under the Cyprus flag
Photo by Bengt Sjöström

21.5.1959:	Launched by Fr. Lürssen Werft, Bremen-Vegesack (#13301), and named MANJA DAN by Mrs. P. Blankholm.
5.11.1959:	Completed and delivered to Rederiet Ocean A/S, (J. Lauritzen), Esbjerg.
24.6.1968:	Acquired by Ab R. Nordström & Co Oy, Loviisa / Lovisa (527), and renamed TAINA.
29.12.1970:	Shares of Ab R. Nordström & Co Oy acquired from Kansallis-Osake-Pankki by Enso-Gutzeit Oy.
1.1.1971:	Management of the vessels of Ab R. Nordström & Co Oy assigned to Oy Finnlines Ltd.
20.4.1971:	Renamed FINNRIVER by Ab R. Nordström & Co Oy, Loviisa.
23.4.1971:	Owners' name registered as Oy Enso-Chartering Ab as per EGM resolution on Jan. 22.
25.7.1973:	Sold to Maritime Enterprises Ltd., Famagusta, Cyprus, (c/o Dalex Shipping Co. S.A., Piraeus), and renamed NENI.
1974:	Sold to Ios Maritime Co. Ltd., Famagusta. Managers remained Dalex Shipping Co. S.A., Piraeus.
1975:	Home port changed to Limassol, Cyprus.
7.1976:	Sold to Parthenon Compania Naviera S.A., (George Dalacouras), (c/o Dalex Shipping Co. S.A.), Piraeus. (As per Lloyd's Register 1978)
1976:	Converted to open/closed shelterdecker with following particulars: 2,129/3,260 GRT, 1,188/2,022 NRT, – /4,344 dwt
1.1978:	Renamed NASSIOUKA by Parthenon Cia. Nav. S.A., (c/o Armada Marine S.A.), Piraeus. (As per Lloyd's Registers 1979–1980) *(Owners in 1976–1979 reported by Greek sources as Eros Shipping Co. S.A., Piraeus, instead of Parthenon Cia. Nav. S.A.)*

ms SIN HOCK CHEW ex FINNRIVER at Singapore
Photo from K. Brzoza

1979:	Sold to Capitol Maritime Inc., (c/o Armada Marine S.A., [A.S. Manes]), Piraeus.	12.1986:	Reported as sold to Taiwan shipbreakers, but the sale did not materialize.
1980:	Acquired by West Pacific Shipping Pte. Ltd., (Singapore), but registered in Nuku'alofa, Tonga, and renamed PACIFIC SKY.	1988:	Home port changed to Port Kelang.
		1990:	Sold to Trimhua Shipping Sendirian Berhad, Kuching, Malaysia, and renamed SENG SOON CHEW.
1982:	Sold to Hua Yu Shipping Sendirian Berhad, Penang, Malaysia, (c/o Leong Shen Shipping (Singapore) Pte. Ltd., Singapore), and renamed SIN HOCK CHEW.	1990:	Sank on Dec. 5 off the coast of Sarawak in the South China Sea, in position 03.22 N, 111.50 E after collision with Malaysian ms Johan.

61. VELI   1971–1971

General Cargo Steamer, two decks – Closed Shelterdecker
Call: OGKZ Ice class: I A

3,560 GRT, 1,923 NRT, 4,318 dwt
97.79 x 14.20 x 6.51 m

Compound Steam Engine 3 cy. (1 HP- and 2 LP-cylinders)
by Maskinfabrikken Atlas A/S, København
2,100 IHP   13 knots

ss SILJA DAN, later VELI
Photo from World Ship Photo Library

15.11.1950: Launched by Aalborg Værft A/S, Aalborg (#87), and named SILJA DAN by Mrs. Abildgaard.

6.4.1951: Completed and delivered to Rederiet Ocean A/S, (J. Lauritzen), Esbjerg.

1.7.1964: Acquired by Lovisa Rederi Ab, (Ab R. Nordström & Co Oy), Loviisa / Lovisa (518), and renamed VELI.

5.5.1969: Owners' amalgamation with the parent company Ab R. Nordström & Co. Oy registered as per EGM resolutions on Sep. 30, 1968.

29.12.1970: Shares of Ab R. Nordström & Co Oy acquired from Kansallis-Osake-Pankki by Enso-Gutzeit Oy.

1.1.1971: Management of the vessels of Ab R. Nordström & Co Oy assigned to Oy Finnlines Ltd.

1971: Fire broke out in her engine room under the port side boiler on Jan. 23 in position 61.07 N, 19.26 E, when 22 miles from Finngrundet in the Gulf of Bothnia, while on voyage from Hamina /Fredrikshamn via Pietarsaari /Jakobstad to Barrow-in-Furness with woodpulp. All 25 crew members safely abandoned ship, being rescued from lifeboats by ms Outokumpu, which took them to Mariehamn. The blazing ship was towed by the Swedish salvage vessel Poseidon on Jan. 24 to Rauma /Raumo, where fire was finally extinguished on Feb. 5. Declared a constructive total loss and sold on May 14 by Vakuutus Oy Pohjola (Pohjola Insurance Co. Ltd.) to Ilmari Tuuli, Helsinki /Helsingfors, who resold her to Helsingin Romuliike, omistaja Martti Kilpi. Arrived in tow on May 27 in Helsinki for demolition.

ss VELI
Photo by Bertil Zandelin

62. FINN-AMER
CONCORDIA AMER
FINN-AMER

1971–1977
1977–1977
1977–1981

RoRo/ Container/ General Cargo Motorship, two decks – Open/Closed Shelterdecker, "Universal Superliner", Stern door and 3 side doors
Call: OGYK   Ice class: I B

7,785/16,963 GRT, 4,069/11,437 NRT, 10,470/14,270 dwt, 440 TEU
173.74 x 25.45 x 7.94/9.15 m

Diesel Engine 2 SA 6 cy. Sulzer 6RND90
by Sulzer Bros. Ltd., Winterthur
11,768 kW / 16,000 BHP   20 knots

ms FINN-AMER
Photo from FG-Shipping Oy Ab

19.12.1970: Launched by Rheinstahl Nordseewerke G.m.b.H., Emden (#421), and named FINN-AMER by Mrs. Aune Heikkilä.

12.5.1971: Completed and delivered to Amer-Tupakka Oy, (c/o Oy Finnlines Ltd), Helsinki /Helsingfors (1431). Employed on Finnlines liner service to USEC.

ms IMPERIAL ex FINN-AMER
Photo from Donald Mac Fie

27.9.1973: Owners' name registered as Amer-Yhtymä Oy as per EGM resolution on Sep. 19.

31.12.1974: Sold to Amer-Sea Oy, the shipping subsidiary of Amer-Yhtymä Oy.

15.12.1976: Owners' amalgamation with the parent company, Amer-Yhtymä Oy, registered.

3.6.1977: Renamed CONCORDIA AMER for duration of charter to D/S A/S Idaho, (Concordia Line), Haugesund.

30.11.1977: Name reverted to FINN-AMER after redelivery from charter.

7.1979: Moved to Mideastcargo liner service to the Middle East.

14.4.1981: Sold to New Sun Shipping Co. S.A., Monrovia, (Compañia Sud Americana de Vapores, Valparaiso), (c/o Wallem Shipmanagement Ltd., Hong Kong), and renamed IMPERIAL when delivered on May 12.

1981: Sold to Imperial Ocean Shipping Co. S.A., Monrovia, (c/o Southern Shipmanagement [Chile] Ltd., Valparaiso).

1984: Registered as closed shelterdecker with following tonnages:
17,605 GRT, 6,997 NRT, 14,499 dwt

1987: Sold to Newton International Enterprises Inc., Monrovia, (Compañia Sud Americana de Vapores, Valparaiso). Managers remained Southern Shipmanagement (Chile) Ltd., Valparaiso.

1992: Sold to Bangladesh shipbreakers and arrived at Chittagong Roads on June 6 and beached there on June 23 for demolition.

63. KAIPOLA (II) 1971–1975
FINNOAK (I) 1975–1987

General Cargo Motorship, two decks – Open/Closed Shelterdecker
Call: OGYM Ice class: I A

3,095/5,689 GRT, 1,880/3,144 NRT, 5,511/7,214 dwt
118.25 x 18.04 x 6.42/7.43 m

Diesel Engine 2 SA 6 cy. Sulzer 6RD56
by the Shipbuilders
3,678 kW / 5,000 BHP   14.8 knots

ms KAIPOLA
Photo from Oy Wärtsilä Ab Turku

ms FINNOAK
Photo by Sea-Foto

ms KIMOLOS ex FINNOAK
Photo by K. Brzoza

19.4.1971:	Launched by Oy Wärtsilä Ab, Turku Shipyard, Turku /Åbo (#1195), and named KAIPOLA by Mrs. Bertta Tiainen.
5.8.1971:	Completed and delivered to Yhtyneet Paperitehtaat Oy, (United Paper Mills Ltd.), Rauma /Raumo (619). Managed and operated by Oy Finnlines Ltd.
1.12.1975:	Acquired by Oy Torlines Ab, (Tor Johansson), Tammisaari /Ekenäs (117), and renamed FINNOAK. Managers remained Oy Finnlines Ltd.
1.1.1976:	Time-chartered to Oy Finncarriers Ab, Helsinki / Helsingfors.
4.8.1980:	Registration changed to Hanko /Hangö (258) due to the closure of the Tammisaari registry.
17.2.1987:	Sold to Huel Shipping – A Limited Partnership, Panama, (c/o Tor K. Husjord Shipping A/S, Narvik), and renamed TRAMARCO CARRIER for duration of charter to Transmarine Chartering Inc., Cold Spring Harbor, N.Y. Delivered on Feb. 27.
7.1990:	Sold to Rex Shipping Co. Ltd., Panama, (Jorma Saarinen, Helsinki), and renamed AQUILA-I.
6.1991:	Sold to Reefer & General Shipping Co. Inc., Panama, (Société de Gestion Evge S.A., Piraeus), (c/o Reefer and General Ship Management Co. Inc., Piraeus), and renamed KIMOLOS.
1994:	Remeasured in accordance with the 1969 Convention as follows: 5,523 GT, 2,967 NT, 5,511 dwt

64. FINNBUILDER   1971–1977
CONCORDIA BUILDER   1977–1978
FINNBUILDER   1978–1981

RoRo/ Container/ General Cargo Motorship, two decks – Open/Closed Shelterdecker, "Universal Superliner", Stern door and 3 side doors
Call: OGYL Ice class: I B

7,785/16,963 GRT, 4,069/11,437 NRT, 10,470/14,270 dwt, 440 TEU
173.74 x 25.45 x 7.94/9.15 m

Diesel Engine 2 SA 6 cy. Sulzer 6RND90
by Sulzer Bros. Ltd., Winterthur
11,768 kW / 16,000 BHP   20 knots

ms FINNBUILDER
Photo from FG-Shipping Oy Ab

5.6.1971:	Launched by Rheinstahl Nordseewerke G.m.b.H., Emden (#422), and named FINNBUILDER by Mrs. Liisa Ketola.
22.10.1971:	Completed and delivered to Rakennustoimisto, Jussi Ketola, (c/o Oy Finnlines Ltd), Helsinki /Helsingfors (1445). Employed on Finnlines liner service to USEC.
13.12.1972:	Owners re-organised as Ky Jussi Ketola & Co.
3.6.1977:	Renamed CONCORDIA BUILDER for duration of charter to D/S A/S Idaho, (Concordia Line, Christian Haaland), Haugesund.
18.1.1978:	Name reverted to FINNBUILDER after redelivery from charter.
8.1979:	Moved to Mideastcargo liner service to the Middle East.
24.3.1981:	Sold to New Sun Shipping Co. S.A., Monrovia, (c/o Wallem Shipmanagement Ltd., Hong Kong), and renamed NORTHERN SAPPHIRE when delivered on Apr. 3.
6.1981:	Renamed COPIAPO by New Sun Shipping Co. S.A., Monrovia, when chartered to Compañia Sud-Americana de Vapores (CSAV). Management taken over by Southern Shipmanagement (Chile) Ltd., Valparaiso.
1984:	Registered as closed shelterdecker with following tonnages: 17,605 GRT, 6,997 NRT, 15,098 dwt
1987:	Sold to Hunter Shipping Operations Inc., Monrovia, (Compañia Sud-Americana de Vapores, Valparaiso). Managers remained Southern Shipmanagement (Chile) Ltd., Valparaiso.
1992:	Sold to Bangladesh shipbreakers and having left Singapore on Apr. 8, beached at Chittagong on abt. May 1 for demolition.

ms CONCORDIA-BUILDER in Jeddah
Photo by Matti Pietikäinen

65. FINNSAILOR (II)   1972–1976
CONCORDIA SAILOR   1976–1978
FINNSAILOR (II)   1978–1981

RoRo/ Container/ General Cargo Motorship, two decks – Open/Closed Shelterdecker, "Universal Superliner", Stern door and 3 side doors
Call: OGZQ Ice class: I B

7,785/16,963 GRT, 4,069/11,437 NRT, 10,470/14,270 dwt, 440 TEU
173.74 x 25.45 x 7.94/9.15 m

Diesel Engine 2 SA 6 cy. Sulzer 6RND90
by Sulzer Bros. Ltd., Winterthur
11,768 kW / 16,000 BHP   20 knots

ms FINNSAILOR at Khor al Fakkan, the Sultanate of Oman
Photo from FG-Shipping Oy Ab

24.9.1971:	Launched by Rheinstahl Nordseewerke G.m.b.H., Emden (#423), and named FINNSAILOR by Mrs. Armi Valleala.
28.1.1972:	Completed and delivered to Enso-Gutzeit Oy, Hamina /Fredrikshamn (264), (c/o Oy Finnlines Ltd., Helsinki/Helsingfors). Employed on Finnlines liner service to USEC.
31.8.1972:	Sold to Merivienti Oy, Hamina, (Enso-Gutzeit Oy), (c/o Oy Finnlines Ltd, Helsinki).
1.4.1976:	Renamed CONCORDIA SAILOR for duration of charter to D/S A/S Idaho, (Concordia Line, Christian Haaland), Haugesund.
7.2.1978:	Name reverted to FINNSAILOR after redelivery from charter.
1978:	In collision on Mar. 29 in fog near the entrance to Gothenburg with Swedish ms Skagern, which sank with loss of three crew members.

ms ACONCAGUA ex FINNSAILOR in Philadelphia
Photo from K. Brzoza

8.1979:	Moved to Mideastcargo liner service to the Middle East.
11.5.1981:	Sold to New Sun Shipping Co. S.A., Monrovia, (c/o Wallem Shipmanagement Ltd., Hong Kong), and renamed ACONCAGUA.
1981:	Sold to Compañia Sud-Americana de Vapores (CSAV), (c/o Southern Shipmanagement (Chile) Ltd.), Valparaiso.
1983:	Registered as closed shelterdecker with following tonnages: 14,704 GRT, 8,872 NRT, 15,200 dwt
10.1993:	Sold to Mediterranean Spirit S.A., Panama, (c/o Regal Agencies Corp., Piraeus), and renamed ACONCAGUA 1.
1993:	Remeasured in accordance with the 1969 Convention as follows: 17,585 GT, 8,560 NT, 15,200 dwt
1994:	Sold to Windle Shipping Co. Ltd., Panama. Managers remained Regal Agencies Corp., Piraeus.
1995:	Sold to Indian shipbreakers and anchored off Alang on Apr. 7 and beached there on Apr. 16 for demolition.

66. FINNPINE (II)   1972–1986

General Cargo Motorship, two decks – Open /Closed Shelterdecker
Call: OGYN Ice class: I A

3,690/6,616 GRT, 1,452/2,965 NRT, 5,302/8,050 dwt
129.38 x 19.45 x 6.47/8.04 m

Diesel Engine 2 SA 6 cy. B&W 6K62EF
by Valmet Oy, Rautpohjan Tehdas, Jyväskylä
6,105 kW / 8,300 BHP   17 knots

29.11.1971:	Launched by Valmet Oy, Helsingin Telakka, Helsinki /Helsingfors (#268) for Enso-Gutzeit Oy, Kotka, and named FINNPINE by Mrs. Elina Keino.
4.5.1972:	Newbuilding contract handed over to Merivienti Oy, a new subsidiary of Enso-Gutzeit Oy.
12.5.1972:	Completed and delivered to Merivienti Oy, (Enso-Gutzeit Oy), Kotka (583). Managed and operated by Oy Finnlines Ltd. Employed on Finnlines Mediterranean service.
1.1.1976:	Time-chartered to Oy Finncarriers Ab, Helsinki.

ms FINNPINE
Photo by Sea-Foto

1.10.1982:	Acquired by Neste Oy, Naantali /Nådendal (69), without change of name. Managers remained Oy Finnlines Ltd.
3.4.1986:	Sold to Hebei Province Subcorporation China Ocean Shipping Co. (COSCO HEBEI), and renamed AN GUO.
1986:	Owners listed as Shanghai Ocean Shipping Company (COSCO SHANGHAI).
1988:	Owners amended to China Ocean Shipping Company (COSCO), Qinhuangdao.
1990:	Owners reverted to Hebei Province Subcorporation China Ocean Shipping Co. (COSCO HEBEI), Qinhuangdao.
1994:	Remeasured in accordance with the 1969 Convention as follows: 7,076 GT, 2,157 NT, 8,942 dwt

67. VALKEAKOSKI   1972–1977
FINNKRAFT (II)   1977–1982
CLIO   1982–1989

General Cargo Motorship, two decks – Open/Closed Shelterdecker
Call: C6CN5 ex OIAI   Ice class: I A

3,095/5,689 GRT, 1,838/3,102 NRT, 5,511/7,214 dwt
118.25 x 18.04 x 6.42/7.43 m

Diesel Engine 2 SA 6 cy. Sulzer 6RD56
by the Shipbuilders
3,678 kW / 5,000 BHP   14.8 knots

ms VALKEAKOSKI
Photo by Skyfotos

ms FINNKRAFT at Kotka
Photo by Bengt Sjöström

ms CLIO at Turku
Photo by K. Brzoza

8.3.1972:	Launched by Oy Wärtsilä Ab, Turku Shipyard, Turku /Åbo (#1196), and named VALKEAKOSKI by Mrs. Kristiina Hakkarainen.
22.6.1972:	Completed and delivered to Yhtyneet Paperitehtaat Oy, (United Paper Mills Ltd.), Rauma /Raumo (620). Managed and operated by Oy Finnlines Ltd.
1.1.1976:	Time-chartered to Oy Finncarriers Ab, Helsinki / Helsingfors.
15.9.1977:	Sold to Merivienti Oy, (Enso-Gutzeit Oy), Helsinki (1586), and renamed FINNKRAFT. Managers remained Oy Finnlines Ltd.
1.10.1982:	Sold to Oy Suomi Line / Finland Line Ab, (Effoa – Finska Ångfartygs Ab / Effoa – Suomen Höyrylaiva Oy / Effoa – Finland Steamship Co. Ltd.), Helsinki, and renamed CLIO. Still managed by Oy Finnlines Ltd.
27.4.1983:	Acquired by Oy Torlines Ab, (Tor Johansson), Tammisaari /Ekenäs (Hanko /Hangö 267), with charter back to previous owners without change of name and managers. Delivered on Apr. 28.
9.2.1987:	Flagged out by a sale to Oak Shipping Ltd., a subsidiary of Oy Torlines Ab in George Town, Cayman Islands, but registered in Nassau, Bahamas. Managers remained Oy Finnlines Ltd.
7.1989:	Sold to China Ocean Shipping Company Jiangshu Branch, Nanjing /Nanking, and renamed LU SHAN when delivered on July 21.
1989:	Renamed YUE LU SHAN by Jiangsu Ocean Shipping Company (COSCO JIANGSU), Nanjing / Nanking.
1990:	Registered as closed shelterdecker with following tonnages: 5,689 GRT, 3,102 NRT, 7,214 dwt
12.1997:	*New GT and NT in accordance with the 1969 Convention not yet reported to Lloyd's Register.*

68. FINNMASTER (II)   1972–1982
CORONA   1982–1986

General Cargo Motorship, two decks – Open/Closed Shelterdecker
Call: OIAO Ice class: I A

2,066/4,045 GRT, 1,242/2,467 NRT, 3,649/5,919 dwt
106.64 x 17.04 x 5.46/7.06 m

Diesel Engine 2 SA 8 cy. Werkspoor 8TM410
by Stork-Werkspoor Diesel N.V., Amsterdam
3,236 kW / 4,400 BHP   14 knots

ms FINNMASTER
Photo by FotoFlite

28.5.1970:	Order placed by Ab R. Nordström & Co. Oy, Loviisa /Lovisa, with Kleven Mekaniske Verksted A/S.
29.12.1970:	Shares of Ab R. Nordström & Co Oy acquired from Kansallis-Osake-Pankki by Enso-Gutzeit Oy.
29.4.1972:	Launched by Kleven Mekaniske Verksted A/S, Ulsteinvik (#23), without naming ceremonies.
28.7.1972:	Christened FINNMASTER by Mrs. Marianne Andresen.
11.8.1972:	Completed and delivered to Oy Enso-Chartering Ab, (Enso-Gutzeit Oy), Loviisa (534), (c/o Oy Finnlines Ltd, Helsinki /Helsingfors). Employed on Finnlines liner service from Finland to England.
3.11.1975:	Owners' amalgamation with the parent company Enso-Gutzeit Oy registered as per AGM resolutions on Apr. 11.
1.1.1976:	Time-chartered to Oy Finncarriers Ab, Helsinki.
1.6.1979:	Sold to Merivienti Oy, (Enso-Gutzeit Oy), Loviisa.
1.10.1982:	Acquired by Oy Suomi Line / Finland Line Ab, (Effoa – Finska Ångfartygs Ab / Effoa – Suomen Höyrylaiva Oy / Effoa – Finland Steamship Co. Ltd.), Helsinki (1678), and renamed CORONA. Managers remained Oy Finnlines Ltd.
4.6.1986:	Owners' amalgamation with the parent company Effoa – Finland Steamship Co. Ltd. registered as per EGM resolutions on Nov. 14, 1985.
12.11.1986:	Sold to Ocean Mercury Shipping S.A., Panama, (c/o Wah Tung Shipping Agency Co. Ltd., Hong Kong), and renamed OCEAN MERCURY.
1.1987:	Sold to China Ocean Shipping Co. (COSCO), and renamed JIA FA.
1990:	Transferred to Xiamen Special Economic Zone Shipping Co. Ltd., Xiamen /Amoy.

ms CORONA on arrival at Helsinki
Photo by Matti Pietikäinen

1992: Owners' name amended to Xiamen Jia He Shipping Co. Ltd., Xiamen /Amoy.

1996: Remeasured in accordance with the 1969 Convention as follows: 4,275 GT, 2,400 NT, 5,919 dwt

1996: Transferred to Tianjin Hailong Shipping Co., Tianjin, and renamed JIN TAI.

69. HANS GUTZEIT   1972–1982
CAPELLA   1982–1985
CAPELLA AV STOCKHOLM   1985–1988
FINNMAID (III)   1988–

RoRo Cargo /Passenger Motor Ferry, four decks
Two stern doors, side door
Passengers: 48 berths
Call: OJFZ ex SLNQ ex OIAL Ice class: I A Super

13,730 GT, 4,119 NT, 5,300 dwt, 1,000 lane metres
137.34 x 24.57 x 6.10 m

2 Vee Diesel Engines 4 SA each 14 cy. Pielstick 14PC2-5V-400
by the Shipbuilders
2 x 5,150 kW / 2 x 7,000 BHP
Total 10,300 kW / 2 x 14,000 BHP   19.3 knots Twin screw

27.4.1972: Launched by Oy Wärtsilä Ab, Turku Shipyard, Turku /Åbo (#1204), and named HANS GUTZEIT by Mrs. Aura Lindblom.

7.9.1972: Completed and delivered to Merivienti Oy, (Enso-Gutzeit Oy), Kotka (586), (c/o Oy Finnlines Ltd, Helsinki /Helsingfors). Employed on Southern Finland – Lübeck roro service.

1.1.1976: Time-chartered to Oy Finncarriers Ab, Helsinki.

ms HANS GUTZEIT
Photo by Matti Pietikäinen

1.10.1982: Sold to Oy Suomi Line / Finland Line Ab, (Effoa – Finska Ångfartygs Ab / Effoa – Suomen Höyrylaiva Oy / Effoa – Finland Steamship Co. Ltd.), Helsinki (1676), and renamed CAPELLA. Managers remained Oy Finnlines Ltd.

12.11.1984: Acquired by Thomesto Oy, Helsinki, and delivered the same day without change of name. Still managed by Oy Finnlines Ltd. Chartered back for 3 years to Oy Finncarriers Ab, the operative subsidiary of Effoa.

18.12.1985: Flagged out by a sale to And. Smith Rederi AB, Stockholm, the Swedish shipping subsidiary of Thomesto Oy, and renamed CAPELLA AV STOCKHOLM when delivered on Dec. 30. Technical management by Oy Finnlines Ltd and personnel by Gorthons Rederi AB, Helsingborg.

30.9.1988: Sold to Partrederiet för Finnmaid, (c/o AB Finnlines Ltd.), Stockholm, and renamed FINNMAID. Technical management by Oy Finnlines Ltd and personnel by BN Management AB.

2.1.1989: Chartered to Oy Finnlink Ab, Helsinki, and inaugurated a ferry service between Uusikaupunki /Nystad and Hargshamn.

1.7.1989: Technical managers' name changed to FG-Shipping Oy Ab.

1989: Fitted in September with a side door and a new stern ramp by Howaldtswerke – Deutsche Werft, Kiel. Returned to service after rebuilding on Oct. 2.

19.1.1990: Sold to Artos Förvaltnings AB, (Investment AB Develop), Stockholm. Bareboat-chartered back to Oy Finnlink Ab. Managers remained as previously.

ms CAPELLA
Photo by Matti Pietikäinen

ms FINNMAID
Photo by K. Brzoza

8.2.1990:	Owners' name changed to Finnmaid AB and home port to Hargshamn.	1.11.1993:	New national reg.no. 11561.
30.8.1993:	Acquired by Laivanisännistöyhtiö Finnmaid (Part Owners Finnmaid), (c/o FG-Shipping Oy Ab), Helsinki (1873), and delivered the same day. Continued on Finnlink roro service between Uusikaupunki and Hargshamn.	16.2.1994:	Remeasured in accordance with the 1969 Convention as above in the heading. Her previous tonnages were: 6,299 GRT, 2,108 NRT, 5,300 dwt
		1.4.1997:	Moved to Naantali /Nådendal – Kapellskär line by Oy Finnlink Ab.
7.9.1993:	Entered in the Finnish parallel Register of Merchant Vessels engaged in International Trade.	30.6.1997:	Sold to Finnlines Oy / Finnlines Ab / Finnlines Ltd / Finnlines AG, Helsinki, and was delivered the same day.

70. FINNWOOD (II) 1972–1982
CARELIA 1982–1983

General Cargo Motorship, two decks – Open/Closed Shelterdecker
Call: OIAM Ice class: I A

3,690/6,616 GRT, 1,452/2,965 NRT, 5,302/8,123 dwt
129.38 x 19.45 x 6.47/8.05 m

Diesel Engine 2 SA 6 cy. B&W 6K62EF
by Valmet Oy, Rautpohjan Tehdas, Jyväskylä
6,105 kW / 8,300 BHP   17 knots

15.1.1970:	Order placed by Enso-Gutzeit Oy, Kotka, but newbuilding handed over to Merivienti Oy, a new subsidiary of Enso-Gutzeit Oy, while on the stocks.	18.9.1972:	Completed and delivered to Merivienti Oy, (Enso-Gutzeit Oy), Kotka (587). Managed and operated by Oy Finnlines Ltd. Employed on Finnlines Mediterranean service.
19.4.1972:	Launched by Valmet Oy, Helsingin Telakka, Helsinki /Helsingfors (#269), and named FINNWOOD by Mrs. Margareta Grönhagen.	1.1.1976:	Time-chartered to Oy Finncarriers Ab, Helsinki.

ms FINNWOOD
Photo by Skyfotos

ms CARELIA in Helsinki
Photo by Matti Pietikäinen

1.10.1982:	Acquired by Effoa – Finska Ångfartygs Ab / Effoa – Suomen Höyrylaiva Oy / Effoa – Finland Steamship Co. Ltd.), Helsinki (1679), and renamed CARELIA. Managers remained Oy Finnlines Ltd.	11.6.1986:	Flagged out by a sale to Cat Shipping Ltd., Limassol, a Cyprian subsidiary of Ab Borgå Sjötransport Oy. Delivered without change of name.
8.4.1983:	Sold to Skop-rahoitus Oy – Skop-finans Ab and leased to Ab Borgå Sjötransport Oy, Porvoo /Borgå (588). Chartered back to previous owners without change of name.	2.1991:	Sold to Hilho Shipping Ltd., Valletta, (Ab Borgå Sjötransport Oy, Porvoo).
		1992:	Sold to J. Master Shipping Co. Ltd., Kingstown, St. Vincent & the Grenadines, (c/o Jiang Tong Co. Ltd., Hong Kong), and renamed J. SISTER.
2.12.1985:	Purchased by Ab Borgå Sjötransport Oy, Porvoo, from the leasing company, Skop-rahoitus Oy.	1994:	Remeasured in accordance with the 1969 Convention as follows: 6,982 GT, 3,292 NT, 8,123 dwt
		1995:	Sold to Jiangsu Ocean Shipping Company (COSCO JIANGSU), Nanjing /Nanking, and renamed JI XI.

71. TUIRA   1972–1989
FINNOAK (II)   1989–1993

General Cargo Motorship, two decks – Open/Closed Shelterdecker
Call: C6CZ9 ex OIAJ Ice class: I A Super

3,095/5,689 GRT, 1,837/3,098 NRT, 5,511/7,214 dwt
118.25 x 18.04 x 6.42/7.43 m

Diesel Engine 2 SA 6 cy. Sulzer 6RD56
by the Shipbuilders
3,678 kW / 5,000 BHP   14.8 knots

ms TUIRA
Photo by Seppo Kaksonen

ms FINNOAK
Photo by Didier Noirel

10.8.1972: Launched by Oy Wärtsilä Ab, Turku Shipyard, Turku /Åbo (#1200), and named TUIRA by Mrs. Annikki Tähtinen.

17.11.1972: Completed and delivered to Oulu Oy, Oulu /Uleåborg (522). Managed and operated by Oy Finnlines Ltd.

1.1.1976: Time-chartered to Oy Finncarriers Ab, Helsinki / Helsingfors.

27.11.1986: Owners' amalgamation with the parent company, Veitsiluoto Oy, Kemi, registered as per EGM resolutions on June 10. Home port remained Oulu.

30.6.1987: Flagged out by a sale to Oulu Shipping Ltd., a subsidiary of Veitsiluoto Oy in George Town, Cayman Islands. Bareboat-chartered back to Veitsiluoto Oy. Managers remained Oy Finnlines Ltd.

ms BALTIC STONE ex FINNOAK
Photo by Bengt Sjöström

13.3.1989: Acquired by Oak Shipping Ltd., a subsidiary of Oy Torlines Ab, (Tammisaari /Ekenäs), in George Town, Cayman Islands, and renamed FINNOAK when delivered on Mar. 17 and registered in Nassau, Bahamas. Managers remained Oy Finnlines Ltd.

19.5.1993: Sold to Sea Carrier Investment Ltd., Nassau, (c/o Bogazzi Servizi Navali S.r.l., Avenza, Italy), and renamed BALTIC STONE.

1994: Remeasured in accordance with the 1969 Convention as follows:
5,877 GT, 3,075 NT, 7,214 dwt

72. **FINNTRADER (II)**   1972–1982
CASTOR   1982–1985

General Cargo Motorship, two decks – Open/Closed Shelterdecker
Call: OIAN Ice class: I A

3,689/6,616 GRT, 1,450/2,962 NRT, 5,302/8,123 dwt
129.38 x 19.45 x 6.47/8.04 m

Diesel Engine 2 SA 6 cy. B&W 6K62EF
by Valmet Oy Rautpohjan Tehdas, Jyväskylä
6,105 kW / 8,300 BHP   17 knots

ms FINNTRADER
Photo by Sea-Foto

ms CASTOR in Helsinki
Photo by Matti Pietikäinen

15.1.1970:	Order placed by Enso-Gutzeit Oy, Kotka, but newbuilding handed over to Merivienti Oy, a new subsidiary of Enso-Gutzeit Oy, while on the stocks.
24.8.1972:	Launched by Valmet Oy, Helsingin Telakka, Helsinki /Helsingfors (#270), and named FINNTRADER by Mrs. Eeva-Liisa Sormanto.
28.12.1972:	Completed and delivered to Merivienti Oy, (Enso-Gutzeit Oy), Kotka (589). Managed and operated by Oy Finnlines Ltd. Employed on Finnlines Mediterranean service.
1.1.1976:	Time-chartered to Oy Finncarriers Ab, Helsinki.
1.10.1982:	Acquired by Effoa – Finska Ångfartygs Ab / Effoa – Suomen Höyrylaiva Oy / Effoa – Finland Steamship Co. Ltd., Helsinki (1680), and renamed CASTOR. Managers remained Oy Finnlines Ltd.
21.5.1985:	Sold to China Ocean Shipping Co. (COSCO), Jiangsu Branch, Nanjing /Nanking, and renamed SU LIN when delivered on May 28.
1986:	Owners' name re-styled as Jiangsu Ocean Shipping Company (COSCO JIANGSU).
12.1997:	*New GT and NT in accordance with the 1969 Convention not yet reported to Lloyd's Register.*

73. KOITELI   1972–1989
FINNELM   1989–1990

General Cargo Motorship, two decks – Open/Closed Shelterdecker
Call: OIZO ex C6CN9 ex OIAK Ice class: I A Super

3,095/5,689 GRT, 1,837/3,098 NRT, 5,511/7,214 dwt
118.25 x 18.04 x 6.42/7.43 m

Diesel Engine 2 SA 6 cy. Sulzer 6RD56
by the Shipbuilders
3,678 kW / 5,000 BHP   14.8 knots

4.10.1972:	Launched by Oy Wärtsilä Ab, Turku Shipyard, Turku /Åbo (#1201), and named KOITELI by Mrs. Elsa Pelkonen.
29.12.1972:	Completed and delivered to Oulu Oy, Oulu /Uleåborg (523). Managed and operated by Oy Finnlines Ltd.
1.1.1976:	Time-chartered to Oy Finncarriers Ab, Helsinki / Helsingfors.
27.11.1986:	Owners' amalgamation with the parent company, Veitsiluoto Oy, Kemi, registered as per EGM resolutions on June 10. Home port remained Oulu.

ms KOITELI at Kemi
Photo by Kari Riutta

ms FINNELM at Hamina
Photo by Matti Pietikäinen

ms SALAMA ex FINNELM
Photo by Kari Mäkirinta, coll. K. Brzoza

30.6.1987: Flagged out by a sale to Oulu Shipping Ltd., a subsidiary of Veitsiluoto Oy in George Town, Cayman Islands, but registered in Nassau, Bahamas. Bareboat-chartered back to Veitsiluoto Oy. Managers remained Oy Finnlines Ltd.

29.3.1989: Acquired by Oy Torlines Ab, (Kirsti Johansson), Tammisaari /Ekenäs (Hanko /Hangö 286), and renamed FINNELM when delivered on Apr. 7. Managers remained Oy Finnlines Ltd.

1.7.1989:	Managers' name changed to FG-Shipping Oy Ab.	10.1992:	Sold to Egyptian Reefer and General Cargo Shipping Co. S.A.S., Alexandria, and renamed SALAMA. Managers remained Reefer and General Ship Management Co. Inc., Piraeus.
10.12.1990:	Sold to Reefer & General Shipping Co. Inc., Panama, (Société de Gestion Evge S.A., Piraeus), (c/o Reefer and General Ship Management Co. Inc., Piraeus) and renamed APOLLONIA V when delivered on Dec. 12.	1994:	Remeasured in accordance with the 1969 Convention as follows: 5,877 GT, 3,075 NT, 7,329 dwt

74. FINNPARTNER (II)   1973–1976
OLAU FINN   1976–1982

Passenger /RoRo Cargo Motor Ferry, two decks with intermediate deck, stern door
Passengers: 494 berths, 314 pullman chairs, total capacity 1,400 pass.
Call: OIBT Ice class: I C

7,977 GRT, 3,539 NRT, 2,750 dwt
140.85 x 20.76 x 5.52 m

4 Diesel Engines 4 SA each 6 cy. Pielstick 6PC2L-400
by the Shipbuilders
4 x 1,853 kW / 4 x 2,520 BHP
Total 7,412 kW / 10,080 BHP   18 knots Twin Screw

ms SAGA, later FINNPARTNER
Photo from Tomas Johannesson

18.10.1965:	Launched by Ab. Lindholmens Varv, Göteborg (#1093), and named SAGA by Princess Christina of Sweden.	2.5.1966:	Completed and delivered to Rederi ab. Svenska Lloyd, (Kjell Andersén), Göteborg (10683). Entered Gothenburg – Hull service and sailed on her maiden trip on May 6 for Hull. Moved on Oct. 6 to Gothenburg – Tilbury line.

ms FINNPARTNER
Photo from Thomproperties Oy

ms OLAU FINN
Photo from Krister Bång

7.2.1972:	Sold to Stena Ab., (Sten A. Olsson), Göteborg, and renamed STENA ATLANTICA.
1972:	While being rebuilt in February–March the forward cargo hold was replaced by new cabins increasing the capacity from 408 to 494 berths. In addition a dormitory was built on the sun deck for 314 passengers. Started on Mar. 13 a liner service from Gothenburg to Kiel and opened on Sep. 4 a new line from Gothenburg to Copenhagen.
13.3.1972:	Owners' name changed to Stena Line Ab., (Sten A. Olsson), Göteborg.
8.3.1973:	Acquired by Thomesto Oy, Helsinki /Helsingfors (1489), (c/o Oy Finnlines Ltd) and delivered on Mar. 13 in Gothenburg.
7.4.1973:	Placed after rebuilding at Valmet Oy, Helsinki shipyard, as FINNPARTNER on Helsinki – Nynäshamn – Travemünde service of Finnlines. The dormitory was replaced by a pool and a department for 314 pullman chairs. In addition to the Baltic service, she operated during the winters 1973–74 and 1974–75 as a cruise ship making trips mainly from Las Palmas, Gran Canaria, to West Africa.
1.12.1975:	Laid up in Helsinki while replaced in cruise traffic by ms Bore Star.
20.4.1976:	Chartered to Olau Line A/S, (Ole Lauritzen), København, and renamed OLAU FINN when started her cross-channel service from Flushing (Vlissingen) to Sheerness.
1.1.1978:	Chartered to Olau Line (U.K.) Ltd., Sheerness, (c/o TT-Linie G.m.b.H. & Co., Hamburg), and continued on the same line.
15.5.1982:	Redelivered from the charter after having made 4,286 channel crossings.

*ms FOLKLINER ex OLAU FINN
approaching Gefle
Photo by Matti Pietikäinen*

*ms FESTOS ex OLAU FINN at Piraeus
Photo by Matti Pietikäinen*

27.5.1982:	Sold to PSP-rahoitus Oy, (PSP-finance Ltd.), Helsinki, which then leased her to Oy Folkline Ab, Kaskinen /Kaskö (66). Opened the following day as FOLKLINER a new line from Kaskinen to Gefle.
1.10.1982:	Registration moved from Kaskinen to Vaasa /Vasa (256) due to the closure of the registry at Kaskinen.
12.1983:	Reported as sold to Minoan Lines Shipping S.A., Iraklion, and to be renamed FESTOS, but the sale did not materialize due to the refusal of the Bank of Greece.
24.8.1984:	Oy Folkline Ab went into liquidation and the vessel was laid up on Sep. 8 at Turku /Åbo awaiting sale. PSP-rahoitus Oy handed over the management to Oy Finnlines Ltd.
30.10.1984:	Sold to Minoan Lines Shipping S.A., Iraklion, and renamed FESTOS when delivered on Nov. 8. After repairs employed on Piraeus – Iraklion, Crete service.
1994:	Remeasured in accordance with the 1969 Convention as follows: 12,374 GT, 4,802 NT, 2,794 dwt

75. FINNALPINO (II) — 1973–1983

General Cargo Motorship, two decks – Open/Closed Shelterdecker
Call: OIBR Ice class: I A

3,689/6,616 GRT, 1,450/2,962 NRT, 5,302/8,123 dwt
129.38 x 19.45 x 6.47/8.04 m

Diesel Engine 2 SA 6 cy. B&W 6K62EF
by Valmet Oy, Rautpohjan Tehdas, Jyväskylä
6,105 kW / 8,300 BHP   17 knots

ms FINNALPINO
Photo by Sea-Foto

15.1.1970: Order placed by Enso-Gutzeit Oy, Kotka, but newbuilding handed over to Merivienti Oy, a new subsidiary of Enso-Gutzeit Oy, while on the stocks.

12.12.1972: Launched by Valmet Oy, Helsingin Telakka, Helsinki/Helsingfors (#271), and named FINNALPINO by Countess Mariuccia Gilberti.

6.4.1973: Completed and delivered to Merivienti Oy, (Enso-Gutzeit Oy), Kotka (590). Managed and operated by Oy Finnlines Ltd. Employed on Finnlines Mediterranean service.

1.1.1976: Time-chartered to Oy Finncarriers Ab, Helsinki.

1.10.1982: Acquired by Neste Oy, Naantali /Nådendal (71), without change of name. Managers remained Oy Finnlines Ltd.

15.11.1983: Sold to Gainvir Transport Ltd., Hamilton, Bermuda, (Kent Line Ltd., [J.D. Irving Ltd.], Saint John, N.B.), and renamed IRVING FOREST when delivered on Nov. 16.

ms IRVING FOREST ex FINNALPINO
Photo by FotoFlite

1990: Abandoned by her crew on Jan. 11 after taking on a heavy list in high seas and gale-force winds whilst on voyage from St. John, N.B. to Rouen. All 19 crew members rescued from liferafts by mt BT Nestor. As per last report shortly afterwards, drifting in position 46.58 N, 28.27 W, but has not been seen since.

76. FINNFELLOW   1973–

RoRo Cargo/Passenger Motor Ferry, four decks
Stern door and side door
Passengers: 48 berths
Call: OIBS Ice class: I A Super

14,297 GT, 4,290 NT, 4,995 dwt, 1,000 lane metres
137.34 x 24.57 x 6.12 m

2 Vee Diesel Engines 4 SA each 14 cy. Pielstick 14PC2-5V-400 by the Shipbuilders
2 x 5,149 kW / 2 x 7,000 BHP
Total 10,298 kW / 14,000 BHP   19.3 knots Twin screw

ms FINNFELLOW in 1987
Photo by Matti Pietikäinen

ms FINNFELLOW in 1992
Photo by Matti Pietikäinen

2.1.1973:	Launched by Oy Wärtsilä Ab, Turku Shipyard, Turku /Åbo (#1205), and named FINNFELLOW by Mrs. Elisabeth Holma.
21.5.1973:	Completed as roro cargo/passenger ferry and delivered to Merivienti Oy, (Enso-Gutzeit Oy), Helsinki /Helsingfors (1492). Managed and operated by Oy Finnlines Ltd, Helsinki. Employed on Helsinki – Kotka – Felixstowe roro service. Tonnages when completed were: 6,291 GRT, 2,109 NRT, 4,995 dwt
1.1.1976:	Time-chartered to Oy Finncarriers Ab, Helsinki.
30.1.1976:	Transferred to Helsinki – Lübeck roro service by Oy Finncarriers Ab.
1.10.1982:	Sold to Neste Oy, Naantali /Nådendal (72), without change of name. Managers remained Oy Finnlines Ltd.
27.2.1986:	Acquired by Oy Finnlines Ltd., Helsinki (1492), as their first own ship.
30.9.1988:	Sold to Laivanisännistöyhtiö Finnfellow, (Part Owners Finnfellow), Uusikaupunki /Nystad (414). Managers remained Oy Finnlines Ltd.
1989:	Arrived on June 6 at Howaldtswerke – Deutsche Werft A.G., Kiel, for conversion to a roro cargo rail vehicles/passenger ferry. Fitted with rails and the hull heightened by 80 cm to accommodate up to 26 railway waggons. Delivered by the shipyard on Aug. 26. Tonnages after new measurement: 6,304 GRT, 2,084 NRT, 4,995 dwt
1.7.1989:	Managers' name changed to FG-Shipping Oy Ab.
4.9.1989:	Chartered to Oy Finnlink Ab, Helsinki, and inaugurated on Sep. 7 a train ferry service between Uusikaupunki /Nystad and Hargshamn.
19.1.1990:	Sold to Oy Finnlink Ab, Helsinki, and immediately the same day further to Laivanisännistöyhtiö Railfellow, (Part Owners Railfellow), Helsinki (1492). Managers remained FG-Shipping Oy Ab.
7.1.1992:	Entered in the Finnish parallel Register of Merchant Vessels engaged in International Trade.
1.11.1993:	New national reg.no. 10789.
28.3.1994:	Remeasured in accordance with the 1969 Convention as above in the heading.
1996:	Went aground on Dec. 9 at Isomatala in position 60.47 N, 21.13 E and sustained considerable damage while on voyage from Hargshamn to Uusikaupunki with trailers. Refloated on Dec. 15 with assistance of two tugs, but ran aground again in bad weather and sustained further damage. Refloated on Dec. 18 and towed to Naantali /Nådendal for repairs by Turun Korjaustelakka Oy / Turku Repair Yard Ltd. At the same time converted back to a roro cargo/passenger ferry by new stern ramp installations. Resumed service on Mar. 9 on her old line.
1.4.1997:	Transferred to Naantali – Kapellskär roro line by Oy Finnlink Ab.
30.9.1997:	Sold to Finnlines Oy / Finnlines Ab / Finnlines Ltd / Finnlines AG, Helsinki, and was delivered the same day.

77. FINNTIMBER

1975–1987

Motor Bulk /Container Carrier, Singledecker
Call: ZHD2009 ex OIEG Ice class: I A

15,646 GRT, 9,064 NRT, 23,323 dwt
177.04 x 22.91 x 10.09 m

Diesel Engine 2 SA 8 cy. MAN K8Z 70/120
by VEB Dieselmotorenwerk Rostock (DMR), Rostock
8,238 kW / 11,200 BHP   15.5 knots

ms FINNTIMBER
Photo by Skyfotos

25.4.1970:	Ordered by I/S Lars Rej Johansen & Knut A. Knutsen, Oslo.	20.6.1974:	Launched by VEB Mathias-Thesen-Werft, Wismar (#104), and named FINNTIMBER by Mrs. Kata Jouhki.
29.9.1971:	Newbuilding contract purchased by Thomesto Oy, Helsinki /Helsingfors.	7.3.1975:	Completed and delivered to Thomesto Oy, (c/o Oy Finnlines Ltd), Helsinki (1527). Entered on Mar. 8 Scanscot worldwide bulk service.

ms SILVER FAITH ex FINNTIMBER in Durban
Photo from K. Brzoza

17.6.1985: Flagged out by a sale to Timber Shipping Ltd., a subsidiary of Thomesto Oy in George Town, Cayman Islands. Delivered on July 8. Managers remained Oy Finnlines Ltd.

6.4.1987: Sold to Icon Shipping and Trading Co. Ltd., Piraeus, (c/o Estamar Ship Management Inc., Athens). Renamed GOOD FAITH when delivered on Apr. 10.

9.1988: Sold to Marine Victory S.A., Nassau, (c/o Silver Carriers S.A., Piraeus), and renamed SILVER FAITH.

5.1992: Sold to Gagich Shipping Co. Ltd., Valletta, (c/o Silver Carriers S.A., Piraeus), and renamed GAGICH.

1994: Remeasured in accordance with the 1969 Convention as follows: 16,314 GT, 8,984 NT, 23,698 dwt

1995: Having arrived on July 20 in Hong Kong, an order was issued on July 31 by Hong Kong Supreme Court for vessel's enforced sale. Reported as renamed HELSINKI while detained in Hong Kong. Tenders to buy vessel had to be with the Court by Oct. 18 and a week later a decision was announced.

1995: Sold to Transcontinental Transport & Trading Pte. Ltd., Singapore, and renamed FEIYU.

78. FINLANDIA   1975–1978
FINNSTAR (II)   1978–1981

Passenger / RoRo Cargo Motor Ferry, three decks
Bow and stern doors
Passengers: 237 de luxe cabins with 576 berths
Call: OGTA Ice class: I A

10,311 GRT, 5,597 NRT, 1,715 dwt
153.00 x 20.00 x 5.80 m

4 Diesel Engines 2 SA each 9 cy. Sulzer 9ZH 40/48
by Oy Wärtsilä Ab, Vaasa /Vasa.
4 x 3,016 kW / 4 x 4,100 BHP
Total 12,064 kW / 16,400 BHP   22 knots Twin screw

ms FINLANDIA
Photo by Rolf Mieritz

ms FINNSTAR
Photo from Matti Pietikäinen

25.8.1966: Launched by Oy Wärtsilä Ab, Helsinki Shipyard, Helsinki /Helsingfors (#383), and named FINLANDIA by Mrs. Louise Ehrnrooth.

10.5.1967: Completed and delivered to Suomen Höyrylaiva Oy – Finska Ångfartygs Ab, Helsinki (1369), with following particulars:
8,583 GRT, 4,383 NRT, 1,715 dwt
Passengers: 254 first and 393 tourist class berths, totalling 1,000 pass.
Entered on May 25 Helsinki – Copenhagen – Travemünde service.

16.6.1975: Sold to Enso-Gutzeit Oy, (c/o Oy Finnlines Ltd), Helsinki. Exchanged for ms Polaris ex Finncarrier. Continued on Helsinki – Travemünde line.

5.9.1978: Conversion to a cruise ferry started by Oy Wärtsilä Ab at Turku /Åbo.

26.9.1978: Renamed FINNSTAR by Enso-Gutzeit Oy.

3.1.1979: Delivered after rebuilding and conversion at Turku. Exterior changed by removing the dummy central funnel and by modifying the exhaust pipes in the stern. New cabins built on upper car deck. Bow door sealed. Particulars after conversion as in the heading. Commenced international cruising in the Mediterranean and on the west coast of Africa.

1980: Arrived on Sep. 14 at Toulon, where laid up.

27.5.1981: Sold to Loke Shipping (Bahamas) Ltd., Nassau, (c/o I.M. Skaugen Management Co. A/S, Oslo), and renamed INNSTAR for the trip from Toulon, where laid up, to Aalborg with arrival on Aug. 18.

4.1982: Delivered after extensive conversion by Aalborg Vaerft A/S. 101 new de luxe cabins installed on lower car deck and a penthouse with 14 suites. Stern door sealed and fitted with a bulbous bow and sponsons aft.
New tonnage: 12,456 GRT, 7,332 NRT, 1,830 dwt
Registered as a passenger ship. Passenger capacity: 515 berths in de luxe cabins.
Renamed PEARL OF SCANDINAVIA and managed by Scanasia Management Ltd., Hongkong. Operated by Pearl Cruises of Scandinavia, San Francisco, Cal.,

ms PEARL OF SCANDINAVIA ex FINN-STAR
Photo by Airfoto

	making from Hongkong 14, 28, and 42 day cruises in the Far East.
1.9.1983:	I.M. Skaugen withdrew from the joint venture and J. Lauritzen A/S took over the management.
4.1987:	Pearl Cruises of Scandinavia was sold to 2000 Corporation, the parent company of Ocean Cruise Lines.
1988:	Refitted and lengthened by a streamlined bow section of 3.65 metres at Sembawang Shipyard, Singapore, where arrived on Jan. 5. The exhaust pipes were covered by an aluminium funnel. New particulars: 12,475 GRT, 7,382 NRT, 1,830 dwt and length 156.67 m
14.2.1988:	Renamed OCEAN PEARL by H.R.H. Princess Galyani Vadhana of Thailand in Bangkok. Still owned by Loke Shipping (Bahamas) Ltd., but operated by Ocean Cruise Lines (UK) Ltd., London.
4.1990:	Croisières Paquet, jointly owned by Paris-based Chargeurs S.A. and Accor S.A. acquired 2000 Corporation and together with it Ocean Cruise Lines.
6.1990:	Reported as sold to Sendumar S.A., Nassau. Operators remained Ocean Cruise Lines (UK) Ltd., London.
1992:	Sold to Sodimarit S.A., Nassau, (c/o Croisières Paquet – Compagnie Française de Croisières).
7.1993:	Chargeurs S.A. and Accor S.A. became owners of Costa Crociere S.p.A.
2.1994:	Renamed PEARL by Sodimarit S.A. after the absorption of Croisières Paquet by Costa Crociere.
1994:	Remeasured in accordance with the 1969 Convention as follows: 12,704 GT, 4,637 NT, 1,830 dwt
1995:	Sailed on Sep. 14 from Singapore for Genoa with arrival on Oct. 18 to undergo refurbishment by Mariotti shipyard. Left Genoa on Nov. 12 being renamed COSTA PLAYA for Puerto Plata, Dominican Republic, where she arrived on Nov. 28. Started as the first ship after the Cold War cruises calling at Cuban ports Santiago de Cuba, Havana, and Baia Nipe.
1995:	Sold to Prestige Cruises N.V., Nassau, (c/o Prestige Cruises Management S.A.M., Monaco).

79. RAUTARUUKKI (I)   1976–1985

Motor Bulk Carrier, Singledecker
Call: OIGN   Ice class: I A

7,439 GRT, 4,573 NRT, 10,935 dwt
143.36 x 18.58 x 7.53 m

Diesel Engine 2 SA 9 cy. MaK 9M551AK
by MaK Maschinenbau G.m.b.H., Kiel
4,413 kW / 6,000 BHP   14.5 knots

ms RAUTARUUKKI at Raahe
Photo by Kari Riutta

ms NORDEN ex RAUTARUUKKI
Photo from K. Brzoza

18.11.1975:	Launched by Gebr. Schürenstedt K.G. Schiffswerft, Bardenfleth a.d. Weser (#1366), without naming ceremonies.
12.3.1976:	Christened RAUTARUUKKI by Mrs. Aune Haavisto and delivered to Rautaruukki Oy, Raahe /Brahestad (317), (c/o Oy Finnlines Ltd, Helsinki /Helsingfors).
20.12.1985:	Sold to Rederi Ab Engship, (Kaj Engblom), Nauvo / Nagu (Turku /Åbo 1633), and renamed NORDEN when delivered on Dec. 20. Chartered back to the previous owners.
9.1.1992:	Entered in the Finnish parallel Register of Merchant Vessels engaged in Internation Trade.
1.11.1993:	New national reg.no. 10014.
11.7.1994:	Remeasured in accordance with the 1969 Convention as follows: 7,764 GT, 4,374 NT, 10,935 dwt

80. KUURTANES 1976–1981

Motor Bulk Carrier, Singledecker
Call: OIGO   Ice class: I A

7,430 GRT, 4,550 NRT, 10,935 dwt
143.36 x 18.58 x 7.53 m

Diesel Engine 2 SA 9 cy. MaK 9M551AK
by MaK Maschinenbau G.m.b.H., Kiel
4,413 kW / 6,000 BHP   14.5 knots

ms KUURTANES
Photo from Matti Pietikäinen

ms MADZY ex KUURTANES
Photo by FotoFlite

30.3.1976:	Launched by Gebr. Schürenstedt K.G. Schiffswerft, Bardenfleth a.d. Weser (#1367), without naming ceremonies.
10.9.1976:	Christened KUURTANES by Mrs. Kirsti Paloluoma and delivered to Alavuden Puunjalostustehdas Oy, (c/o Oy Finnlines Ltd), Helsinki /Helsingfors (1565).
15.5.1981:	Sold to Partrederiet för ms Madzy, Kristen Kristensson m.fl., Donsö, and renamed MADZY when delivered on May 27. Operated by Thunbolaget, Lidköping. (SKCP)
4.8.1982:	Managing owner changed to Lars Kristensson, Donsö.
19.12.1986:	Sold to Donsöshipping K/B, Donsö. Still operated by Thunbolaget, Lidköping.
1994:	Remeasured in accordance with the 1969 Convention as follows: 7,490 GT, 4,429 NT, 11,065 dwt

81. FINNJET — 1977–1989

Passenger/ RoRo Cargo TGT and TD-E Ferry, four decks, Bow and stern doors
Passengers: 1,631 berths
Call: OIHH   Ice class: I A Super

25,908 GRT, 11,202 NRT, 2,728 dwt
212.96 x 24.45 x 6.50 m

2 Gas Turbines Pratt & Whitney FT4C-1DLF
by Turbo Power & Marine Systems, Farmington, Ct.
2 x 27,600 kW / 2 x 37,500 SHP
Total 55,200 kW / 75,000 SHP 30 knots Twin screw

2 Vee Diesel Engines 4 SA each 18 cy. Vaasa 18V32
by Oy Wärtsilä Ab, Vaasa /Vasa
2 x 5,760 kW / 2 x 7,750 BHP
Total 11,520 kW / 15,500 BHP   18.5 knots
connected with 2 Strömberg generators each 6,500 kVA

gts FINNJET in original colours
Photo by Matti Pietikäinen

28.3.1976:	Launched by Oy Wärtsilä Ab, Helsinki Shipyard, Helsinki /Helsingfors (#407), as the fastest ever built passenger /cargo ferry, without naming ceremonies.
28.4.1977:	Christened FINNJET by Mrs. Annikki Mattila and delivered to Enso-Gutzeit Oy, (c/o Oy Finnlines Ltd), Helsinki (1576). Entered on May 13 Helsinki – Travemünde liner service.
12.1981:	Fitted by Amsterdamse Droogdok Maatshappij bv in Amsterdam in 45 days with a diesel-electric propulsion incl. the above Diesel engines, 2 generators and 2 electric motors of 5,300 kW each, in order to save in bunker consumption during low season. Returned to service on Dec. 13.
1.1.1983:	Marketing and operation assigned to Oy Finnjet-Line Ltd, Helsinki.
1986:	Arrived on Jan. 12 at Oy Wärtsilä Ab, Helsinki Shipyard, for installation of 29 Commodore class cabins on the former sun deck. Back on service on Feb. 8.
3.6.1986:	Acquired by Effoa – Finska Ångfartygs Ab / Effoa – Suomen Höyrylaiva Oy / Effoa – Finland Steamship Co. Ltd., Helsinki, without change of name. Technical managers remained Oy Finnlines Ltd, but operation and manning taken over by Oy Silja Line Ab.

gts FINNJET in Silja Line livery
Photo by Matti Pietikäinen

gts FINNJET on her last regular visit at Travemünde on Sep. 14, 1997
Photo by Matti Pietikäinen

20.3.1987:	Sold to Oy Efjon Trading Ab, (Effoa – Finska Ångfartygs Ab / Effoa – Suomen Höyrylaiva Oy / Effoa – Finland Steamship Co. Ltd.), Helsinki. *(In the Finnish Merchant Marine -register books 1988–1990 the owners erroneously stated as Oy Effoa-Trading Ab.)*
17.2.1988:	Owners' name changed to Rederi Ab Effjohn / Varustamo Oy Effjohn.
1.5.1989:	Whole management incl. technical matters taken over by Oy Silja Line Ab.
15.12.1989:	Sold to Partrederiet för GTS Finnjet, (c/o Oy Silja Line Ab), Helsinki. Partners were Effoa Cruise and Ferry Oy Ab – 61 % and Johnson Cruise and Ferries AB – 39 %.
27.12.1991:	Sold to Effdo 1 Oy, (c/o Oy Silja Line Ab), Helsinki.
13.1.1993:	Home port changed to Mariehamn (1378).
23.6.1993:	Owners' amalgamation with the parent company, Oy Silja Line Ab, registered.
1.11.1993:	New Åland reg.no. 50258.
7.4.1994:	Arrived at Howaldtswerke – Deutsche Werft A.G., Kiel, for installation of new gear boxes to be able to use simultaneously both gas turbines and D/E-machinery. Back on service on May 1.
27.4.1994:	Remeasured in accordance with the 1969 Convention as follows: 32,940 GT, 17,284 NT, 2,728 dwt
11.11.1996:	Sold to Sally Ab, Mariehamn, (Silja Line Oy Ab, Helsinki).
1997:	Returned on Sep. 16 to Helsinki on her last regular trip from Travemünde. Thereafter rebuilt and refurbished at Cityvarvet, Gothenburg. Commenced on Oct. 9 Helsinki – Tallinn (Muuga) daily service.

82. LOTILA (II) — 1977–1995

General Cargo Motorship, two decks – Tweendecker
Call: OJFO ex C6CS5 ex ZHEJ8 ex OIGP Ice class: I A Super

12,409 GT, 4,868 NT, 14,931 dwt
159.22 x 21.00 x 9.13 m

Diesel Engine 2 SA 6 cy. Sulzer 6RND68
by Astilleros Españoles S.A., Factoria de Sestao, Bilbao
7,281 kW / 9,900 BHP   16 knots

ms LOTILA
Photo from FG-Shipping Oy Ab

29.7.1976:	Launched by S.A. Juliana Constructora Gijonesa, Gijon (#252), after having been named LOTILA the previous day by Mrs. Irma Pöyhönen.
25.11.1977:	Completed and delivered to Yhtyneet Paperitehtaat Oy, (United Paper Mills Ltd.), Rauma /Raumo (627), (c/o Oy Finnlines Ltd, Helsinki /Helsingfors).
13.1.1983:	Joined F-ships pool transatlantic contract service to/from USEC and Canada as a vessel of Neste Oy.
22.5.1986:	Flagged out by a sale to Lotila Shipping Ltd., a subsidiary of United Paper Mills Ltd. in George Town, Cayman Islands. Delivered and hoisted Cayman flag on June 11. Bareboat-chartered back to United Paper Mills Ltd. Managers remained Oy Finnlines Ltd.
13.4.1987:	Transferred to Bahamas flag with Nassau as home port.
31.5.1989:	Sold to FCRS-Shipping Ltd., Nassau, (Finncarriers Oy Ab, Helsinki) and delivered on June 3. Managers remained Oy Finnlines Ltd, which on July 1 was renamed FG-Shipping Oy Ab. Continued on F-ships pool service.

19.2.1993:	Sold to Amer-Yhtymä Oy, Helsinki (1869), and delivered on Feb. 24. Bareboat-chartered to Finnlines Oy and further to Finncarriers Oy Ab. Managers remained FG-Shipping Oy Ab and still employed in F-ships pool.	15.11.1993:	Remeasured in accordance with the 1969 Convention as above in the heading. Her previous particulars as open/closed shelterdecker were: 6,786/12,410 GRT, 3,487/6,423 NRT, 8,770/14,931 dwt 159.22 x 21.04 x 6.86/9.13 m
29.3.1993:	Entered in the Finnish parallel Register of Merchant Vessels engaged in International Trade.	27.7.1995:	Sold to Atlas Navigation Co. Ltd., Panama, (c/o Regal Agencies Corp., [T.A. Tsakiri], Piraeus), and renamed CLIPPER FAME when delivered on Aug. 3. Remained, however, on F-ships pool service until Feb. 23, 1996.
1.11.1993:	New national reg.no. 10170.		

83. WALKI   1978–1980
FINNOCEANIS   1980–1988

General Cargo Motorship, two decks – Open/Closed Shelterdecker
Call: C6CR7 ex ZHED7 ex OIGQ   Ice class: I A Super

6,783/12,407 GRT, 3,486/6,422 NRT, 8,770/14,931 dwt
159.22 x 21.04 x 6.86/9.13 m

Diesel Engine 2 SA 6 cy. Sulzer 6RND68
by Astilleros Españoles S.A., Factoria de Sestao, Bilbao
7,281 kW / 9,900 BHP   16 knots

ms WALKI
Photo from FG-Shipping Oy Ab

22.11.1976:	Launched by S.A. Juliana Constructora Gijonesa, Gijon (#253), and named WALKI by Mrs. Annikki Mäkinen.		Managed by Oy Finnlines Ltd, Helsinki/Helsingfors.
31.5.1978:	Completed and delivered to Yhtyneet Paperitehtaat Oy, (United Paper Mills Ltd.), Rauma/Raumo (630).	17.6.1980:	Acquired by Thomesto Oy, Helsinki (1629), and renamed FINNOCEANIS when delivered on June 24. Managers remained Oy Finnlines Ltd.

ms FINNOCEANIS
Photo by Skyfotos

ms ATLANTA
Photo from K. Brzoza

16.12.1982:	Joined F-ships pool transatlantic contract service to/from USEC and Canada.
21.3.1986:	Flagged out by a sale to Timber Shipping Ltd., a subsidiary of Thomesto Oy in George Town, Cayman Islands. Delivered and hoisted Cayman flag on Apr. 30. Bareboat-chartered back to Thomesto Oy. Managers remained Oy Finnlines Ltd.
21.4.1987:	Transferred to Bahamas flag with Nassau as home port.

4.1.1988:	Sold to Oy Gustav Paulig Ab, Helsinki (1629), (c/o Oy Crossline Ab Ltd., Porvoo /Borgå), and renamed ATLANTA when delivered on Jan. 12. Continued in F-ships pool, but from now on as a vessel of Finncarriers Oy Ab.	31.12.1991:	Left F-ships pool.
2.1.1989:	Administration taken over by Navicon Oy Ab, Helsinki, a subsidiary of Effoa, but managers remained Oy Crossline Ab Ltd.	1.1992:	Renamed ATLANTA FOREST by Marefin Ltd., when chartered to Kent Line Ltd., Saint John, N.B.
		1994:	Remeasured in accordance with the 1969 Convention as follows: 12,582 GT, 3,774 NT, 14,931 dwt
4.5.1989:	Sold to Turicus Oy Ab, (Agrofin Oy Ab), Helsinki, (c/o Navicon Oy Ab & Oy Crossline Ab Ltd).	7.1995:	Sold to Promitor Shipping Co., Limassol, (c/o Regal Agencies Corp., Piraeus), and renamed CLIPPER FOREST. Charter to Kent Line Ltd. continued.
2.4.1991:	Flagged out by a sale to Marefin Ltd., a subsidiary of Turicus Oy Ab in Valletta. Same managers remained and the vessel continued in F-ships pool.	1996:	Renamed KENT FOREST by Promitor Shipping Co. while on charter to Kent Line Ltd.

84. FINNBEAVER 1978–1988

Motor Bulk Carrier, Singledecker
Call: ZHET ex OIDI   Ice class: II

19,905 GRT, 13,798 NRT, 34,995 dwt
196.02 x 24.20 x 11.14 m

Diesel Engine 2 SA 7 cy. Sulzer 7RND68
by Astilleros Españoles S.A., Factoria de Sestao, Bilbao
8,496 kW / 11,550 BHP   15 knots

ms MATAI, later FINNBEAVER
Photo by Airfoto

19.10.1974:	Launched by Astilleros Españoles S.A., Factoria de Sevilla, Sevilla (#173), and named MATAI by Mrs. Lene Ahlström.	6.1.1975:	Completed and delivered to Oy Pulpships Ab, (c/o Oy Henry Nielsen Ab), Helsinki /Helsingfors (1522).

ms FINNBEAVER
Photo from FG-Shipping Oy Ab

20.12.1977:	Owners went into liquidation and the vessel was laid up in Helsinki.	22.11.1985:	Flagged out by a sale to Beaver Shipping Ltd., a subsidiary of Ky Jussi Ketola & Co. in George Town, Cayman Islands. Delivered and hoisted Cayman flag on Dec. 7. Managers remained Oy Finnlines Ltd.
9.2.1978:	Purchased at auction by the main creditors, Helsingin Osakepankki, (Bank of Helsinki), on behalf of a company under formation, Helsinki.	1987:	Transferred to Bahamas flag with Nassau as home port.
14.3.1978:	Transferred to Oy Hermes Ship Ltd., (Helsingin Osakepankki), (c/o Oy Henry Nielsen Ab), Helsinki, and renamed PASSAD.	1.3.1988:	Management taken over by Sun Enterprises Ltd., (S. Livanos (Hellas) S.A.), Piraeus.
10.8.1978:	Acquired by Ky Jussi Ketola & Co., (c/o Oy Finnlines Ltd), Helsinki, and renamed FINNBEAVER.	5.1991:	Sold to Nereid Shipping Corp., (Uniship Maritime Inc.), Piraeus, and renamed DELFINI.
		1994:	Remeasured in accordance with the 1969 Convention as follows: 19,307 GT, 12,435 NT, 34,995 dwt

85. FINNFURY   1978–1988

Motor Bulk Carrier, Singledecker
Call: ZHEN ex OIDK Ice class: II

19,907 GRT, 13,796 NRT, 34,995 dwt
196.02 x 24.20 x 11.15 m

Diesel Engine 2 SA 7 cy. Sulzer 7RND68
by Astilleros Españoles S.A., Factoria de Sestao, Bilbao
8,496 kW / 11,550 BHP   15 knots

ms FINNFURY
Photo from FG-Shipping Oy Ab

ms LACERTA ex FINNFURY
Photo by FotoFlite

28.3.1975: Launched by Astilleros Españoles S.A., Factoria de Sevilla, Sevilla (#175), and named FORANO by Mrs. Ebba Lindahl.

15.7.1975: Completed and delivered to Oy Pulpships Ab, (c/o Oy Henry Nielsen Ab), Helsinki /Helsingfors (1545).

20.12.1977: Owners went into liquidation and the vessel was laid up in Helsinki.

9.2.1978: Purchased at auction by the main creditors, Helsingin Osakepankki, (Bank of Helsinki), on behalf of a company under formation, Helsinki.

14.3.1978:	Transferred to Oy Mare Ship Ltd., (Helsingin Osakepankki), (c/o Oy Henry Nielsen Ab), Helsinki, and renamed MONSUN.	1.3.1988:	Management taken over by Sun Enterprises Ltd., (S. Livanos (Hellas) S.A.), Piraeus, and transferred to Cyprus flag with Limassol as home port.
7.8.1978:	Acquired by Ky Jussi Ketola & Co., (c/o Oy Finnlines Ltd), Helsinki, and renamed FINNFURY.	4.1988:	Sold to Bella Shipping Co. Ltd., Valletta, (Drytank S.A., Piraeus), and renamed LACERTA.
22.10.1985:	Flagged out by a sale to Fury Shipping Ltd., a subsidiary of Ky Jussi Ketola & Co. in George Town, Cayman Islands. Delivered and hoisted Cayman flag on Nov. 1. Managers remained Oy Finnlines Ltd.	9.1991:	Sold to Seadomain Shipping Ltd., Valletta, (Drytank S.A., Piraeus), and renamed MILAGRO.
		1994:	Remeasured in accordance with the 1969 Convention as follows: 19,559 GT, 12,925 NT, 34,995 dwt
		1997:	Owners amended to Bella Shipping Co. Ltd. Managers remained Drytank S.A.

86. KAIPOLA (III)   1978–1979
FINNFIGHTER (II)   1979–

General Cargo Motorship, two decks – Tweendecker
Call: OJGY ex C6KM4 ex OIGR   Ice class: I A Super

12,582 GT, 5,258 NT, 14,931 dwt
159.22 x 21.01 x 9.13 m

Diesel Engine 2 SA 6 cy. Sulzer 6RND68
by Astilleros Españoles S.A., Factoria de Sestao, Bilbao
7,281 kW / 9,900 BHP   15.5 knots

ms KAIPOLA at Rauma with ms LOTILA
Photo by Foto Tammelin

3.5.1977:	Launched by S.A. Juliana Constructora Gijonesa, Gijon (#254), and named KAIPOLA by Mrs. Arnevi Lassila.	6.10.1978:	Completed and delivered to Yhtyneet Paperitehtaat Oy, (United Paper Mills Ltd.), Rauma /Raumo (631), (c/o Oy Finnlines Ltd, Helsinki /Helsingfors).
		17.10.1979:	Acquired by Merivienti Oy, (Enso-Gutzeit Oy), Kotka (605), (c/o Oy Finnlines Ltd, Helsinki), and renamed FINNFIGHTER.

ms FINNFIGHTER
Photo by Rolf Mieritz

1.10.1982:	Sold to Neste Oy, Naantali /Nådendal (70). Managers remained Oy Finnlines Ltd.
3.1.1983:	Joined F-ships pool transatlantic contract service to/from USEC and Canada.
6.6.1988:	Sold to Palkkiyhtymä Oy, Helsinki (1755). Managers remained Oy Finnlines Ltd.
1.7.1989:	Managers' name changed to FG-Shipping Oy Ab.
27.9.1991:	Flagged out by a sale to Puhos Shipping Ltd., a subsidiary of Palkkiyhtymä Oy in George Town, Cayman Islands. Registered in Nassau, Bahamas, when delivered on Oct. 1 and bareboat-chartered back to Palkkiyhtymä Oy. Managers remained FG-Shipping Oy Ab.
1994:	Remeasured in accordance with the 1969 Convention as above in the heading. Her previous particulars as open/closed shelterdecker were: 6,766/12,390 GRT, 3,502/6,434 NRT, 8,770/14,931 dwt 159.22 x 21.04 x 6.86/9.13 m
20.7.1995:	Purchased back by Palkkiyhtymä Oy, (c/o FG-Shipping Oy Ab), Helsinki (#11810). Delivered on July 28 and entered the same day in the Finnish parallel Register of Merchant Vessels engaged in International Trade. Still employed in F-ships pool.

87. WALKI PAPER   1979–1979

General Cargo Motorship, two decks – Open/Closed Shelterdecker
Call: OIGS Ice class: I A Super

6,766/12,390 GRT, 3,502/6,434 NRT, 8,700/14,861 dwt
159.22 x 21.04 x 6.86/9.13 m

Diesel Engine 2 SA 6 cy. Sulzer 6RND68
by Astilleros Españoles S.A., Factoria de Sestao, Bilbao
7,281 kW / 9,900 BHP   16 knots

13.10.1977:	Launched by S.A. Juliana Constructora Gijonesa, Gijon (#255), and named WALKI PAPER by Lady Susan Hussey.
23.3.1979:	Completed and delivered to Yhtyneet Paperitehtaat Oy, (United Paper Mills Ltd.), Rauma /Raumo (632). Managed and operated by Oy Finnlines Ltd, Helsinki /Helsingfors.

*ms WALKI PAPER at Rauma with ms WALKI
Photo by Foto Tammelin*

*ms SALLA at Hamina
Photo by Matti Pietikäinen*

13.12.1979:	Acquired by Oy Suomi Line / Finland Line Ab, (Suomen Höyrylaiva Oy – Finska Ångfartygs Ab), Helsinki (1619), and renamed SALLA.
13.2.1981:	Parent company's name registered as Effoa – Finska Ångfartygs Ab / Effoa – Suomen Höyrylaiva Oy / Effoa – Finland Steamship Co. Ltd. as per EGM resolutions on Nov. 12 and Dec. 12, 1980.
1985:	Severely damaged as a result of a collision on Apr. 6 near Kalbådagrund Lighthouse in the Gulf of Finland with the Russian Abakanles during a voyage from Hamina /Fredrikshamn to Bremen with pulp and general cargo. After the collision she took a heavy list and before being beached was abandoned by her crew. Further damaged by fire, which broke out and gutted her accommodation. Later refloated and arrived on Apr. 16 in tow at Helsinki, where discharged.
14.6.1985:	Declared a constructive total loss and taken over by Vakuutus Oy Pohjola, (Pohjola Insurance Co. Ltd.), Helsinki. Offered for sale "as lies" in Helsinki.
10.7.1985:	Sold to K/S Resalla & Fekete & Co. A/S, (Fekete & Co. A/S), Tønsberg, and renamed RESALLA. – Left Helsinki on July 13 in tow by ms Kronö for Norway.
7.1985:	Sold further to A/S Tambur, (Fosen Mek. Verksteder A/S), Rissa. – Arrived on July 31 in tow at Fevaag, where she was to be reconstructed.
10.1986:	Completed after extensive repairs by Fosen Mek. Verksteder A/S. – Reported as renamed FRENGENFJORD, but the change of name was never registered. On the contrary she made her trial trip with SALLA still painted on the bows.
10.10.1986:	Sold to Peto Shipping Ltd., Panama, (c/o T.K. Husjord, Narvik), and renamed TRAMARCO

ms AUNG MINGALA ex WALKI PAPER
Photo from Krister Bång

	TRADER for duration of charter to Transmarine Chartering Inc., Cold Spring Harbor, N.Y.
3.1988:	Sold to Bernice Shipping Ltd., Nassau, Bahamas, (Mineral Shipping USA Inc., Tampa, Fla.), and renamed BERNICE.
11.1989:	Sold to Burma Navigation Corp., Yangon, Union of Myanmar, and renamed AUNG MINGALA, but still operated by Mineral Shipping USA Inc.
3.1993:	Purchased back by Bernice Shipping Ltd., Nassau, (Mineral Shipping (Pte.) Ltd., Singapore), and the name reverted to BERNICE.
1994:	Remeasured in accordance with the 1969 Convention as follows: 12,691 GT, 4,664 NT, 14,467 dwt
2.2.1995:	Acquired by Rederi Ab Engship, (Kaj Engblom), Nauvo /Nagu (#11771), and renamed BRAVADEN. (Call: OJGQ)
7.2.1995:	Entered in the Finnish parallel Register of Merchant Vessels engaged in International Trade.

88. FINNFOREST (II)   1979–1982
CANOPUS   1982–1992

RoRo Cargo Motor Ferry, two decks, stern door
Call: OIIG Ice class: I A Super

4,817 GRT, 1,833 NRT, 6,565 dwt
142.22 x 19.27 x 7.02 m

4 Diesel Engines 4 SA each 8 cy. MWM TBD501-8
by Motoren-Werke Mannheim A.G., Mannheim
4 x 2,207 kW / 4 x 3,000 BHP
Total 8,828 kW / 12,000 BHP   18 knots Twin screw

4.6.1977:	Launched by Oy Navire Ab, Naantali /Nådendal (#59) as a nameless sub-contract hull for A/S Fredriksstad Mek. Verksted, and towed to Fredrikstad.	3.10.1977:	Completed by A/S Fredriksstad Mek. Verksted, Fredrikstad (#432), and delivered to Oy Navire Ab, Parainen /Pargas (Turku /Åbo 1529), (c/o Höyrylaiva Oy Bore – Ångfartygs Ab Bore, Turku).
30.9.1977:	Christened ROLITA by Mrs. Rakel Jalkanen.		

ms ROLITA, later FINNFOREST, in Jeddah
Photo by Matti Pietikäinen

ms FINNFOREST
Photo by FotoFlite

4.9.1979: Renamed FINNFOREST by Oy Navire Ab. (Permission to change the name.)

10.10.1979: Management taken over by Oy Finnlines Ltd, Helsinki /Helsingfors.

ms CANOPUS
Photo by K. Brzoza

ms CUPRIA ex FINNFOREST
Photo from Krister Bång

20.12.1979: Acquired by Merivienti Oy, (Enso-Gutzeit Oy), Kotka (606), while chartered to Oy Finncarriers Ab.

1.10.1982: Sold to Effoa – Finska Ångfartygs Ab / Effoa – Suomen Höyrylaiva Oy / Effoa – Finland Steamship Co. Ltd., Helsinki (1677), and renamed CANOPUS. Managers remained Oy Finnlines Ltd.

31.12.1986: Sold to Oy Finncarriers Ab, Helsinki, the operational subsidiary of Effoa.

13.5.1987: Owners' name registered as Finncarriers Oy Ab as per EGM resolution on Dec. 31, 1986.

18.4.1989: Owners' name changed to Finnlines Group Oy Ab.

30.4.1989: A new Finncarriers Oy Ab was established by Finnlines Group Oy Ab and in accordance with the demerger principle of the Business Taxation Act, the parent company transferred the assets of the old Finncarriers including ms Canopus to the new Finncarriers Oy Ab.

1.7.1989: Managers' name changed to FG-Shipping Oy Ab.

7.1.1992: Entered in the Finnish parallel Register of Merchant Vessels engaged in International Trade.

10.4.1992: Sold to B & N, Bylock & Nordsjöfrakt AB, Skärhamn, and renamed CUPRIA when delivered on Apr. 14. (SDIN)

1994: Remeasured in accordance with the 1969 Convention as follows: 10,279 GT, 3,083 NT, 6,671 dwt

4.1995: Renamed NORCOVE when chartered to North Sea Ferries for Zeebrügge – Middlesbrough service.

1996: Owners' name changed to B & N Rederi AB. Managed by B & N Sea Partner AB.

89. VARJAKKA (II)　　　　　　　　　　　　　　　　　　　　　　1979–1996

General Cargo Motorship, two decks – Tweendecker
Call: OJFR ex C6CO5 ex ZHED5 ex OIGT　Ice class: I A Super

12,409 GT, 4,868 NT, 14,938 dwt
159.22 x 21.00 x 9.15 m

Diesel Engine 2 SA 6 cy. Sulzer 6RND68
by Astilleros Españoles S.A., Factoria de Sestao, Bilbao
7,281 kW / 9,900 BHP　　15 knots

ms VARJAKKA
Photo by FotoFlite

10.3.1978:　Launched by S.A. Juliana Constructora Gijonesa, Gijon (#256), and named VARJAKKA by Mrs. Eila Merikanto.

6.11.1979:　Completed and delivered to Oulu Oy, Oulu /Uleåborg (532), (c/o Oy Finnlines Ltd, Helsinki /Helsingfors).

177

27.1.1983:	Joined F-ships pool transatlantic contract service to/from USEC and Canada.	29.4.1993:	Entered in the Finnish parallel Register of Merchant Vessels engaged in International Trade.
2.9.1986:	Flagged out by a sale to Oulu Shipping Ltd., a subsidiary of Oulu Oy in George Town, Cayman Islands. Delivered on Sep. 22 and bareboat-chartered back to Oulu Oy. Managers remained Oy Finnlines Ltd.	1.11.1993:	New national reg.no. 10179.
		1993:	Remeasured in accordance with the 1969 Convention as above in the heading. Her previous particulars as open/closed shelterdecker were: 6,762/12,385 GRT, 3,494/6,428 NRT, 8,774/14,938 dwt 159.22 x 21.04 x 6.86/9.13 m
27.11.1986:	Parent company's amalgamation with Veitsiluoto Oy, Kemi, registered as per EGM resolutions on June 10. Veitsiluoto Oy now became the new parent company and bareboat-charterers.	7.9.1995:	Parent company Veitsiluoto Oy amalgamated with Enso-Gutzeit Oy, forming a new parent company named Enso Oy.
12.3.1987:	Transferred to Bahamas flag with Nassau as home port.	2.1.1996:	Sold to B & N Rederi AB, (B & N, Bylock & Nordsjöfrakt AB), Skärhamn, and renamed WESTÖN when delivered on Jan. 5. Managed by B & N Sea Partner AB. (SDOT) Continued on F-ships service as a vessel of B & N Rederi AB.
21.4.1993:	Purchased back by Lumi Shipping Oy, Kemi (436), a Finnish subsidiary of Veitsiluoto Oy and delivered on Apr. 27. Managed by FG-Shipping Oy Ab, Helsinki, and continued in F-ships pool.		
		4.6.1997:	Flagged out by a sale to B & N, Bylock & Nordsjöfrakt AS, Oslo, NIS-register, (c/o Bylock & Nordsjöfrakt Sea Partner AS, Sarpsborg), and delivered on June 16.

90. PUHOS   1980–1993

Motor Bulk Carrier, Singledecker
Call: C6CS7 ex ZHEF ex OIDW Ice class: I C

16,988 GRT, 11,558 NRT, 30,242 dwt
189.49 x 22.85 x 10.68 m

Diesel Engine 2 SA 7 cy. Sulzer 7RND68
by Astilleros Españoles S.A., Factoria de Manises, Valencia
8,496 kW / 11,550 BHP   15 knots

ms PUHOS
Photo by Kari Riutta

ms KAMARI I ex PUHOS at Valletta
Photo by Michael Cassar

26.2.1977:	Launched by Astilleros Españoles S.A., Factoria de Sevilla, Sevilla (#195), and named PUHOS by Mrs. Aune Mauranen.
2.6.1977:	Completed and delivered to Palkkiyhtymä Oy, (c/o Oy Henry Nielsen Ab), Helsinki /Helsingfors (1583).
1.1.1980:	Management taken over by Oy Finnlines Ltd, Helsinki.
10.9.1985:	Flagged out by a sale to Puhos Shipping Ltd., a subsidiary of Palkkiyhtymä Oy in George Town, Cayman Islands. Delivered and hoisted Cayman flag on Sep. 16. Managers remained Oy Finnlines Ltd.
10.4.1987:	Transferred to Bahamas flag with Nassau as home port.
1.7.1989:	Managers' name changed to FG-Shipping Oy Ab.
7.5.1993:	Sold to Waterguardian Ship Ltd., Limassol, (Drytank S.A., Piraeus), and renamed KAMARI when delivered on May. 12. The name was, however, already registered in Cyprus and therefore amended to KAMARI I.
1993:	Managers changed to Cardiff Marine Inc., Piraeus.
1994:	Remeasured in accordance with the 1969 Convention as follows: 16,810 GT, 10,203 NT, 30,242 dwt
8.1995:	Sold to Bridem Shipping Ltd., Limassol (c/o M. Odysseos Shipmanagement Ltd., Nicosia), and renamed BLUEBILL.

91. POKKINEN   1980–1996

General Cargo Motorship, two decks – Tweendecker
Call: OJFQ ex C6CO4 ex ZHEO6 ex OIGU   Ice class: I A Super

12,409 GT, 4,868 NT, 14,883 dwt
159.22 x 21.00 x 9.13 m

Diesel Engine 2 SA 6 cy. Sulzer 6RND68
by Astilleros Españoles S.A., Factoria de Sestao, Bilbao
7,281 kW / 9,900 BHP   16 knots

ms POKKINEN
Photo from FG-Shipping Oy Ab

16.9.1978:	Launched by S.A. Juliana Constructora Gijonesa, Gijon (#257), after having been named POKKINEN the previous day by Mrs. Helka Hannunkari. Launch was delayed due to heavy wind.
30.1.1980:	Completed and delivered to Oulu Oy, Oulu /Uleåborg (533), (c/o Oy Finnlines Ltd, Helsinki /Helsingfors).
17.3.1983:	Joined F-ships pool transatlantic contract service to/from USEC and Canada.
27.11.1986:	Owners' amalgamation with the parent company, Veitsiluoto Oy, Kemi, registered as per EGM resolutions on June 10. Home port remained Oulu.
11.12.1986:	Flagged out by a sale to Oulu Shipping Ltd., a subsidiary of Veitsiluoto Oy in George Town, Cayman Islands. Delivered the same day and bareboat-chartered back to Veitsiluoto Oy. Managers remained Oy Finnlines Ltd.
17.2.1987:	Transferred to Bahamas flag with Nassau as home port.
21.4.1993:	Purchased back by Lumi Shipping Oy, Kemi (437), a Finnish subsidiary of Veitsiluoto Oy. Delivered on May 7 and entered the same day in the Finnish parallel Register of Merchant Vessels engaged in International Trade. Managed by FG-Shipping Oy Ab, Helsinki, and continued on F-ships pool service.
1.11.1993:	New national reg.no. 11521.
3.12.1993:	Remeasured in accordance with the 1969 Convention as above in the heading. Her previous particulars as open/closed shelterdecker were: 6,762/12,385 GRT, 3,495/6,430 NRT, 8,741/14,883 dwt 159.22 x 21.04 x 6.86/9.13 m
7.9.1995:	Parent company Veitsiluoto Oy amalgamated with Enso-Gutzeit Oy, forming a new parent company named Enso Oy.
25.1.1996:	Sold to B & N Rederi AB, (B & N, Bylock & Nordsjöfrakt AB), Skärhamn, and renamed TOFTÖN when delivered on Jan. 31. Managed by B & N Sea Partner AB. (SDNV) Chartered to Finncarriers Oy Ab and continued on F-ships service.
21.5.1997:	Flagged out by a sale to B & N, Bylock & Nordsjöfrakt AS, Oslo, NIS-register (c/o Bylock & Nordsjöfrakt Sea Partner AS, Sarpsborg), and delivered on May 26.

92. FINNARCTIS   1980–1991

General Cargo Motorship, two decks – Open/Closed Shelterdecker
Call: C6CR2 ex ZHED6 ex OIGV   Ice class: I A Super

6,752/12,385 GRT, 3,495/6,430 NRT, 8,744/14,906 dwt
159.22 x 21.04 x 6.86/9.13 m

Diesel Engine 2 SA 6 cy. Sulzer 6RND68
by Astilleros Españoles S.A., Factoria de Sestao, Bilbao
7,281 kW / 9,900 BHP   16 knots

ms FINNARCTIS at Raahe
Photo by Matti Pietikäinen

29.12.1978:	Launched by S.A. Juliana Constructora Gijonesa, Gijon (#258), without naming ceremonies.
27.11.1980:	Christened FINNARCTIS by Mrs. Leena Honkasalo.
28.11.1980:	Delivered to Thomesto Oy, Helsinki /Helsingfors (1643). Managed by Oy Finnlines Ltd. Time-chartered for 4 years to Outokumpu Oy.
22.11.1984:	After redelivery from time-charter joined F-ships pool transatlantic contract service to/from USEC and Canada.
21.3.1986:	Flagged out by a sale to Timber Shipping Ltd., a subsidiary of Thomesto Oy in George Town, Cayman Islands. Delivered on Apr. 26 and hoisted Cayman flag. Bareboat-chartered back to Thomesto Oy. Managers remained Oy Finnlines Ltd.
11.3.1987:	Transferred to Bahamas flag with Nassau as home port.
21.6.1989:	Bareboat-chartered to Finncarriers Oy Ab, Helsinki.
9.8.1989:	Sold to FCRS-Shipping Ltd., Nassau, (Finnlines Group Oy Ab, Helsinki) and delivered without change of name on Aug. 12. Managers FG-Shipping Oy Ab, Helsinki. Continued on F-ships pool service on bareboat-charter to Finncarriers Oy Ab.
24.4.1991:	Sold to Bektransport 1 KS, (c/o Paal Wilson Management A/S), Bergen (NIS-1082), and renamed CHIMO when delivered on May 6. However, remained on F-ships pool service until Oct. 31.
11.1992:	Managers changed to Continental Ship Management AS, Bergen.

ms CHIMO ex FINNARCTIS
Photo by FotoFlite

1993:	Remeasured in accordance with the 1969 Convention as follows: 12,688 GT, 4,284 NT, 14,241 dwt	3.1995:	Transferred to AFG Alouette Arrow Ltd. Partnership c/o American Finance, Boston, but home port and managers remained unchanged.
21.12.1994:	Sold to Chantal Shipping Corp., Monrovia, but home port remained Bergen. Renamed ALOUETTE ARROW. Managers Westfleet Management A/S, Fyllingsdalen.	1996:	Managers changed to Kristian Gerhard Jebsen Skipsrederi A/S, Bergen.

93. KEMIRA   1981–

Motor Bulk Carrier /Sulphur Acid Tanker, Singledecker
Call: OINR Ice class: I A Super

5,582 GT, 2,257 NT, 8,145 dwt
112.65 x 17.50 x 8.23 m

Diesel Engine 4 SA 8 cy. Sulzer 8ZL40/48
by Oy Wärtsilä Ab, Turku /Åbo
4,119 kW / 5,600 BHP   14.8 knots

ms KEMIRA
Photo from FG-Shipping Oy Ab

30.8.1980:	Launched by Kleven Mekaniske Verksted A/S, Ulsteinvik (#34), and named KEMIRA by Mrs. Liisa Pessi.	7.1.1992:	Entered in the Finnish parallel Register of Merchant Vessels engaged in International Trade.
12.1.1981:	Completed and delivered to Kemira Oy, Uusikaupunki /Nystad (391). Managed by Oy Finnlines Ltd.	1.11.1993:	New national reg.no. 11183.
		15.4.1994:	Remeasured in accordance with the 1969 Convention as above in the heading. Her previous tonnages were: 5,547 GRT, 2,510 NRT, 8,145 dwt
1.7.1989:	Managers' name changed to FG-Shipping Oy Ab.	1.1.1994:	Sold to Kemira Chemicals Oy, Uusikaupunki.

94. FINNPOLARIS   1981–1991

General Cargo Motorship, two decks – Open/Closed Shelterdecker
Call: C6CD9 ex ZHED8 ex OIGW   Ice class: I A Super

6,762/12,385 GRT, 3,495/6,430 NRT, 8,744/14,907 dwt
159.22 x 21.04 x 6.86/9.13 m

Diesel Engine 2 SA 6 cy. Sulzer 6RND68
by Astilleros Españoles S.A., Factoria de Sestao, Bilbao
7,281 kW / 9,900 BHP   16 knots

ms FINNPOLARIS on the coast of Dronning Maud Land in Antarctica
Photo by Kalevi Sundqvist

6.9.1979:	Launched by S.A. Juliana Constructora Gijonesa, Gijon (#259), without naming ceremonies.	8.1983:	Chartered to Indian Govt. for an Antarctic expedition trip. Crane No. 3 removed and replaced by a helicopter deck and accommodation containers placed on the tweendeck of hold No. 3. Sailed via Goa and Port Louis, Mauritius, to Dronning Maud Land, Antarctica, where "berthed" on Dec. 27 in position 69.57 S, 12.49 E as the first Finnish ship ever in Antarctica. Made the following winter another trip for Indian Govt. to Dronning Maud Land and then in 1986–87
25.9.1981:	Christened FINNPOLARIS by Mrs. Marjatta Jouhki and delivered to Thomesto Oy, Helsinki /Helsingfors (1653). Managed by Oy Finnlines Ltd.		
22.1.1983:	Joined F-ships pool transatlantic contract service to/from USEC and Canada.		

ms FINNPOLARIS in Terra Nova Bay on the coast of the Ross Sea in Antarctica
Photo by Kalevi Sundqvist

	and 1987–88 two trips for Italian Govt. to Terra Nova Bay in Ross Sea in position 74.43 S, 164.10 E.
21.3.1986:	Flagged out by a sale to Timber Shipping Ltd., a subsidiary of Thomesto Oy in George Town, Cayman Islands. Delivered on Apr. 26 and hoisted Cayman flag. Bareboat-chartered back to Thomesto Oy. Managers remained Oy Finnlines Ltd.
6.10.1986:	Transferred to Bahamas flag with Nassau as home port.
21.5.1989:	Bareboat-chartered to Finncarriers Oy Ab, Helsinki.
9.8.1989:	Sold to FCRS-Shipping Ltd., Nassau, (Finnlines Group Oy Ab, Helsinki) and delivered without change of name on Aug. 12. Managers FG-Shipping Oy Ab, Helsinki. Continued on F-ships pool service on bareboat-charter to Finncarriers Oy Ab.
1991:	Struck on Aug. 11 an iceberg about 90 miles SW of Upernavik, Greenland, in position 71.59.3 N, 59.52.7 W in Baffin Bay, while on voyage from Nanisivik, Baffin Island, to Darrow, La. with zink concentrate. Sank early the following day in depth of 450 m. Crew rescued from lifeboat by the Danish mt Sofie Theresa.

95. **FINNHAWK (II)**   1981–1989

RoRo Cargo Motor Ferry, two decks, two stern doors
Call: C6BJ6 ex OIPE Ice class: I C

13,341 GRT, 5,457 NRT, 18,451 dwt, 1,132 TEU
192.59 x 27.03 x 8.40 m

2 Diesel Engines 2 SA each 6 cy. Sulzer 6RND68M
by "H. Cegielski" Z.P.M., Poznan
2 x 7,943 kW / 2 x 10,800 BHP
Total 15,886 kW / 21,600 BHP   19 knots Twin screw

17.10.1978:	Order placed with AB Oskarshamns Varv, Oskarshamn, by Lars Johansson, Skärhamn.	27.6.1980:	Leased by AB Skärhamns Oljetransport for 5 years to Merivienti Oy with a purchase option.
21.5.1979:	Order transferred to AB Skärhamns Oljetransport, Skärhamn.	13.8.1980:	Launched by AB Oskarshamns Varv, Oskarshamn (#429), without naming ceremonies.

ms FINNHAWK
Photo by FotoFlite

ms MALMÖ LINK ex FINNHAWK
Photo by Tomas Johannesson

12.12.1980:	Completed and delivered as FINNHAWK to AB Skärhamns Oljetransport, (OT-Rederierna), Skärhamn. (SICE) Never christened. – Operated by Atlantic Cargo Services AB, Göteborg.
30.12.1981:	Acquired by Merivienti Oy, (Enso-Gutzeit Oy), Helsinki /Helsingfors (1658), due to the financial difficulties of the previous owners and delivered the same day. Managed by Oy Finnlines Ltd. Continued in Atlanticargo service.
31.12.1982:	Sold to the parent company, Enso-Gutzeit Oy, Helsinki. Managers remained Oy Finnlines Ltd.
27.8.1985:	Sold to South Atlantic Cargo Shipping N.V., Curaçao, but registered in Nassau, Bahamas. Still in Atlanticargo liner service. Technical management by Oy Finnlines Ltd and manning by Billabong Ship Management A/S & Co., Bergen.
21.10.1989:	Sold to Windspoint Shipping Co. Ltd., Gibraltar, (Rederi AB Nordö-Link, Malmö), and delivered the same day without change of name. It was planned to convert the vessel to a passenger/car cruise ferry by cutting away all old structure 4.5 metres above the main deck and constructing new facilities. Intended to employ the rebuilt ferry for 1,800 passengers and 500 cars in the summer 1990 on Malmö – Lübeck cruise service. The plans were, however, found too expensive and uneconomic. Therefore decided to make a smaller conversion to a combi-roro ferry.
1.12.1989:	Arrived at Gdynia for conversion to a passenger/roro and rail cargo motor ferry.
6.4.1990:	Sold to Rederi AB Nordö-Link, Malmö, and was deleted on Apr. 11 from Bahamas ship register.
6.5.1990:	Delivered by Stocznia Marynarki Wojennej, (Naval Shipyard), Gdynia, as renamed MALMÖ LINK after conversion to a passenger/roro and rail cargo motor ferry with a new deckhouse for 214 berths for passengers. Stern doors sealed. Fitted with a new guillotine-type bow door and two side doors on starboard side. – Entered Malmö – Travemünde service. (SICE) Remeasured after conversion in accordance with the 1969 Convention as follows: 33,163 GT, 17,966 NT, 10,600 dwt, 3,400 lane metres, of which 900 rail metres – 192.48 x 27.03 x 6.75 m.

96. FINNROSE (II)   1981–1989

RoRo Cargo Motor Ferry, two decks, two stern doors
Call: C6BJ1 ex OIPF Ice class: I C

13,375 GRT, 5,487 NRT, 18,541 dwt, 1,132 TEU
192.59 x 27.03 x 8.40 m

2 Diesel Engines 2 SA each 6 cy. Sulzer 6RND68M
by "H. Cegielski" Z.P.M., Poznan
2 x 7,943 kW / 2 x 10,800 BHP
Total 15,886 kW / 21,600 BHP   19 knots Twin screw

17.10.1978:	Order placed with AB Oskarshamns Varv, Oskarshamn, by Lars Johansson, Skärhamn.
21.5.1979:	Order transferred to AB Skärhamns Oljetransport, Skärhamn.
22.1.1980:	Launched by AB Oskarshamns Varv, Oskarshamn (#428), without naming ceremonies.
24.6.1980:	Christened FINNROSE by Mrs. Liisa Lanu.
27.6.1980:	Leased by AB Skärhamns Oljetransport for 5 years to Merivienti Oy with a purchase option as per a Letter of Intent signed on Apr. 10.
27.7.1980:	Completed and delivered to AB Skärhamns Oljetransport, (OT-Rederierna), Skärhamn. (SICD) – Operated by Atlantic Cargo Services AB, Göteborg.
29.12.1981:	Acquired by Merivienti Oy, (Enso-Gutzeit Oy), Helsinki /Helsingfors (1659), due to the financial difficulties of the previous owners and delivered the

ms FINNROSE
Photo from Krister Bång

ms LÜBECK LINK ex FINNROSE
Photo by Tomas Johannesson

                same day. Managed by Oy Finnlines Ltd. Continued in Atlanticargo service.

31.12.1982: Sold to the parent company, Enso-Gutzeit Oy, Helsinki. Managers remained Oy Finnlines Ltd.

2.9.1985: Sold to South Atlantic Cargo Shipping N.V., Curaçao, but registered in Nassau, Bahamas. Still in Atlanticargo liner service. Technical management by Oy Finnlines Ltd and manning by Billabong Ship Management A/S & Co., Bergen.

20.9.1989: Sold to Windspoint Shipping Co. Ltd., Gibraltar, (Rederi AB Nordö-Link, Malmö), and delivered the same day without change of name.
It was planned to convert the vessel to a passenger/car cruise ferry by cutting away all old structure 4.5 metres above the main deck and constructing new facilities. Intended to employ the rebuilt ferry for 1,800 passengers and 500 cars in the summer 1990 on Malmö – Lübeck cruise service. The plans were, however, found too expensive and uneconomic. Therefore decided to make a smaller conversion to a combi-roro ferry.

23.12.1989: Arrived at Gdynia for conversion to a passenger/roro and rail cargo motor ferry.

6.4.1990: Sold to Rederi AB Nordö-Link, Malmö, and was deleted on Apr. 11 from Bahamas ship register.

23.4.1990: Delivered by Stocznia Marynarki Wojennej, (Naval Shipyard), Gdynia, as renamed LÜBECK LINK after conversion to a passenger/roro and rail cargo motor ferry with a new deckhouse for 214 berths for passengers. Stern doors sealed. Fitted with a new

guillotine-type bow door and two side doors on starboard side. – Entered Malmö – Travemünde service. (SICD)
Remeasured after conversion in accordance with the 1969 Convention as follows:

33,163 GT, 17,966 NT, 10,600 dwt, 3,400 lane metres, of which 900 rail metres – 192.48 x 27.03 x 6.75 m.

97. FINNMERCHANT (II)   1982–

RoRo Cargo Motor Ferry, two decks, two stern doors
Passengers: 12 berths
Call: OIPZ Ice class: I A Super

21,195 GT, 6,359 NT, 13,090 dwt, 2,170 lane metres, 608 TEU
154.90 x 25.11 x 6.46 m

2 Vee Diesel Engines 4 SA each 12 cy. Sulzer 12ZV40/48
by Oy Wärtsilä Ab, Turku /Åbo
2 x 6,600 kW / 2x 8,973 BHP
Total 13,200 kW / 17,946 BHP   18.5 knots Single screw

ms FINNMERCHANT in original colours
Photo by Matti Pietikäinen

11.6.1982:	Launched by Rauma-Repola Oy, Rauman Telakka, Rauma /Raumo (#271) for Merivienti Oy, (Enso-Gutzeit Oy), Helsinki /Helsingfors, without naming ceremonies.
1.10.1982:	Sold while fitting out to Neste Oy, Naantali /Nådendal.
10.12.1982:	Christened FINNMERCHANT by Mrs. Marjatta Roos.
16.12.1982:	Delivered to Neste Oy, Naantali (73), (c/o Oy Finnlines Ltd, Helsinki).
27.12.1982:	Completed by Rauma-Repola Oy, Rauman Telakka and left Rauma on Jan. 3, 1983 for Helsinki. Entered Finncarriers roro service from Helsinki and Turku to Purfleet.
7.9.1988:	Sold to Laivanisännistöyhtiö Finnmerchant (Part Owners Finnmerchant), Helsinki (1758). Partners were Thomesto Oy, Finncarriers Oy Ab, and Oy Finnlines Ltd. Managers remained Oy Finnlines Ltd.
1.7.1989:	Managers' name changed to FG-Shipping Oy Ab.
10.1990:	Moved to Southern Finland – Lübeck roro service of Finncarriers Oy Ab.

ms FINNMERCHANT in Finncarriers green livery
Photo by Rolf Mieritz

7.1.1992:	Entered in the Finnish parallel Register of Merchant Vessels engaged in International Trade.	15.3.1994:	Sold to Finnlines Oy / Finnlines Ab / Finnlines Ltd / Finnlines AG, Helsinki. Managers remained FG-Shipping Oy Ab.
1.11.1993:	New national reg.no. 10620.	5.7.1994:	Remeasured in accordance with the 1969 Convention as above in the heading. Her previous tonnages were: 8,425 GRT, 3,314 NRT, 13,025 dwt

98. FOSSEAGLE   1983–1985
FINNEAGLE (II)   1985–1987

RoRo Cargo Motor Ferry, two decks, two stern doors
Call: C6CU2 ex OIPB Ice class: II

9,074 GRT, 4,756 NRT, 14,763 dwt, 2500 lane metres, 840 TEU
183.14 x 24.04 x 8.48 m

Diesel Engine 2 SA 6 cy. Sulzer 6RND76
by "H. Cegielski" Z.P.M., Poznan
8,826 kW / 12,000 BHP   17 knots

ms FOSSEAGLE
Photo from Krister Bång

ms FINNEAGLE
Photo from Krister Bång

ms BORAC ex FINNEAGLE in Rotterdam
Photo by Matti Pietikäinen

1974:	Order placed as a 55,000 dwt product tanker by OT-Rederierna, Skärhamn, with AB Oskarshamns Varv, Oskarshamn (#419), for delivery in 1979.
20.4.1976:	Order converted to a 13,800 dwt roro vessel by OT-Rederierna.
3.8.1977:	Launched by AB Oskarshamns Varv, Oskarshamn (#424), without naming ceremonies.
9.12.1977:	Order transferred to AB Skärhamns Oljetransport, (OT-Rederierna).
7.2.1978:	Completed and delivered as EMIRATES EXPRESS to AB Skärhamns Oljetransport, (OT-Rederierna), (Lars G. Johansson), Skärhamn. (SDHV) Never christened. – Entered OT Express Line service to the Middle East.
7.9.1981:	Renamed ABUJA EXPRESS by AB Skärhamns Oljetransport, when moved to OT Africa Line service to West Africa.
8.12.1981:	Acquired by Kansallisrahoitus Oy (Kansallis Finance Ltd.), Helsinki /Helsingfors, and leased to Ab Vasa Shipping Oy, Vaasa /Vasa (250). After delivery on Dec. 10 continued without change of name on her previous liner service to West Africa.
3.11.1983:	Ab Vasa Shipping Oy went into liquidation and Kansallisrahoitus Oy handed over the management of the vessel to Oy Finnlines Ltd.
8.11.1983:	Renamed FOSSEAGLE by Kansallisrahoitus Oy for duration of charter to FOSS Shipping Ltd., London. Name painted on Nov. 29. Moved back to Middle East liner service.
29.11.1984:	Home port changed to Helsinki (1701).
8.1.1985:	Renamed FINNEAGLE after redelivery from charter.
16.4.1987:	Flagged out by a sale to Eagle Shipping Ltd., a subsidiary of Thomesto Oy in George Town, Cayman Islands. Delivered on Apr. 22 and registered in

Nassau, Bahamas. Bareboat-chartered back to Kansallisrahoitus Oy. Managers remained Oy Finnlines Ltd.

30.7.1987: Sold to Jasper Park Shipping Inc., Manila (Monrovia), (c/o Fred. Olsen & Co., Oslo), and renamed BORAC.

28.6.1989: Transferred to NIS-register under Norwegian flag by Jasper Park Shipping Inc. (NIS-605). Home port changed to Oslo.

1994: Remeasured in accordance with the 1969 Convention as follows:
20,165 GT, 6,049 NT, 14,763 dwt

99. FINNFALCON   1984–1988

Motor Bulk Carrier, Singledecker
Call: ZHD2002 ex OISA   Ice class: II

21,625 GT, 11,107 NT, 32,813 dwt
195.30 x 25.30 x 10.63 m

Diesel Engine 2 SA 6 cy. Sulzer 6RLB66
by Sulzer Bros. Ltd., Winterthur
8,164 kW /11,100 BHP   14.8 knots

ms FINNFALCON
Photo from K. Brzoza

ms BERGEN FALCON ex FINNFALCON
Photo from K. Brzoza

3.8.1983:	Launched by Stocznia Szczecinska im. Adolfa Warskiego, Szczecin (#B537/1), without naming ceremonies.
18.8.1984:	Completed and delivered to Ky Jussi Ketola & Co., (c/o Oy Finnlines Ltd), Helsinki /Helsingfors (1714).
28.10.1984:	Christened FINNFALCON at sea in the Mediterranean while on voyage from Algeciras to Istanbul.
17.4.1985:	Flagged out by a sale to Falcon Shipping Ltd., a subsidiary of Ky Jussi Ketola & Co. in George Town, Cayman Islands. Delivered on Apr. 26. Managers remained Oy Finnlines Ltd.
1.3.1988:	Management taken over by Sun Enterprises Ltd., (S. Livanos (Hellas) S.A.), Piraeus.
5.5.1990:	Sold to KS Bergen Falcon, (Bergen Bulk Carriers AS), Bergen (NIS-944), and renamed BERGEN FALCON.
30.8.1995:	Sold to Brand Shipping Co. Ltd., Panama, (c/o Kapelco Maritime Services Ltd., Piraeus), and renamed BERGA FALCON.

100. FINNWHALE — 1985–1988

Motor Bulk Carrier, Singledecker
Call: C6CR4 ex ZHD2003 ex OISO Ice class: II

21,625 GT, 11,107 NT, 32,813 dwt
195.30 x 25.30 x 10.63 m

Diesel Engine 2 SA 6 cy. Sulzer 6RLB66
by "H. Cegielski" Z.P.M., Poznan
8,164 kW /11,100 BHP   14.8 knots

ms FINNWHALE
Photo by FotoFlite

16.3.1984:	Launched by Stocznia Szczecinska im. Adolfa Warskiego, Szczecin (#B537/2), without naming ceremonies.	1.3.1988:	Management taken over by Sun Enterprises Ltd., (S. Livanos (Hellas) S.A.), Piraeus.
11.1.1985:	Completed and delivered as FINNWHALE to Ky Jussi Ketola & Co., (c/o Oy Finnlines Ltd), Helsinki / Helsingfors (1723). Never christened, but sponsored by Mrs. Vappu Ketola.	30.4.1990:	Sold to North Atlantic Cargo Shipping N.V., Curacao, (c/o Wallem Shipmanagement (Isle of Man) Ltd., Douglas, IoM). Registered in Nassau, Bahamas, without change of name.
17.4.1985:	Flagged out by a sale to Whale Shipping Ltd., a subsidiary of Ky Jussi Ketola & Co. in George Town, Cayman Islands. Delivered on May 9. Managers remained Oy Finnlines Ltd.	23.11.1994:	Sold to KS Bergen Pride, (Bergen Bulk Carriers AS), Bergen (NIS), and renamed BERGEN PRIDE.
		27.9.1995:	Sold to Domain Shipping Co. Ltd., Panama, (c/o Kapelco Maritime Services Ltd., Piraeus), and renamed BERGA PRIDE.
6.4.1987:	Transferred to Bahamas flag with Nassau as home port.		

101. PARA-CHARLIE   1985–1993

Non-propelled RoLo Deck Cargo Barge, one deck, side ramp
Call: –

2,039 GT, 612 NT, 4,500 dwt
81.90 x 20.00 x 5.00 m

Barge PARA-CHARLIE in tow by ms HURTIG
Photo by Rolf Mieritz

18.6.1984:	Launched by Rauma-Repola Oy, Uudenkaupungin Telakka, Uusikaupunki /Nystad (#320), without naming ceremonies.	1.7.1989:	Managers' name changed to FG-Shipping Oy Ab.
		18.3.1993:	Management taken over by Paratug Ltd Oy, Parainen /Pargas.
29.6.1984:	Christened PARA-CHARLIE by Mrs. Hilppa Sjöström and delivered to Ra-Shipping Ltd. Oy, (Rainer Sjöström), (c/o Paratug Ltd Oy), Parainen / Pargas (Turku /Åbo 1623).	1.11.1993:	New national reg.no. 10852.
		18.3.1994:	Sold to Rakennusliike Sillanpää Oy, Naantali / Nådendal, and renamed CHARLIE.
2.5.1985:	Management taken over by Oy Finnlines Ltd.		

1996: Capsized on Jan. 22 in the North Sea while on voyage from Larvik to Lowestoft towed by ms Towing Witch. Towed upside down on Jan. 24 to Europoort to be righted.

22.4.1996: Sold to Oceanwide Shipping Ltd., Gibraltar.

102. PARA-ALFA   1985–1992

Non-propelled RoLo Deck Cargo Barge, one deck, side ramp
Call: –

2,039 GT, 612 NT, 4,500 dwt
81.90 x 20.00 x 5.00 m

Barge PARA-ALFA
Photo by K. Brzoza

18.11.1983: Launched by Rauma-Repola Oy, Uudenkaupungin Telakka, Uusikaupunki /Nystad (#318), without naming ceremonies.

1.12.1983: Christened PARA-ALFA by Mrs. Carola Kiviluoto, and delivered the following day to Paratug Ltd Oy, (Mikko Kiviluoto), Parainen /Pargas (Turku /Åbo 1613).

4.5.1985: Management taken over by Oy Finnlines Ltd.

1.7.1989: Managers' name changed to FG-Shipping Oy Ab.

31.8.1992: Sold to Olskrokens Sten AB, Göteborg, and renamed ALFA-ROCK. (SEOA)

30.1.1995: Sold to Kari Laitsalmi Ky, Naantali /Nådendal (#11762), and renamed ALFA.

3.12.1996: Sold to Trond A. Kittilsen Shipping A/S, Trosvik, Norway, and renamed FOKUS BARGE.

103. PARA-BRAVO   1985–1992
PARA-DUO   1992–1995

Non-propelled RoLo Deck Cargo Push-Barge, one deck, side ramp
Call: –   Ice Class: I B

2,826 GT, 847 NT, 6,100 dwt
89.70 x 19.96 x 5.10 m

Schottel Bow Thruster

Barge PARA-DUO
Photo by Raimo A. Wirrankoski

6.4.1984:	Launched by Rauma-Repola Oy, Uudenkaupungin Telakka, Uusikaupunki /Nystad (#319), without naming ceremonies.
27.4.1984:	Christened PARA-BRAVO by Mrs. Gunvor Sjöström and delivered to Ra-Shipping Ltd. Oy, (Rainer Sjöström), (c/o Paratug Ltd Oy), Parainen /Pargas (Turku /Åbo 1621).
5.5.1985:	Management taken over by Oy Finnlines Ltd.
1.7.1989:	Managers' name changed to FG-Shipping Oy Ab.
7.1.1992:	Management taken over by Paratug Ltd Oy, Parainen.
7.11.1991:	Rebuilding contract signed between Ra-Shipping Ltd. Oy, Uudenkaupungin Telakka Oy, and Laivanisännistöyhtiö Proomu 343.
7.5.1992:	Launched after conversion from an ordinary barge to a push-barge by Uudenkaupungin Telakka Oy, Uusikaupunki /Nystad (#343). Her previous particulars were: 2,041 GT, 613 NT, 4,500 dwt 81.90 x 20.00 x 5.00 m
25.5.1992:	Christened PARA-DUO by Mrs. Carola Kiviluoto.
9.6.1992:	Delivered to Laivanisännistöyhtiö Proomu 343, (Part Owners Barge 343), Turku, (Paratug Ltd Oy, Parainen).
10.6.1992:	Time-chartered to Finncarriers Oy Ab and employed on F-ships Baltic bulk services. Managed again by FG-Shipping Oy Ab.
1.11.1993:	New national reg.no. 10846.
2.5.1995:	Management taken over by Paratug Ltd Oy, Parainen, but time-charter to Finncarriers continued.

104. **PARA-DELTA** 1985–1993

Non-propelled RoLo Deck Cargo Barge, one deck, side ramp
Call: –

2,039 GT, 612 NT, 4,500 dwt
81.90 x 20.00 x 5.00 m

Barge PARA-DELTA
Photo by Rolf Mieritz

8.3.1985:	Launched by Rauma-Repola Oy, Uudenkaupungin Telakka, Uusikaupunki /Nystad (#323), without naming ceremonies.
22.3.1985:	Christened PARA-DELTA by Mrs. Carola Kiviluoto and delivered to Travans Oy, (Mikko Kiviluoto), (c/o Paratug Ltd Oy), Parainen /Pargas (Turku /Åbo 1630).
27.5.1985:	Management taken over by Oy Finnlines Ltd.
1.7.1989:	Managers' name changed to FG-Shipping Oy Ab.
20.10.1993:	Management taken over by Paratug Ltd Oy, Parainen.
1.11.1993:	New national reg.no. 10848.

105. **JALINA** 1985–1987
FINNROVER (II) 1987–1988

RoRo Cargo Motor Ferry, two decks, two stern doors
Passengers: 12 berths
Call: C6CT5 ex OIQY   Ice class: I A

4,301 GRT, 1,373 NRT, 5,710 dwt, 324 TEU, 1,269 lane metres
137.45 x 22.34 x 6.60 m

2 Diesel Engines 4 SA each 9 cy. Werkspoor 9TM410
by Stork-Werkspoor Diesel N.V., Amsterdam
2 x 3,861 kW / 2 x 5,275 BHP
Total 7,722 kW / 10,550 BHP   18 knots Twin screw

ms KOTKA LILY, later JALINA, in Helsinki
Photo by Matti Pietikäinen

ms JALINA
Photo from FG-Shipping Oy Ab

26.5.1972:	Launched by Rauma-Repola Oy, Rauman Telakka, Rauma /Raumo (#206), and named ANTARES by Mrs. Elina Keino.
30.10.1972:	Completed and delivered to Suomen Höyrylaiva Oy – Finska Ångfartygs Ab, Helsinki /Helsingfors (1478). Entered Helsinki – Kotka – Hamburg liner service. (Call: OIBS)
8.8.1975:	Renamed RHEINFELS for duration of charter to Deutsche Dampfschiffahrts Ges. Hansa, Bremen, and employed on Germany – Persian Gulf service.
4.1.1977:	Sold to N.V. Nederlandsche Scheepvaart Unie, Rotterdam, and assigned to Koninklijke Nedlloyd B.V., (N.S.U. Scheepvaart B.V.), Rotterdam. Delivered on Jan. 13. Renamed NEDLLOYD ROCKANJE and employed on USEC – Middle East service.
1978:	Transferred to Nedlloyd Lijnen B.V., (Koninklijke Nedlloyd Groep N.V.), Rotterdam.
20.10.1983:	Acquired by Kotka Line Ky, (Paavo Haveri), Kotka (627), (c/o Oy Henry Nielsen Ab, Helsinki), and renamed KOTKA LILY. Entered liner service from Kotka and Helsinki via Bremerhaven to Chatham and Blyth.
28.6.1984:	Owners reorganized as Kotka Line Oy.
2.1.1985:	Owners went into liquidation and the vessel was laid up in Helsinki.
8.8.1985:	Sold at auction to Kansallis-Osake-Pankki, the main creditors of the previous owners. (BoS 27.8.1985)
21.8.1985:	Management taken over by Oy Finnlines Ltd, Helsinki, but home port remained Kotka.
27.8.1985:	Renamed JALINA for duration of charter to I/S Jahre Line, Oslo, and employed on Oslo – Kiel liner service.
19.3.1987:	Renamed FINNROVER after redelivery from charter.
30.3.1987:	Flagged out by a sale to Rover Shipping Ltd., a subsidiary of Thomesto Oy in George Town, Cayman Islands. Delivered on Mar. 31 and registered in

ms FINNROVER at Esbjerg
Photo by Matti Pietikäinen

ms SEAHORSE ex FINNROVER
Photo from Krister Bång

Nassau, Bahamas. Bareboat-chartered back to Kansallis-Osake-Pankki. Managers remained Oy Finnlines Ltd. Chartered to Elbe Humber Roline for Esbjerg – Hull liner service.

20.6.1988: Sold to K/S A/S Bulk Venture I, (c/o Nils Hugo Sand, [Goliath Shipping A/S]), Oslo (NIS-263), and renamed SEAHORSE when delivered on June 29.

2.1992: Renamed DANA CORONA by K/S A/S Bulk Venture I when chartered to DFDS A/S for Immingham – Cuxhaven service.

1994: Remeasured in accordance with the 1969 Convention as follows:
12,110 GT, 3,633 NT, 5,710 dwt

106. FINNTRADER (III)   1986–1990

Motor Bulk /Container Carrier, Singledecker
Call: C6CR6 ex ZHEI2 ex OITO Ice class: I C

21,305 GT, 10,412 NT, 30,975 dwt
184.86 x 27.60 x 10.33 m

Diesel Engine 2 SA 6 cy. Sulzer 6RTA58
by Sulzer Bros. Ltd., Winterthur
7,080 kW / 9,600 BHP   14.4 knots

ms FINNTRADER
Photo from Krister Bång

ms BALTIC SKOU ex FINNTRADER in Hamburg
Photo by Matti Pietikäinen

26.4.1985:	Launched by Stocznia Gdanska im. Lenina, Gdansk (#B539/1), and named FINNTRADER by Mrs. Kirsti Airikkala.	3.12.1990:	Sold to Baltic Skou A/S, (c/o Skou International A/S), København, and renamed BALTIC SKOU when delivered on Dec. 7. – Continued on Scanscot service.
31.12.1985:	Taken over while still fitting-out by Thomesto Oy, Helsinki /Helsingfors (not reg.). Managed by Oy Finnlines Ltd.	1.1.1991:	Managers' name changed to SITE International A/S.
		1.1.1994:	Managers' name changed to Tschudi & Eitzen International A/S.
30.1.1986:	Completed by Stocznia Gdanska im. Lenina. – Entered on Feb. 1 Scanscot worldwide bulk/container service.	16.11.1995:	Sold to Panartic Shipping Co., Ltd., Valletta, Malta, (c/o Antares Shipping Co. Ltd., London), and renamed NORTH VISCOUNTESS when delivered on Dec. 4.
21.3.1986:	Flagged out by a sale to Timber Shipping Ltd., a subsidiary of Thomesto Oy in George Town, Cayman Islands. Delivered on Apr. 25 and bareboat-chartered back to Thomesto Oy. Managers remained Oy Finnlines Ltd.	1996:	Managers changed to Palmyra Management S.A., Montreux, Switzerland.
		1996:	Renamed CIELO DI SIENA by Panartic Shipping Co., Ltd., due to charter to Medbulk, (d'Amico Societa di Navigazione, S.p.A., Palermo).
2.4.1987:	Transferred to Bahamas flag with Nassau as home port.		

107. RAUTARUUKKI (II) 1986–

Motor Pusher Tug, three decks
Call: OJHM ex SBMC ex OITU Ice class: I A Super

1,554 GT, 467 NT, 150 dwt
41.70 x 14.36 x 6.70 m

2 Diesel Engines 4 SA each 6 cy. Sulzer 6ZAL40
by Oy Wärtsilä Ab, Turku /Åbo
2 x 3,840 kW / 2 x 5,200 BHP
Total 7,680 kW / 10,400 BHP   15 knots
Single screw

ms RAUTARUUKKI under construction in June 1986 at Rauma
Photo by K. Brzoza

20.12.1985:	Launched by Hollming Oy, Rauma /Raumo (#262), without naming ceremonies.	30.10.1989:	Flagged out by a sale to Partrederiet för ms Rautaruukki, Rautaruukki Rör AB m.fl., Stockholm. Technical managers remained FG-Shipping Oy Ab, but manning by AB Finnlines Ltd, Stockholm. (SBMC)
31.10.1986:	Christened RAUTARUUKKI by Mrs. Pirjo-Riitta Kivimäki and delivered to Rautaruukki Oy, Raahe / Brahestad (322), (c/o Oy Finnlines Ltd, Helsinki / Helsingfors). Employed as pusher for push-barges Kalla and Tasku.		
		27.12.1996:	Sold to Merita Rahoitus Oy (Merita Finance Ltd), Helsinki (#11900), and bareboat-chartered to Oy JIT-Trans Ltd, Raahe.
1.7.1989:	Managers' name changed to FG-Shipping Oy Ab.	8.1.1997:	Entered in the Finnish parallel Register of Merchant Vessels engaged in International Trade.

108. KALLA 1986–

Non-propelled RoLo Deck Cargo Push-Barge, one deck, side ramp
Call: – ex SBMB Ice class: I A Super

9,066 GT, 2,720 NT, 14,002 dwt
159.10 x 27.20 x 6.70 m

Bow Thruster with 680 kW electric motor

Push-barge KALLA
Photo from FG-Shipping Oy Ab

15.5.1986:	Launched by Setenave – Estaleiros Navais de Setubal E.P., Setubal (#B126), as a sub-delivery for Hollming Oy, Rauma /Raumo. Towed to Uusikaupunki /Nystad for fitting out by Rauma-Repola Oy, Uudenkaupungin Telakka as sub-contractors.	31.10.1986:	Completed by Hollming Oy, Rauma (#258), as KALLA for Rautaruukki Oy, Raahe /Brahestad (323), (c/o Oy Finnlines Ltd, Helsinki /Helsingfors).
		1.7.1989:	Managers' name changed to FG-Shipping Oy Ab.

FINNPUSKU-combination KALLA and RAUTARUUKKI
Photo by Klaus Koszubatis

30.10.1989: Flagged out by a sale to Partrederiet för Kalla, Rautaruukki Rör AB m.fl., Stockholm. Managers remained FG-Shipping Oy Ab. (SBMB)

27.12.1996: Sold to Merita Rahoitus Oy (Merita Finance Ltd), Helsinki (#11901), and bareboat-chartered to Oy JIT-Trans Ltd, Raahe.

109. TASKU   1986–

Non-propelled RoLo Deck Cargo Push-Barge, one deck, side ramp
Call: – ex SBME Ice class: I A Super

9,066 GT, 2,720 NT, 14,002 dwt
159.10 x 27.20 x 6.70 m

Bow Thruster with 680 kW electric motor

Push-barge TASKU
Photo by K. Brzoza

22.6.1986:	Launched by Setenave – Estaleiros Navais de Setubal E.P., Setubal (#B127), as a sub-delivery for Hollming Oy, Rauma /Raumo. Towed to Uusikaupunki /Nystad for fitting out by Rauma-Repola Oy, Uudenkaupungin Telakka as sub-contractors.	1.7.1989:	Managers' name changed to FG-Shipping Oy Ab.
		1.11.1989:	Flagged out by a sale to Partrederiet för Tasku, Rautaruukki Rör AB m.fl., Stockholm. Managers remained FG-Shipping Oy Ab. (SBME)
31.10.1986:	Completed by Hollming Oy, Rauma (#259) as TASKU for Rautaruukki Oy, Raahe /Brahestad (324), (c/o Oy Finnlines Ltd, Helsinki /Helsingfors).	27.12.1996:	Sold to Merita Rahoitus Oy (Merita Finance Ltd), Helsinki (#11902), and bareboat-chartered to Oy JIT-Trans Ltd, Raahe.

110. LAPPONIA   1986–1990

Motor Bulk Carrier, Singledecker
Call: C6CP5 ex ZHEP6   Ice class: I A

12,804 GRT, 5,401 NRT, 17,190 dwt
163.96 x 22.94 x 8.65 m

Diesel Engine 2 SA 6 cy. MAN K6Z 70/120E
by Kawasaki Heavy Industries Ltd., Kobe
6,841 kW / 9,300 BHP   15.5 knots

ms LAPPONIA in Montreal
Photo from K. Brzoza

26.8.1977:	Launched by Hyundai Shipbuilding & Heavy Industries Co. Ltd., Ulsan (#1660), without naming ceremonies.	1.1.1984:	Management handed over to Oy Finncarriers Ab, Helsinki, a subsidiary of Effoa – Finland Steamship Co. Ltd.
3.9.1977:	Christened ASTREA by Mrs. Eva-May Åberg.	29.10.1986:	Flagged out by a sale to EFF-Shipping Ltd., a subsidiary of Effoa – Finland Steamship Co. Ltd. in George Town, Cayman Islands. Renamed LAPPONIA when delivered on Nov. 3. Bareboat-chartered back to Effoa – Finland Steamship Co. Ltd. Managed by Oy Finnlines Ltd.
15.3.1978:	Completed and delivered to Suomen Höyrylaiva Oy – Finska Ångfartygs Ab, Helsinki /Helsingfors (1593). (Call: OIHZ)		
13.2.1981:	Owners' name registered as Effoa – Finska Ångfartygs Ab / Effoa – Suomen Höyrylaiva Oy / Effoa – Finland Steamship Co. Ltd. as per EGM resolutions on Nov. 12 and Dec. 12, 1980.	4.11.1986:	Joined F-ships pool transatlantic contract service to/ from USEC and Canada.

ms STRILBERG ex LAPPONIA in the River Elbe
Photo by Matti Pietikäinen

17.2.1987:	Transferred to Bahamas flag with Nassau as home port.
12.1.1988:	Left F-ships pool.
3.1.1990:	Sold to Oy Gustav Paulig Ab, (c/o Navicon Oy Ab), Helsinki (1777), without change of name when delivered on Jan. 8. (Call: OJCI)
25.2.1991:	Flagged out by a sale to Lapponia Shipping Co. Ltd., Valletta, a subsidiary of Oy Gustav Paulig Ab. Managers remained Navicon Oy Ab, Helsinki.
1994:	Remeasured in accordance with the 1969 Convention as follows: 16,788 GT, 9,395 NT, 17,190 dwt
23.12.1994:	Sold to Simon Møkster Shipping A/S, Stavanger (NIS), and renamed STRILBERG.
1995:	Converted to a self-unloading bulk carrier.

111. TELLUS   1987–1988

General Cargo Motorship, two decks – Tweendecker
Call: C6CK6   Ice class: I C

24,869 GT, 11,897 NT, 37,425 dwt, 1,104 TEU
182.51 x 29.50 x 11.53 m

Diesel Engine 2 SA 6 cy. Sulzer 6RLB66
by Sumitomo Heavy Industries Ltd., Tamashima
9,429 kW /12,820 BHP   15 knots

ms TELLUS
Photo from Krister Bång

12.9.1983:	Launched by Nippon Kokan K.K., Tsu Works (#85), without naming ceremonies.
13.1.1984:	Completed and delivered as TELLUS to Effoa – Finska Ångfartygs Ab / Effoa – Suomen Höyrylaiva Oy / Effoa – Finland Steamship Co. Ltd., Helsinki / Helsingfors (1708). Managed by Oy Finncarriers Ab, Helsinki, the operational subsidiary of Effoa – Finland Steamship Co. Ltd. (Call: OIPV)
5.4.1984:	Christened traditionally TELLUS by Mrs. Meri Lahermaa in Helsinki.
15.1.1987:	Flagged out by a sale to EFF-Shipping Ltd., a subsidiary of Effoa – Finland Steamship Co. Ltd. in George Town, Cayman Islands. Delivered on Feb. 2 and registered in Nassau, Bahamas. Bareboat-chartered back to Effoa – Finland Steamship Co. Ltd. Managed by Oy Finnlines Ltd.
8.1.1988:	Sold to Argonaut Shipping Inc., Panama, (c/o South African Marine Corp. Ltd. [SAFMARINE], Cape Town), and renamed RECIFE. Chartered to SAFMARINE.
1996:	Renamed NTABENI by Argonaut Shipping Inc. Converted to general cargo tar motorship with following tonnages: 25,005 GT, 10,741 NT, 37,425 dwt

112. FENNIA   1987–1992
FINNMASTER (III)   1992–

RoRo Cargo Motor Ferry, two decks, two stern doors
Passengers: 12 berths
Call: OJFH ex C6CT5 Ice class: I A

11,839 GT, 3,552 NT, 5,710 dwt, 324 TEU, 1,269 lane metres
137.45 x 22.28 x 6.64 m

2 Diesel Engines 4 SA each 9 cy. Werkspoor 9TM410
by Stork-Werkspoor Diesel N.V., Amsterdam
2 x 3,861 kW / 2 x 5, 275 BHP
Total 7,722 kW / 10,550 BHP   17 knots Twin screw

ms FENNIA on charter to Kent Line
Photo from A. Duncan

15.12.1972:	Launched by Rauma-Repola Oy, Rauman Telakka, Rauma /Raumo (#208), without naming ceremonies.
5.4.1973:	Christened SIRIUS by Mrs. Camilla Dettman and delivered to Suomen Höyrylaiva Oy – Finska Ångfartygs Ab, Helsinki /Helsingfors (1490). (Call: OIBW)

ms FINNMASTER
Photo by Matti Pietikäinen

13.2.1981: Owners' name registered as Effoa – Finska Ångfartygs Ab / Effoa – Suomen Höyrylaiva Oy / Effoa – Finland Steamship Co. Ltd. as per EGM resolutions on Nov. 12 and Dec. 12, 1980.

1.1.1984: Management handed over to Oy Finncarriers Ab, Helsinki, the operational subsidiary of Effoa – Finland Steamship Co. Ltd.

22.4.1987: Flagged out by a sale to EFF-Shipping Ltd., a subsidiary of Effoa – Finland Steamship Co. Ltd. in George Town, Cayman Islands. Renamed FENNIA when delivered on Apr. 24 and registered in Nassau, Bahamas. Bareboat-chartered back to Effoa – Finland Steamship Co. Ltd. Managed by Oy Finnlines Ltd.

1.7.1989: Managers' name changed to FG-Shipping Oy Ab.

19.10.1989: Sold to Fennia-Shipping Ltd., Nassau, (Finncarriers Oy Ab, Helsinki). Managers remained FG-Shipping Oy Ab.

11.12.1992: Acquired by Finnlines Oy / Finnlines Ab / Finnlines Ltd / Finnlines AG, Helsinki (1868), and renamed FINNMASTER when delivered on Dec. 21. Managed by FG-Shipping Oy Ab.

23.12.1992: Entered in the Finnish parallel Register of Merchant Vessels engaged in International Trade.

1.11.1993: New national reg.no. 10621.

10.12.1993: Remeasured in accordance with the 1969 Convention as above in the heading. Her previous particulars were: 4,469 GRT, 1,478 NRT, 5,660 dwt 137.45 x 22.34 x 6.60 m

113. FINN STEEL

1987–1991
1991–

Motor Tug Pusher, three decks
Call: OIVR Ice class: I A Super

1,562 GT, 469 NT, 431 dwt
41.70 x 14.36 x 6.70 m

2 Diesel Engines 4 SA each 6 cy. Sulzer 6ZAL40
by Oy Wärtsilä Ab, Turku /Åbo
2 x 3,840 kW / 2 x 5,200 BHP
Total 7,680 kW / 10,400 BHP   13.4 knots Single screw

ms FINN at Raahe
Photo by Raimo A. Wirrankoski

FINNPUSKU-combination FINN and BULK
Photo by Rolf Mieritz

7.11.1986:	Launched by Hollming Oy, Rauma /Raumo (#263), without naming ceremonies.
28.4.1987:	Christened FINN by Mrs. Marjatta Roos and delivered to Laivanisännistöyhtiö Puskija (Part Owners Pusher), (Oy Finnlines Ltd), Helsinki /Helsingfors (1740). Working as pusher for push-barges Baltic, Board, and Bulk.
30.6.1988:	Rautaruukki Oy and their subsidiary Oy JIT-Trans Ltd. took over the shares of the other partners.
1.7.1989:	Managing owner's name changed to FG-Shipping Oy Ab.
1990:	Capsized off Hanko /Hangö on Dec. 27 during heavy weather while pushing the barge Baltic, which also capsized, from Luleå via Raahe /Brahestad to Koverhar. Seven crew members and the pilot lost their lives.
1991:	Righted on Jan. 31 by crane ship Stanislav Yudin and towed to Hanko. After examination left Hanko in tow and arrived on Mar. 21 at Hollming shipyard, Rauma, for repairs.
23.10.1991:	Renamed STEEL and owners' name registered as Laivanisännistöyhtiö Steel (Part Owners Steel). Home port changed to Raahe /Brahestad (327).

17.11.1991:	Returned to service after completed repairs.	1.9.1993:	Owners' name changed to Suomen Asiakasrahoitus Oy (Finnish Customer Finance Ltd).
7.1.1992:	Entered in the Finnish parallel Register of Merchant Vessels engaged in International Trade.	1.11.1993:	New national reg.no. 10594.
28.12.1992:	Sold to Suomen Yritysrahoitus Oy / Finska Företagsfinans Ab / Finnish Corporate Finance Ltd, Helsinki (1740), and bareboat-chartered to Oy JIT-Trans Ltd, Raahe.	2.8.1995:	Owners' name changed to Merita Rahoitus Oy (Merita Finance Ltd).

114. BALTIC   1987–1991
BOTNIA   1991–

Non-propelled RoLo Deck Cargo Push-Barge, one deck, side ramp
Call: – Ice class: I A Super

9,066 GT, 2,720 NT, 14,000 dwt
159.10 x 27.20 x 6.70 m

Bow Thruster with 680 kW electric motor

Push-barge BALTIC at Rauma
Photo by Matti Pietikäinen

11.10.1986:	Launched by Setenave – Estaleiros Navais de Setubal E.P., Setubal (#B128), as a sub-delivery for Hollming Oy, Rauma /Raumo. Towed to Rauma for fitting out by Rauma-Repola Oy, Rauman Telakka as sub-contractors.	30.6.1988:	Rautaruukki Oy and their subsidiary Oy JIT-Trans Ltd. took over the shares of the other partners.
		1.7.1989:	Managing owner's name changed to FG-Shipping Oy Ab.
28.4.1987:	Completed by Hollming Oy, Rauma (#257), as BALTIC for Laivanisännistöyhtiö Proomu I, (Part Owners Barge I), (Oy Finnlines Ltd), Helsinki / Helsingfors (1742).	1990:	Capsized off Hanko /Hangö on Dec. 27 during heavy weather while pushed by the tug Finn, which also capsized, from Luleå via Raahe /Brahestad to Koverhar with iron ore.

1991:	Rightened on Jan. 31 by crane ship Stanislav Yudin and towed to Hanko. After examination left Hanko in tow and arrived on Mar. 21 at Hollming shipyard, Rauma, for repairs.	28.12.1992:	Sold to Suomen Yritysrahoitus Oy / Finska Företagsfinans Ab / Finnish Corporate Finance Ltd, Helsinki (1742), and bareboat-chartered to Oy JIT-Trans Ltd, Raahe.
23.10.1991:	Renamed BOTNIA and owners' name registered as Laivanisännistöyhtiö Botnia (Part Owners Botnia). Home port changed to Raahe /Brahestad (329).	1.9.1993:	Owners' name changed to Suomen Asiakasrahoitus Oy (Finnish Customer Finance Ltd).
17.11.1991:	Returned to service after completed repairs.	1.11.1993:	New national reg.no. 10581.
		2.8.1995:	Owners' name changed to Merita Rahoitus Oy (Merita Finance Ltd).

115. BOARD   1987–

Non-propelled RoLo Deck Cargo Push-Barge, one deck, side ramp
Call: – Ice class: I A Super

9,066 GT, 2,720 NT, 14,000 dwt
159.10 x 27.20 x 6.70 m

Bow Thruster with 680 kW electric motor

Push-barge BOARD with pusher FINN
Photo by K. Brzoza

27.11.1986:	Launched by Setenave – Estaleiros Navais de Setubal E.P., Setubal (#B129), as a sub-delivery for Hollming Oy, Rauma /Raumo. Towed to Rauma for fitting out by Rauma-Repola Oy, Rauman Telakka as sub-contractors.	23.10.1991:	Owners' name registered as Laivanisännistöyhtiö Board (Part Owners Board) and home port changed to Raahe /Brahestad (330).
28.4.1987:	Completed by Hollming Oy, Rauma (#260), as BOARD for Laivanisännistöyhtiö Proomu II, (Part Owners Barge II), (Oy Finnlines Ltd), Helsinki / Helsingfors (1741).	28.12.1992:	Sold to Suomen Yritysrahoitus Oy / Finska Företagsfinans Ab / Finnish Corporate Finance Ltd, Helsinki (1741), and bareboat-chartered to Oy JIT-Trans Ltd, Raahe.
		1.9.1993:	Owners' name changed to Suomen Asiakasrahoitus Oy (Finnish Customer Finance Ltd).
30.6.1988:	Rautaruukki Oy and their subsidiary Oy JIT-Trans Ltd. took over the shares of the other partners.	1.11.1993:	New national reg.no. 10579.
1.7.1989:	Managing owner's name changed to FG-Shipping Oy Ab.	2.8.1995:	Owners' name changed to Merita Rahoitus Oy (Merita Finance Ltd).

116. BULK   1987–

Non-propelled RoLo Deck Cargo Push-Barge, one deck, side ramp
Call: – Ice class: I A Super

9,066 GT, 2,720 NT, 14,000 dwt
159.10 x 27.20 x 6.70 m

Bow Thruster with 680 kW electric motor

Push-barge BULK with pusher FINN
Photo by Rolf Mieritz

22.12.1986:	Launched by Setenave – Estaleiros Navais de Setubal E.P., Setubal (#B132), as a sub-delivery for Hollming Oy, Rauma /Raumo. Towed to Rauma for fitting out by Rauma-Repola Oy, Rauman Telakka as sub-contractors.	23.10.1991:	Owners' name registered as Laivanisännistöyhtiö Bulk (Part Owners Bulk) and home port changed to Raahe /Brahestad (328).
8.5.1987:	Completed by Hollming Oy, Rauma (#261), as BULK for Laivanisännistöyhtiö Proomu III, (Part Owners Barge III), (Oy Finnlines Ltd), Helsinki / Helsingfors (1743).	28.12.1992:	Sold to Suomen Yritysrahoitus Oy / Finska Företagsfinans Ab / Finnish Corporate Finance Ltd, Helsinki (1743), and bareboat-chartered to Oy JIT-Trans Ltd, Raahe.
30.6.1988:	Rautaruukki Oy and their subsidiary Oy JIT-Trans Ltd. took over the shares of the other partners.	1.9.1993:	Owners' name changed to Suomen Asiakasrahoitus Oy (Finnish Customer Finance Ltd).
		1.11.1993:	New national reg.no. 10582.
1.7.1989:	Managing owner's name changed to FG-Shipping Oy Ab.	2.8.1995:	Owners' name changed to Merita Rahoitus Oy (Merita Finance Ltd).

117. TAURUS 1987–1988

General Cargo Motorship, two decks – Tweendecker
Call: C6CW6 Ice class: I C

24,464 GT, 11,789 NT, 37,425 dwt, 1,104 TEU
182.51 x 29.50 x 11.53 m

Diesel Engine 2 SA 6 cy. Sulzer 6RLB66
by Sumitomo Heavy Industries Ltd., Tamashima
9,429 kW /12,820 BHP   15 knots

ms TAURUS at Kotka
Photo by Matti Pietikäinen

28.2.1983:	Launched by Nippon Kokan K.K., Tsu Works (#84), without naming ceremonies.	1.7.1983:	Christened TAURUS by Mrs. Jane Erkko and delivered to Effoa – Finska Ångfartygs Ab / Effoa – Suomen Höyrylaiva Oy / Effoa – Finland Steamship Co. Ltd., Helsinki /Helsingfors (1692). (Call: OIPU)

ms INFANTA ex TAURUS in Durban
Photo from K. Brzoza

1.1.1984:	Management handed over to Oy Finncarriers Ab, Helsinki, a subsidiary of Effoa – Finland Steamship Co. Ltd.	18.1.1988:	Sold to Argonaut Shipping Inc., Panama, (c/o South African Marine Corp. Ltd. [SAFMARINE], Cape Town), and renamed INFANTA. Chartered to SAFMARINE.
27.5.1987:	Flagged out by a sale to EFF-Shipping Ltd., a subsidiary of Effoa – Finland Steamship Co. Ltd. in George Town, Cayman Islands. Delivered the same day and registered in Nassau, Bahamas. Bareboat-chartered back to Effoa – Finland Steamship Co. Ltd. Managed by Oy Finnlines Ltd.	12.1994:	Sold to Great Trans Shipping Inc., Panama, (c/o Wah Tung Shipping Agency Co. Ltd., Hong Kong), and renamed GREAT TRANS.

118. POLLUX   1987–1988

General Cargo Motorship, two decks – Open/Closed Shelterdecker
Call: C6CU8 Ice class: I A Super

8,687/14,116 GRT, 3,864/6,472 NRT, 11,850/17,160 dwt, 540 TEU
155.80 x 22.50 x 7.59/9.32 m

Diesel Engine 2 SA 6 cy. Sulzer 6RND76
by Sulzer Bros. Ltd., Winterthur
8,827 kW / 12,000 BHP   16 knots

12.3.1977:	Launched by Haugesund Mek. Verksted A/S, Haugesund (#57), without naming ceremonies.	13.2.1981:	Owners' name registered as Effoa – Finska Ångfartygs Ab / Effoa – Suomen Höyrylaiva Oy / Effoa – Finland Steamship Co. Ltd. as per EGM resolutions on Nov. 12 and Dec. 12, 1980.
25.11.1977:	Completed and delivered as POLLUX for Suomen Höyrylaiva Oy – Finska Ångfartygs Ab, Helsinki / Helsingfors (1589). (Call: OIHU)	1.1.1984:	Management handed over to Oy Finncarriers Ab, Helsinki, the operational subsidiary of Effoa – Finland Steamship Co. Ltd.
10.12.1977:	Christened traditionally POLLUX at Hamina / Fredrikshamn by Mrs. Anna Ehrnrooth.		

ms POLLUX
Photo from Krister Bång

ms NOMADIC POLLUX ex POLLUX on F-ships charter
Photo by Bengt Sjöström

23.6.1987:	Flagged out by a sale to EFF-Shipping Ltd., a subsidiary of Effoa – Finland Steamship Co. Ltd. in George Town, Cayman Islands. Delivered the same day and registered in Nassau, Bahamas. Bareboat-chartered back to Effoa – Finland Steamship Co. Ltd. Managed by Oy Finnlines Ltd, Helsinki.
20.7.1988:	Sold to Holy Rosette Marine S.A., Ålesund (NIS-278), (Panama), (c/o Barber International A/S, Oslo), and renamed BALTIKUM.
9.1988:	Remeasured in Norway as follows: 6,360/11,903 GRT, 4,013/7,125 NRT, 11,850/17,161 dwt
2.1989:	Sold to BHT Pollux Shipping Co. Inc., Bergen (NIS), and the name reverted to POLLUX. Managers remained Barber International A/S, Oslo.
4.4.1990:	Renamed NOMADIC POLLUX by BHT Pollux Shipping Co. Inc.
11.1990:	Sold to K/S Nomadic Pollux, Bergen (NIS), (Nomadic Shipping A/S, Minde).
12.1991:	Sold to A/S S/S Mathilda, Bergen (NIS), (c/o Nomadic Management A/S, Minde), without change of name.
1994:	Remeasured in accordance with the 1969 Convention as follows: 14,013 GT, 4,419 NT, 17,161 dwt
1996:	Managers changed to Green Management AS, Minde.
12.12.1996:	Chartered to Finncarriers Oy Ab for F-ships service.

119. PALLAS   1987–1988

General Cargo Motorship, two decks and 3rd deck in Nos. 2 & 3 holds – Open/Closed Shelterdecker
Call: C6CV2   Ice class: I A

5,111/7,890 GRT, 2,282/3,878 NRT, 8,270/10,000 dwt
146.60 x 20.04 x 6.83/7.60 m

Diesel Engine 2 SA 6 cy. B&W 6K62EF
by Valmet Oy, Rautpohjan Tehdas, Jyväskylä
6,105 kW / 8,300 BHP   17.4 knots

ms PALLAS at Kotka
Photo by Bengt Sjöström

26.11.1970: Launched by Rauma-Repola Oy, Rauman Telakka, Rauma /Raumo (#197), and named PALLAS by Mrs. Eine Koski.

22.8.1971: Completed and delivered to Suomen Höyrylaiva Oy – Finska Ångfartygs Ab, Helsinki /Helsingfors (1438). (Call: OGYB)

10.11.1974: Delivered after lengthening by a cargo section of 18.24 metres at Howaldtswerke – Deutsche Werft A.G., Hamburg. Fitted with a sixth deck crane. Her original particulars before lengthening were:
4,233/6,493 GRT, 1,745/3,055 NRT, 6,600/8,330 dwt
128.36 x 20.04 x 6.91/7.84 m

13.2.1981: Owners' name registered as Effoa – Finska Ångfartygs Ab / Effoa – Suomen Höyrylaiva Oy / Effoa – Finland Steamship Co. Ltd. as per EGM resolutions on Nov. 12 and Dec. 12, 1980.

1.1.1984: Management handed over to Oy Finncarriers Ab, Helsinki, the operational subsidiary of Effoa – Finland Steamship Co. Ltd.

17.6.1987: Flagged out by a sale to EFF-Shipping Ltd., a subsidiary of Effoa – Finland Steamship Co. Ltd. in George Town, Cayman Islands. Delivered on July 1 and registered in Nassau, Bahamas. Bareboat-chartered back to Effoa – Finland Steamship Co. Ltd. Managed by Oy Finnlines Ltd.

10.6.1988: Sold to Arctis Enterprises S.A., (c/o Transcontinental Maritime & Trading S.A.), Piraeus, without change of name.

1992: Sold to Conington Shipping Co., Nassau, (c/o Marine Managers Ltd., Haifa).

1993: Managers changed to Bogazzi Servizi Navali S.r.l., Avenza, Italy.

1994: Remeasured in accordance with the 1969 Convention as follows:
7,997 GT, 3,784 NT, 10,160 dwt

120. **PATRIA** 1987–1988

General Cargo Motorship, two decks – Open/Closed Shelterdecker
Call: C6CU9 Ice class: I A Super

8844/14,234 GRT, 3,897/6,584 NRT, 11,850/17,160 dwt, 540 TEU
155.80 x 22.50 x 7.59/9.32 m

Diesel Engine 2 SA 6 cy. Sulzer 6RND76
by Sulzer Bros. Ltd., Winterthur
8,827 kW / 12,000 BHP   16 knots

ms PATRIA at Turku
Photo by K. Brzoza

24.11.1977:	Launched by Haugesund Mek. Verksted A/S, Haugesund (#58), without naming ceremonies.
15.4.1978:	Christened PATRIA by Mrs. Louise Swanljung.
28.4.1978:	Completed and delivered as PATRIA to Suomen Höyrylaiva Oy – Finska Ångfartygs Ab, Helsinki / Helsingfors (1589). (Call: OIHV)
13.2.1981:	Owners' name registered as Effoa – Finska Ångfartygs Ab / Effoa – Suomen Höyrylaiva Oy / Effoa – Finland Steamship Co. Ltd. as per EGM resolutions on Nov. 12 and Dec. 12, 1980.
1.1.1984:	Management handed over to Oy Finncarriers Ab, Helsinki, the operational subsidiary of Effoa – Finland Steamship Co. Ltd.
20.7.1987:	Flagged out by a sale to EFF-Shipping Ltd., a subsidiary of Effoa – Finland Steamship Co. Ltd. in George Town, Cayman Islands. Delivered on July 22 and registered in Nassau, Bahamas. Bareboat-chartered back to Effoa – Finland Steamship Co. Ltd. Managed by Oy Finnlines Ltd.
26.7.1988:	Sold to Holy Lotus Marine S.A., Ålesund (NIS-283), (Panama), (c/o Barber International A/S, Oslo), and renamed UKRAINA.
9.1988:	Remeasured in Norway as follows: 6,407/12,017 GRT, 4,018/7,237 NRT, 11,850/17,160 dwt
2.1989:	Sold to BHT Patria Shipping Co. Inc., Bergen (NIS), and the name reverted to PATRIA. Managers remained Barber International A/S, Oslo.
4.4.1990:	Renamed NOMADIC PATRIA by BHT Patria Shipping Co. Inc.
11.1990:	Sold to K/S Nomadic Patria, Bergen (NIS), (Nomadic Shipping A/S, Minde).

*ms NOMADIC PATRIA ex PATRIA
in Montreal
Photo from K. Brzoza*

12.1991: Sold to Norchem Shipping A/S, Bergen (NIS), (c/o Nomadic Management A/S, Minde), without change of name.

1994: Remeasured in accordance with the 1969 Convention as follows: 14,013 GT, 4,419 NT, 17,161 dwt

1996: Managers changed to Green Management AS, Minde.

14.12.1996: Chartered to Finncarriers Oy Ab for F-ships service.

121. ARIEL 1987–1988

General Cargo Motorship, two decks and 3rd deck in Nos. 2 & 3 holds – Open/Closed Shelterdecker
Call: C6CU7 Ice class: I A

4,887/7,571 GRT, 2,184/3,822 NRT, 7,590/9,530 dwt
145.98 x 19.03 x 6.80/7.70 m

Diesel Engine 2 SA 6 cy. B&W 6K62EF
by the Shipbuilders
6,105 kW / 8,300 BHP   17.5 knots

*ms ARIEL on arrival at Mäntyluoto
Photo by Matti Pietikäinen*

17.9.1970:	Launched by Helsingør Skibsværft og Maskinbyggeri A/S, Helsingør (Elsinore) (#393), and named ARIEL by Mrs. Brita Segercrantz.
29.12.1970:	Completed and delivered to Suomen Höyrylaiva Oy – Finska Ångfartygs Ab, Helsinki /Helsingfors (1423). (Call: OGYA)
1974:	Lengthened by a cargo section of 18.04 metres at Helsingør Værft A/S, Helsingør. Fitted with a sixth deck crane. Her original particulars before lengthening were: 4,061/6,244 GRT, 1,697/3,030 NRT, 5,990/7,960 dwt 127.94 x 19.03 x 6.86/7.95 m
13.2.1981:	Owners' name registered as Effoa – Finska Ångfartygs Ab / Effoa – Suomen Höyrylaiva Oy / Effoa – Finland Steamship Co. Ltd. as per EGM resolutions on Nov. 12 and Dec. 12, 1980.
1.1.1984:	Management handed over to Oy Finncarriers Ab, Helsinki, the operational subsidiary of Effoa – Finland Steamship Co. Ltd.
31.7.1987:	Flagged out by a sale to EFF-Shipping Ltd., a subsidiary of Effoa – Finland Steamship Co. Ltd. in George Town, Cayman Islands. Delivered the same day and registered in Nassau, Bahamas. Bareboat-chartered back to Effoa – Finland Steamship Co. Ltd. Managed by Oy Finnlines Ltd.
2.5.1988:	Sold to Marine Force S.A., (c/o Transcontinental Maritime & Trading S.A.), Piraeus, without change of name.
1991:	Sold to Act Compania Naviera S.A., (c/o Target Marine S.A.), Piraeus.
1992:	Sold to Conington Shipping Co., Nassau, (c/o Marine Managers Ltd., Haifa).
1993:	Managers changed to Bogazzi Servizi Navali S.r.l., Avenza, Italy.
1994:	Remeasured in accordance with the 1969 Convention as follows: 7,661 GT, 4,181 NT, 9,529 dwt.

122. FINNSAILOR (III)   1987–

RoRo Cargo/ Passenger Motor Ferry, three decks, two stern doors, "Combi-RoRo"
Passengers: 119 berths
Call: OIVK Ice class: I A Super

20,783 GT, 6,235 NT, 8,027 dwt, 1,400 lane metres
157.61 x 25.30 x 7.30 m

2 Vee Diesel Engines 4 SA each 12 cy.
Sulzer 12ZAV40
by Oy Wärtsilä Ab, Turku /Åbo
2 x 7,680 kW / 2 x 10,441 BHP
Total 15,360 kW / 20,882 BHP
20.5 knots Twin screw

ms FINNSAILOR in her original navy blue livery
Photo by Matti Pietikäinen

ms FINNSAILOR painted Finncarriers green
Photo by Seppo Kaksonen

ms FINNSAILOR in FinnLink colours
Photo by K. Brzoza

31.10.1986: Launched by Stocznia Gdanska im. Lenina, Gdansk (#B489/1), without naming ceremonies.

12.5.1987: Christened FINNSAILOR by Mrs. Doris Sundström.

21.10.1987: Completed and delivered as roro cargo motor ferry to Neste Oy, Naantali /Nådendal (92), (c/o Oy Finnlines Ltd, Helsinki /Helsingfors). Entered Finncarriers roro service from Helsinki to Lübeck.

26.1.1989: Sold to Laivanisännistöyhtiö Finnsailor, (Part Owners Finnsailor), Helsinki (1764). Managers remained Oy Finnlines Ltd.

1.7.1989: Managers' name changed to FG-Shipping Oy Ab.

7.1.1992: Entered in the Finnish parallel Register of Merchant Vessels engaged in International Trade.

1.11.1993: New national reg.no. 11191.

15.3.1994: Sold to Finnlines Oy / Finnlines Ab / Finnlines Ltd / Finnlines AG, Helsinki. Managers remained FG-Shipping Oy Ab.

1996: Arrived on Feb. 12 at Turun Korjaustelakka Oy / Turku Repair Yard Ltd. for conversion by Luonnonmaa drydock at Naantali /Nådendal to a combi-roro ferry with 119 berths for passengers. New cabins were constructed in an extension at the rear of the deck house. Delivered on Apr. 17 and chartered to Oy Finnlink Ab for Helsinki – Norrköping roro service. Her particulars before the conversion were: 19,919 GT, 5,976 NT, 8,842 dwt, 2,090 lane metres, 12 berths

17.12.1996: Moved to Naantali – Kapellskär line by Oy Finnlink Ab.

1997: Arrived again on Apr. 21 at Turku Repair Yard Ltd., where fitted with a side door on starboard side forward and a new upper stern ramp. Delivered on May 9 and returned to Naantali – Kapellskär service.

123. FINNFOREST (III)   1988–1988
ANTARES   1988–

RoRo Cargo Motor Ferry, three decks, two stern doors
Passengers: 12 berths
Call: OIWI Ice class: I A Super

19,963 GT, 5,989 NT, 8,793 dwt, 2,090 lane metres
157.61 x 25.30 x 7.30 m

2 Vee Diesel Engines 4 SA each 12 cy. Sulzer 12ZAV40S
by Oy Wärtsilä Ab, Turku /Åbo
2 x 7,200 kW / 2 x 9,789 BHP
Total 14,400 kW / 19,578 BHP   20.5 knots Twin screw

ms FINNFOREST in Helsinki awaiting sale
Photo by Matti Pietikäinen

ms ANTARES
Photo by Seppo Kaksonen

30.9.1987:	Launched by Stocznia Gdanska im. Lenina, Gdansk (#B489/2), without naming ceremonies.
31.8.1988:	Completed and delivered as FINNFOREST to Thomesto Oy, (c/o Oy Finnlines Ltd), Helsinki / Helsingfors (1756).
7.9.1988:	Sold to Finncarriers Oy Ab, (Effoa – Finska Ångfartygs Ab / Effoa – Suomen Höyrylaiva Oy / Effoa – Finland Steamship Co. Ltd.), Helsinki, and renamed ANTARES. Managers remained Oy Finnlines Ltd. Entered Finncarriers roro service from Helsinki to Lübeck.
18.4.1989:	Owners' name changed to Finnlines Group Oy Ab.
30.4.1989:	A new Finncarriers Oy Ab was established by Finnlines Group Oy Ab and in accordance with the demerger principle of the Business Taxation Act, the parent company transferred the assets of the old Finncarriers including ms Antares to the new Finncarriers Oy Ab.
1.7.1989:	Managers' name changed to FG-Shipping Oy Ab.
6.9.1989:	Christened traditionally ANTARES by Mrs. Marjatta Jouhki at Rauma.
7.1.1992:	Entered in the Finnish parallel Register of Merchant Vessels engaged in International Trade.
1.11.1993:	New national reg.no. 11192.

124. FINNWOOD (III)   1989–1990
LANKA ABHAYA   1990–1992
FINNWOOD (III)   1992–1997

Motor Bulk /Container Carrier, Singledecker
Call: C6KI9 ex OIZP Ice class: I C

21,305 GT, 10,412 NT, 30,946 dwt
184.86 x 27.50 x 10.33 m

Diesel Engine 2 SA 6 cy. Sulzer 6RTA58
by Sulzer Bros. Ltd., Winterthur
7,080 kW / 9,600 BHP   14.4 knots

ms FINNWOOD
Photo from K. Brzoza

ms FINNWOOD temporarily renamed
LANKA ABHAYA, when chartered to Ceylon
Shipping Corporation
Photo from K. Brzoza

3.6.1981:	Ordered together with ms Finntrader (III) by Thomesto Oy, Helsinki /Helsingfors, from Stocznia Gdanska for delivery in September 1984.	13.9.1984:	Order cancelled by Thomesto Oy due to delayed delivery date.
		12.12.1986:	New order placed by Palkkiyhtymä Oy, Helsinki.

29.10.1988: Launched by Stocznia Gdanska im. Lenina, Gdansk (#B539/2), without naming ceremonies.

18.12.1989: Completed and delivered as FINNWOOD to Palkkiyhtymä Oy, (Pekka Aarnio), Helsinki (1776). Never christened. Managed by FG-Shipping Oy Ab.

8.2.1990: Renamed LANKA ABHAYA for duration of charter to Ceylon Shipping Corporation, Colombo. New name painted on Mar. 20.

30.7.1991: Flagged out by a sale to Puhos Shipping Ltd., a subsidiary of Palkkiyhtymä Oy in George Town, Cayman Islands. Registered in Nassau, Bahamas, when delivered on Aug. 7. Bareboat-chartered back to Palkkiyhtymä Oy. Managers remained FG-Shipping Oy Ab.

12.1991: Name reverted to FINNWOOD after redelivery from charter to Ceylon Shipping Corporation.

13.12.1997: Management taken over by Bibby-Harrison Management Services, Ltd., Liverpool, and the vessel renamed PISCES VENTURER.

125. TALLINK 1989–1992

Passenger /RoRo Cargo Motor Ferry, three decks, bow & stern doors
Passengers: 155 cabins, 422 berths, 405 deck pax
Call: OJCH Ice class: I A

10,341 GT, 3,254 NT, 1,250 dwt
126.93 x 19.50 x 5.20 m

2 Vee Diesel Engines 4 SA each 16 cy. Pielstick 6PC2L-400
by Ch. de l'Atlantique, St. Nazaire
2 x 5,884 kW / 2 x 8,000 BHP
11,768 kW / 16,000 BHP   20 knots Twin screw

ms SVEA REGINA, later TALLINK, in Helsinki
Photo by Matti Pietikäinen

2.1.1970: Ordered by Oy Siljavarustamo – Ab Siljarederiet, but transferred while on the stocks to Stockholms Rederi ab. Svea.

3.12.1971: Launched by Dubigeon-Normandie S.A., Prairie-au-Duc. Nantes (#127), without naming ceremonies.

26.5.1972: Christened SVEA REGINA by Mrs. Ingegerd Hägglöf and delivered to Stockholms Rederi ab. Svea, (Svea-Rederierna), Stockholm (11270). Operated by Oy Silja Line Ab on Helsinki /Helsingfors – Stockholm service until 1975, when moved to Turku /Åbo – Norrtälje line.

ms ODYSSEAS ELYTIS outside Rhodes
Photo by Matti Pietikäinen

ms SCANDINAVIAN SKY at Freeport, Bahamas
Photo by Matti Pietikäinen

22.9.1978:	Sold to Suomen Höyrylaiva Oy – Finska Ångfartygs Ab, Helsinki (1601), and renamed REGINA. (Call: OIIV)
15.10.1978:	Chartered to Polska Zegluga Baltycka (Polish Baltic Shipping Co.), Kolobrzeg, for 6 months with a purchase option.
15.4.1979:	Redelivered by the Polish charterers. Thereafter made a cruise from Kiel to Kirkenes. In the summer employed by Silja Line on Turku – Stockholm service and in the autumn chartered to Brittany Ferries for Portsmouth – St. Malo line.
13.11.1979:	Sold to Transatlantic Navigators Ltd., Piraeus, (Michail Karageorgis [London] Ltd.), and renamed MEDITERRANEAN SUN when delivered on Nov. 29. Employed on Patras – Ancona ferry service.
1980:	Sold to Heritage Shipping Co. Ltd., Limassol, (Michail Karageorgis S.A.), Piraeus.
1982:	Sold to Naftiliaki Eteria Lesvou A.E., (Maritime Co. of Lesvos S.A.), Mytilene, and renamed ODYSSEAS ELYTIS. Sailed on Rhodes – Limassol – Alexandria line.
6.1985:	Sold to Sky Cruises Ltd., Nassau, (SeaEscape Ltd., Miami, Fla.), and renamed SCANDINAVIAN SKY. Left Piraeus on June 10 for Rendsburg, where rebuilt by Werft Nobiskrug. Sailed in July for Miami, Fla., and entered Miami – Bahamas cruise service.
1989:	Transferred to Star Cruises Ltd., Nassau, (SeaEscape Ltd., Miami).
18.12.1989:	Acquired by Palkkiyhtymä Oy, Helsinki (1778), and renamed TALLINK. Managed by FG-Shipping Oy Ab. Employed on Helsinki–Tallinn liner service of Tallink.

ms TALLINK in Helsinki
Photo by Matti Pietikäinen

25.1.1990:	Remeasured in accordance with the 1969 Convention as above in the heading. Her previous tonnages when purchased to Finland were: 7,977 GRT, 3,539 NRT, 2,750 dwt
26.6.1992:	Sold to Tallink Bahamas Ltd., (Nassau), but bareboat-chartered on June 30 to RAS Eesti Merelaevandus, Tallinn, under the Estonian flag. Managed by RAS Eesti Merelaevandus and time-chartered to Tallink, Tallinn, for Tallinn – Helsinki liner service.
1.1.1994:	Time-chartered to AS Eminre, Tallinn, but continued on Tallinn – Helsinki service under marketing name Tallink.
1.3.1995:	Time-chartered to AS Hansatee, Tallinn, but still continued on Tallink passenger/roro service to Helsinki.
18.12.1996:	Laid up in Tallinn due to new strict SOLAS rules and offered for sale.

126. ARCTURUS   1990–1991

RoRo Cargo Motor Ferry, two decks, two stern doors
Passengers: 12 berths
Call: OIPH   Ice class: I A Super

8,425 GRT, 3,314 NRT, 13,090 dwt, 2,170 lane metres, 608 TEU
154.90 x 25.11 x 6.46 m

2 Vee Diesel Engines 4 SA each 12 cy. Pielstick 12PC2-6V-400
by Oy Wärtsilä Ab, Turku /Åbo
2 x 6,600 kW / 2 x 8,973 BHP
Total 13,200 kW / 17,946 BHP   18.5 knots Single screw

18.1.1982:	Launched by Rauma-Repola Oy, Rauman Telakka, Rauma /Raumo (#270), without naming ceremonies.	29.6.1982:	Completed and delivered to Effoa – Finska Ångfartygs Ab / Effoa – Suomen Höyrylaiva Oy / Effoa – Finland Steamship Co. Ltd., Helsinki /Helsingfors (1669). Employed on Finncarriers roro service from Helsinki and Kotka to Purfleet and Rotterdam.
11.6.1982:	Christened ARCTURUS by Mrs. Anna Ehrnrooth.		

ms ARCTURUS
Photo by Matti Pietikäinen

ms AURORA ex ARCTURUS in Oslofjord
Photo by Lars Helge Isdahl

31.12.1986:	Sold to Oy Finncarriers Ab, Helsinki, a fully-owned subsidiary of Effoa – Finland Steamship Co. Ltd.
13.5.1987:	Owners' name registered as Finncarriers Oy Ab as per EGM resolution on Dec. 30, 1986.
18.4.1989:	Owners' name changed to Finnlines Group Oy Ab.
30.4.1989:	A new Finncarriers Oy Ab was established by Finnlines Group Oy Ab and in accordance with the demerger principle of the Business Taxation Act, the parent company transferred the assets of the old Finncarriers including ms Arcturus to the new Finncarriers Oy Ab.
1.1.1990:	Management taken over by FG-Shipping Oy Ab, Helsinki.
23.12.1991:	Sold to Hafslund Transport AS, but handed over to Hafslund Bulk 1 AS, (Hafslund Transport AS), Tønsberg (c/o Barber International A/S), and renamed AURORA when delivered on Dec. 27. (NIS-1160). Time-chartered back to Finncarriers Oy Ab and moved to Kotka/Helsinki – Rostock service.
5.1992:	Owners' name changed to Actinor RoRo AS, (Hafslund Transport AS), Tønsberg. Managers remained Barber International A/S.
1994:	Remeasured in accordance with the 1969 Convention as follows: 20,381 GT, 6,114 NT, 13,090 dwt
1996:	Chartered to Fred. Olsen & Co., Oslo, for Kristiansand S – Europoort service.

127. OIHONNA 1990–

RoRo Cargo Motor Ferry, two decks, two stern doors
Passengers: 12 berths
Call: OISE Ice class: I A Super

20,203 GT, 6,061 NT, 12,870 dwt, 2,070 lane metres, 608 TEU
155.00 x 25.05 x 6.46 m

2 Vee Diesel Engines 4 SA each 12 cy. Pielstick 12PC2-6V-400
by Oy Wärtsilä Ab, Turku /Åbo
2 x 6,600 kW / 2 x 8,973 BHP
Total 13,200 kW / 17,946 BHP   18.5 knots Single screw

ms OIHONNA
Photo by Seppo Kaksonen

21.10.1983: Launched by Rauma-Repola Oy, Rauman Telakka, Rauma /Raumo (#284), without naming ceremonies.

27.4.1984: Christened OIHONNA by Mrs. Leila Rautalahti and delivered to Effoa – Finska Ångfartygs Ab / Effoa – Suomen Höyrylaiva Oy / Effoa – Finland Steamship Co. Ltd., Helsinki /Helsingfors (1709). Employed on Finncarriers roro service from Helsinki to Lübeck.

31.12.1986: Sold to Oy Finncarriers Ab, Helsinki, a fully-owned subsidiary of Effoa – Finland Steamship Co. Ltd.

13.5.1987:	Owners' name registered as Finncarriers Oy Ab as per EGM resolution on Dec. 30, 1986.	1.1.1990:	Management taken over by FG-Shipping Oy Ab, Helsinki.
18.4.1989:	Owners' name changed to Finnlines Group Oy Ab.	7.1.1992:	Entered in the Finnish parallel Register of Merchant Vessels engaged in International Trade.
30.4.1989:	A new Finncarriers Oy Ab was established by Finnlines Group Oy Ab and in accordance with the demerger principle of the Business Taxation Act, the parent company transferred the assets of the old Finncarriers including ms Oihonna to the new Finncarriers Oy Ab.	1.11.1993:	New national reg.no. 10625.

128. ENVIK   1990–1993

Motor Bulk Cement Carrier, Singledecker
Call: OIQS Ice class: I A Super

3,686 GT, 1,106 NT, 3,683 dwt
95.81 x 16.50 x 5.20 m

Diesel Engine 4 SA 8 cy. Wärtsilä 8R32
by Oy Wärtsilä Ab, Vaasa /Vasa
2,890 kW / 3,818 BHP   13.7 knots

ms ENVIK
Photo by Matti Pietikäinen

5.3.1982:	Order placed by Oy Partek Ab with Kleven Mekaniske Verksted A/S, Ulsteinvik (#42), but construction handed over to Kleven Løland A/S.		1615), (c/o Effoa – Finska Ångfartygs Ab / Effoa – Suomen Höyrylaiva Oy / Effoa – Finland Steamship Co. Ltd., Helsinki /Helsingfors).
10.1983:	Launched by Kleven Løland A/S, Leirvik i Sogn (#48), without naming ceremonies.	1.1.1984:	Managers changed to Oy Finncarriers Ab, Helsinki.
2.12.1983:	Christened ENVIK by Mrs. Karin Lehto and delivered to Oy Partek Ab, Parainen /Pargas (Turku /Åbo	1.3.1990:	Management taken over by FG-Shipping Oy Ab, Helsinki.

30.8.1991:	Sold to Partek Sementti Oy / Partek Cement Ab, Parainen.
26.8.1992:	Owners registered as Partek Industrial Minerals Oy Ab, Parainen, as per EGM resolution on Aug. 11.
31.8.1992:	Transferred to the newly-established Partek Sementti Oy / Partek Cement Ab.
1.11.1993:	New national reg.no. 11186.
1.6.1994:	Owners' name registered as Finnsementti Oy / Finncement Ab, Parainen, as per AGM resolution on Apr. 13.
30.6.1994:	Management taken over by the Owners.

129. FARONA 1990–1990
TRANSESTONIA 1990–1992

RoRo Cargo Motor Ferry, two decks, bow and stern doors
Passengers: 12 berths
Call: ESAU ex OJCN Ice class: I A

2,386 GRT, 867 NRT, 4,025 dwt, 175 TEU, 860 lane metres
118.09 x 16.04 x 5.95 m

2 Diesel Engines 4 SA each 9 cy. Pielstick 9PC2L-400
by Oy Wärtsilä Ab, Turku /Åbo
2 x 3,310 kW / 2 x 4,500 BHP
Total 6,620 kW / 9,000 BHP   17 knots Twin screw

ms ARONA at Turku
Photo by K. Brzoza

23.2.1972:	Launched by Hollming Oy, Rauma /Raumo (#200), and named ARONA by Mrs. Eleanor Lindholm.
1.9.1972:	Completed and delivered to Rederi Ab Asta, (Lennart Karlsson), Mariehamn (1184). (Call: OIAR) Employed on United Owners' liner service from Helsinki /Helsingfors and Kotka to Amsterdam.
5.12.1986:	Sold to Bulk Alandica Ab Ltd, (Bror Husell), Mariehamn, and renamed LARONA.
1.6.1987:	Sold to Amstelstraat Management Co BV, (Kustvaartbedrijf Moerman BV), Rotterdam, and renamed LARGO.

ms FARONA under repairs in April 1990 in Helsinki
Photo by Matti Pietikäinen

ms TRANSESTONIA under the Soviet flag
Photo by Matti Pietikäinen

12.1988: Acquired by Selektiv Finans ApS, (Pelle Bentsen), København, and bareboat-chartered to Farøyar Holding Frakt A/S, Torshavn. Renamed FARONA and hoisted Faroes flag. Entered Copenhagen – Aalborg – Torshavn liner service.

4.1989: Transferred by Selektiv Finans ApS to Danish flag (DIS) with København as home port, after the charterers had gone into liquidation due to the economic crisis in the Faroes.

12.6.1989: Time-chartered to Gotlandslinjen for summer service to Gotland. Thereafter laid up at Visby.

30.3.1990: Acquired by Palkkiyhtymä Oy, Helsinki (1781), and docked at Vuosaari in Helsinki for repairs. Managed by FG-Shipping Oy Ab.

18.4.1990: Sold to Laevandusühisettevõte "Tallink", (Shipping Joint Venture "Tallink"), Tallinn, (Partners: RAS Eesti Merelaevandus, Tallinn, and Palkkiyhtymä Oy, Helsinki), and renamed TRANSESTONIA. FG-Shipping Oy Ab remained as technical managers, while crewing was taken over by RAS Eesti Merelaevandus, Tallinn. Employed on Tallinn – Helsinki daily roro service.

20.8.1991: Transferred to Estonian flag (#A-007), when Estonia gained independence. Moved to Tallinn – Rostock – Helsinki roro service.

26.6.1992: Sold to Tallink Bahamas Ltd., (Nassau), but bareboat-chartered on July 1 to RAS Eesti Merelaevandus, Tallinn, under the Estonian flag. Managed by RAS Eesti Merelaevandus and chartered to Tallink for Tallinn – Helsinki – Aarhus roro service.
Owners erroneously stated as Estline, Tallinn, in Lloyd's Registers in 1993–1996, thereafter Estonian Shipping Co. (ESCO), (RAS Eesti Merelaevandus).

1994: Remeasured in accordance with the 1969 Convention as follows: 6,040 GT, 1,812 NT, 4,025 dwt

130. ASTREA 1991–

RoRo Cargo /General Cargo Motor Ferry, two decks, stern door
Call: OJCU Ice class: I A

9,528 GT, 2,858 NT, 6,686 dwt, 824 lane metres, 451 TEU
129.10 x 21.00 6.42 m

Vee Diesel Engine 4 SA 12 cy. Wärtsilä 12V32E
by Wärtsilä Diesel Oy, Vaasa /Vasa
4,860 kW / 6,603 BHP 13.5 knots

ms ASTREA
Photo by Seppo Kaksonen

7.7.1990: Launched by Tangen Verft Kragerø A/S, Kragerø (#150), without naming ceremonies.

14.1.1991: Christened ASTREA by Mrs. Marjatta Härmälä and delivered by Langsten Slip & Båtbyggeri A/S, Tomrefjord (#150) to Finncarriers Oy Ab, Helsinki / Helsingfors (1795). Managed by FG-Shipping Oy Ab. Employed on Finncarriers service from Finland to Biscay.

1.11.1993: New national reg.no. 11176.

131. PARA-UNO 1992–1995

Non-propelled RoLo Deck Cargo Push-Barge, one deck, side ramp
Call: – Ice Class: I B

2,826 GT, 847 NT, 6,100 dwt
89.70 x 19.96 x 5.10 m

Schottel Bow Thruster

Barge PARA-UNO
Photo by Stig Löthner

7.5.1992:	Launched by Uudenkaupungin Telakka Oy, Uusikaupunki /Nystad (#343), without naming ceremonies.
25.5.1992:	Christened PARA-UNO by Mrs. Helena Forsblom.
31.5.1992:	Delivered to Laivanisännistöyhtiö Proomu 342, (Part Owners Barge 342), Turku /Åbo (1734), (Paratug Ltd Oy, Parainen /Pargas).
4.6.1992:	Time-chartered to Finncarriers Oy Ab and employed on F-ships Baltic bulk services. Managed by FG-Shipping Oy Ab.
1.11.1993:	New national reg.no. 10877.
2.5.1995:	Management taken over by Paratug Ltd Oy, Parainen, but time-charter to Finncarriers continued.

132. MEGA — 1993–

Motor Pusher Tug, one deck
Call: OIEV Ice class: I A Super

768 GT, 231 NT, 186 dwt
40.77 x 13.29 x 5.10 m

4 Diesel Engines 4 SA each 8 cy. Wärtsilä 824TS
geared to 2 Strömberg generators
by Oy Wärtsilä Ab, Vaasa /Vasa
4 x 978 kW / 4 x 1,329 BHP
Total 3,912 kW / 5,316 BHP   14 knots Twin screw

ms AATOS as a harbour icebreaker in Helsinki
Photo by Matti Pietikäinen

ms MEGA at Turku
Photo by K. Brzoza

11.6.1974:	Launched by Oy Wärtsilä Ab, Vaasan Tehdas, Vaasa / Vasa, without naming ceremonies. Towed to Helsinki /Helsingfors for fitting out.		va Oy / Effoa – Finland Steamship Co. Ltd., Helsinki /Helsingfors, as per merger arrangement signed on Dec. 7, 1988.

11.6.1974: Launched by Oy Wärtsilä Ab, Vaasan Tehdas, Vaasa / Vasa, without naming ceremonies. Towed to Helsinki /Helsingfors for fitting out.

9.1.1975: Christened TEUVO by Mrs. Ejna Poukka and delivered by Oy Wärtsilä Ab, Helsinki Shipyard, Helsinki (#405), as TEUVO to Helsingin kaupunki, Satamalaitos – Helsingfors stad, Hamnverket (City of Helsinki, Port Authority), Helsinki (1535). Her particulars as harbour icebreaker /tug were:
664 GRT, 0 NRT
39.92 x 12.90 x 5.20 m

17.9.1985: Sold to Oy Hangon Hinaus Ab, Hanko /Hangö (272), and renamed AATOS.

1985: Remeasured in accordance with the 1969 Convention as follows: 680 GT, 204 NT, – dwt

22.11.1989: Owners amalgamated with the parent company, Effoa – Finska Ångfartygs Ab / Effoa – Suomen Höyrylaiva Oy / Effoa – Finland Steamship Co. Ltd., Helsinki /Helsingfors, as per merger arrangement signed on Dec. 7, 1988.

30.12.1991: Sold to Alfons Håkans Oy Ab, Helsinki (1535).

3.6.1993: Acquired by Lumi Shipping Oy, (Veitsiluoto Oy), Kemi (438), and renamed MEGA when delivered the same day. Managed by FG-Shipping Oy Ab, Helsinki.

30.9.1993: Completed by Kvaerner Masa-Yards Oy / Kvaerner Masa-Yards Inc., Turku /Åbo, after conversion from an icebreaker/tug to a pusher. Working as pusher for push-barge Motti.

1.11.1993: New national reg.no. 10260.

7.9.1995: Parent company Veitsiluoto Oy amalgamated with Enso-Gutzeit Oy, forming a new parent company named Enso Oy.

133. MOTTI   1993–

Non-propelled RoLo Deck Cargo Push-Barge, one deck, side ramp
Call: – Ice Class: I A

5,165 GT, 1,550 NT, 8,212 dwt
133.50 x 23.84 x 5.40 m

Bow thruster with 145 kW electric motor

Pusher-barge combination MOTTI and MEGA
Photo by Sea-Foto

14.8.1993:	Launched by Kvaerner Masa-Yards Oy / Kvaerner Masa-Yards Inc., Turku /Åbo (#1324), without naming ceremonies.
1.9.1993:	The pusher-barge combination was named MEGA – MOTTI by Mrs. Arja Pajula.
30.9.1993:	Completed as MOTTI for Lumi Shipping Oy, (Veitsiluoto Oy), Kemi (440). Managed by FG-Shipping Oy Ab, Helsinki. Mainly employed in carrying pulpwood from Southern Finland to Veitsiluoto factories in Kemi and Oulu, pushed by ms Mega.
1.11.1993:	New national reg.no. 11569.
7.9.1995:	Parent company Veitsiluoto Oy amalgamated with Enso-Gutzeit Oy, forming a new parent company named Enso Oy.

134. RAILSHIP I   1994–

RoRo Cargo/ Rail Vehicles Motor Ferry, three decks, stern door
Passengers: 10 berths
Call: OJGC   Ice class: I A Super

17,864 GT, 5,380 NT, 8,970 dwt, 1,708 lane metres, 78 rail waggons
177.20 x 21.60 x 6.32 m

4 Diesel Engines 4 SA each 8 cy. MaK 8M551AK
by Atlas-MaK Maschinenbau, Kiel
4 x 3,680 kW / 4 x 4,935 BHP
Total 14,720 kW / 19,740 BHP   17 knots Twin screw

ms RAILSHIP I
Photo by K. Brzoza

6.9.1974:	Launched by Rickmers Rhederei GmbH, Rickmers Werft, Bremerhaven (#378), without naming ceremonies.
10.2.1975:	Christened RAILSHIP I by Mrs. Daniela Westphal.
11.2.1975:	Completed and delivered to Partenreederei m.s. "Railship I", Lübeck, (c/o H.M. Gehrckens GmbH & Co., Hamburg). Employed on Railship liner service from Travemünde to Hanko.

8.1979:	Lengthened from 150.02 m to 177.20 m at A.G. Weser, Bremen, by an additional cargo section of 27.18 metres. Her original particulars were: 5,322 GRT, 2,425 NRT, 7,210 dwt, 1300 lane metres, 60 rail waggons 150.02 x 22.00 x 6.49 m
5.4.1994:	Acquired by Railship Oy Ab, Hanko /Hangö, (c/o FG-Shipping Oy Ab, Helsinki /Helsingfors) (#11697), and delivered on Apr. 7. Continued on Railship service between Travemünde and Hanko. Entered the same day in the Finnish parallel Register of Merchant Vessels engaged in International Trade.
26.4.1994:	Remeasured in accordance with the 1969 Convention as above in the heading. Her previous tonnages when purchased to Finland were: 6,522 GRT, 3,150 NRT, 8,970 dwt

135. FINNPINE (III)   1994–

StoRo Cargo Motor Ferry, two decks, stern door and two side doors
Call: OJGM   Ice class: I A

8,996 GT, 3,222 NT, 7,700 dwt, 1,184 lane metres, 146 TEU
120.22 x 21.02 x 6.70 m

Vee Diesel Engine 4 SA 16 cy. Wärtsilä 16V32
by Oy Wärtsilä Ab, Vaasa /Vasa
5,700 kW / 7,749 BHP   13.5 knots

ms SOLANO, later FINNPINE, in the Baltic Sea
Photo by Matti Pietikäinen

ms FINNPINE
Photo by Dirk Jankowsky/ coll. K. Brzoza

29.3.1984:	Launched by Rauma-Repola Oy, Rauman Telakka, Rauma /Raumo (#286), and named SOLANO by Mrs. Iris Nielsen.	7.1.1992:	Flagged out by a sale to Henry Nielsen Shipping (Bahamas) Ltd., a subsidiary of Oy Henry Nielsen Ab in Nassau, Bahamas.
24.9.1984:	Completed and delivered to Ab Helsingfors Steamship Co. Ltd., (Oy Henry Nielsen Ab), Helsinki / Helsingfors (1716). (Call: OISI)	7.1.1994:	Sold to Solano Navigation Co. Ltd., Nassau, (c/o Oy Henry Nielsen Ab, Helsinki).
15.9.1987:	Owners' name changed to Oy Nielsen Shipping Services Ltd., (Oy Henry Nielsen Ab), Helsinki.	25.8.1994:	Acquired by Finnlines Oy / Finnlines Ab / Finnlines Ltd / Finnlines AG, Helsinki, and renamed FINNPINE. (#11723) Managed by FG-Shipping Oy Ab. Entered the same day in the Finnish parallel Register of Merchant Vessels engaged in International Trade.
8.8.1991:	Owners' name reverted to Ab Helsingfors Steamship Co. Ltd.		

136. FINNHANSA (II) 1994–

RoRo Cargo/ Passenger Motor Ferry, three decks, stern door, "Combi-RoRo"
Passengers: 114 berths
Call: OJFG Ice class: I A Super

32,534 GT, 9,761 NT, 10,700 dwt, 3,200 lane metres, 423 TEU
183.00 x 28.70 x 7.40 m

4 Diesel Engines 4 SA each 8 cy. Sulzer 8ZAL40S
by "Zgoda" Zaklady Urzadzen Technicznych, Swietochlowice
4 x 5,760 kW / 4 x 7,829 BHP
Total 23,040 kW / 31,316 BHP   20 knots Twin screw

ms FINNHANSA
Photo by Seppo Kaksonen

1.9.1993:	Newbuilding taken over by Finnlines Oy / Finnlines Ab / Finnlines Ltd / Finnlines AG, Helsinki /Helsingfors, and entered in the Finnish ship register.	3.8.1994:	Completed and delivered as FINNHANSA to Finnlines Ltd, Helsinki (#11570). Managed by FG-Shipping Oy Ab. Employed on Finncarriers liner service from Helsinki to Lübeck. Entered the same day in the Finnish parallel Register of Merchant Vessels engaged in International Trade.
14.9.1993:	Launched by Stocznia Gdanska S.A., Gdansk (#B501/01), without naming ceremonies.		
		19.9.1994:	Christened traditionally FINNHANSA by Mrs. Marjatta Jouhki in Helsinki.

137. FINNPARTNER (III) 1995–

RoRo Cargo/ Passenger Motor Ferry, three decks, stern door, "Combi-RoRo"
Passengers: 114 berths
Call: OJGE Ice class: I A Super

32,534 GT, 9,761 NT, 11,600 dwt, 3,200 lane metres, 423 TEU
183.00 x 28.70 x 7.40 m

4 Diesel Engines 4 SA each 8 cy. Sulzer 8ZAL40S
by "Zgoda" Zaklady Urzadzen Technicznych, Swietochlowice
4 x 5,760 kW / 4 x 7,829 BHP
Total 23,040 kW / 31,316 BHP   20 knots Twin screw

ms FINNPARTNER
Photo by Seppo Kaksonen

27.6.1994: Newbuilding taken over by Finnlines Oy / Finnlines Ab / Finnlines Ltd / Finnlines AG, Helsinki /Helsingfors, and entered in the Finnish ship register.

15.7.1994: Launched by Stocznia Gdanska S.A., Gdansk (#B501/02), without naming ceremonies, but in the presence of President Lech Walesa.

12.2.1995: Completed and delivered as FINNPARTNER to Finnlines Ltd, Helsinki (#11719). Managed by FG-Shipping Oy Ab. Employed on Finncarriers liner service from Helsinki to Lübeck.
Entered the same day in the Finnish parallel Register of Merchant Vessels engaged in International Trade.

22.3.1995: Christened traditionally FINNPARTNER by Mrs. Marjatta Härmälä in Helsinki.

138. **FINNTRADER (IV)** 1995–

RoRo Cargo/ Passenger Motor Ferry, three decks, stern door, "Combi-RoRo"
Passengers: 114 berths
Call: OJGF Ice class: I A Super

32,534 GT, 9,761 NT, 11,600 dwt, 3,200 lane metres, 423 TEU
183.00 x 28.70 x 7.40 m

4 Diesel Engines 4 SA each 8 cy. Sulzer 8ZAL40S
by "Zgoda" Zaklady Urzadzen Technicznych, Swietochlowice
4 x 5,760 kW / 4 x 7,829 BHP
Total 23,040 kW / 31,316 BHP   20 knots Twin screw

ms FINNTRADER
Photo by Matti Pietikäinen

31.3.1995:	Newbuilding taken over by Finnlines Oy / Finnlines Ab / Finnlines Ltd / Finnlines AG, Helsinki /Helsingfors, and entered in the Finnish ship register.
7.4.1995:	Launched by Stocznia Gdanska S.A., Gdansk (#B501/04), without naming ceremonies.
26.10.1995:	Completed and delivered as FINNPARTNER to Finnlines Ltd, Helsinki (#11788). Managed by FG-Shipping Oy Ab. Employed on Finncarriers liner service from Helsinki to Lübeck. Entered the same day in the Finnish parallel Register of Merchant Vessels engaged in International Trade.
1.12.1995:	Christened traditionally FINNTRADER by Mrs. Elisa Lagerroos in Helsinki.

139. FINNARROW (II)   1997–

RoRo Cargo/ Passenger Motor Ferry, two decks, stern door, "Combi-RoRo"
Passengers: 188 berths
Call: OJIG   Ice class: I A

25,996 GT, 7,798 NT, 6,124 dwt, 2,400 lane metres
168.15 x 28.30 x 6.60 m

4 Diesel Engines 4 SA each 6 cy. Sulzer 6ZAL40S
by New Sulzer Diesel Singapore Pte. Ltd., Singapore
4 x 4,320 kW / 4 x 5,873 BHP
Total 17,280 kW / 23,492 BHP   20 knots Twin screw

ms GOTLAND, now renamed FINNARROW
Photo by K. Brzoza

28.9.1993:	Launched by P.T. Dok & Perkapalan Kodja Bahari Unit IV, Tanjung Priok, Indonesia (#1005), without naming ceremonies.
19.4.1996:	Christened GOTLAND in Jakarta by Mrs. Marianne Nilsson and delivered to Rederi AB Gotland, Visby. (SIHB) Sailed for final completion to Dunkirk, where arrived on May 20 to be fitted out by ARNO Dunkerque S.A. After delivery in June, laid up at Kappelshamn on Gotland until Feb. 1997 when chartered for two months to Tor Line and employed on Gothenburg – Ghent service.
4.1997:	Chartered to Nordic Trucker Line and inaugurated on Apr. 11 Oxelösund – St. Petersburg roro service.
9.6.1997:	Chartered to SeaWind Line Oy Ab for Turku /Åbo – Stockholm service in exchange for the smaller ms Sea Wind II, which was transferred to Nordic Trucker Line service.
17.12.1997:	Acquired by Finnlines Oy / Finnlines Ab / Finnlines Ltd / Finnlines AG, Helsinki /Helsingfors, and renamed FINNARROW when delivered on Dec. 19. (#11985). Managed by FG-Shipping Oy Ab. Entered the same day in the Finnish parallel Register of Merchant Vessels engaged in International Trade.

140. NB AESA 78 — 1998–

RoRo Cargo/ Passenger Motor Ferry, three decks, bow and stern doors, "Combi-RoRo"
Passengers: 400 berths
Call: OJIC Ice class: I A

30,500 GT, 9,150 NT, 7,000 dwt, 2,500 lane metres
188.30 x 28.70 x 6.30 m

4 Diesel Engines 4 SA each 8 cy. Sulzer 8ZAL40S
by New Sulzer Diesel France S.A., Mantes
4 x 5,760 kW / 4 x 7,829 BHP
Total 23,040 kW / 31,316 BHP   21 knots Twin screw

ms NB AESA 78 as a model named STENA SEAPACER
Photo from Maritime Reporter

6.10.1995: Order placed with Astilleros Españoles S.A., Puerto Real (#78), by Stena Ferries Ltd., London. Project name reported as Stena Seapacer.

25.6.1997: Memorandum of Agreement signed between Stena Ferries Ltd. and Finnlines Oy / Finnlines Ab / Finnlines Ltd / Finnlines AG, Helsinki /Helsingfors, concerning take-over of the newbuilding from the Shipbuilders immediately after delivery in the second quarter of 1998.

141. NB AESA 79   1998–

RoRo Cargo/ Passenger Motor Ferry, three decks, bow and stern doors, "Combi-RoRo"
Passengers: 400 berths
Call: OJID Ice class: I A

30,500 GT, 9,150 NT, 7,000 dwt, 2,500 lane metres
188.30 x 28.70 x 6.30 m

4 Diesel Engines 4 SA each 8 cy. Sulzer 8ZAL40S
by New Sulzer Diesel France S.A., Mantes
4 x 5,760 kW / 4 x 7,829 BHP
Total 23,040 kW / 31,316 BHP   21 knots Twin screw

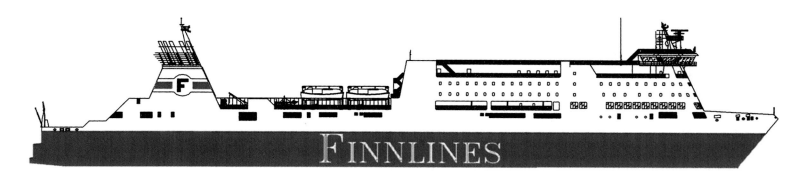

ms NB AESA 79
Drawing from FG-Shipping Oy Ab

6.10.1995: Order placed with Astilleros Españoles S.A., Puerto Real (#79), by Stena Ferries Ltd., London.

25.6.1997: Memorandum of Agreement signed between Stena Ferries Ltd. and Finnlines Oy / Finnlines Ab / Finnlines Ltd / Finnlines AG, Helsinki /Helsingfors, concerning take-over of the newbuilding from the Shipbuilders immediately after delivery in the third quarter of 1998.

Other Ships Connected with Finnlines Having the Prefix "Finn" in Their Names

ms FINN-HEIDE chartered to Finnlines in 1969–1970
Photo from FG-Shipping Oy Ab

FINNEAGLE in 1979–1981 on Atlanticargo service
Photo from FG-Shipping Oy Ab

ms FINNROSE in 1979–1980 on Atlanticargo service
Photo from FG-Shipping Oy Ab

FINNORIENT at Khor al Fakkan, the Sultanate of Oman
Photo by Börje Gustafsson

FINN-HEIDE	9,406/69	**1969–1970**

ex Heide Leonhardt -69. Later 1970 Heide Leonhardt, 1993 Ali S.
Chartered by Partenreederei m.s. Finn-Heide, (Leonhardt & Blumberg), Hamburg, to Oy Finnlines Ltd for U.S. Gulf service.

FINN-LEONHARDT	9,406/69	**1969–1970**

Later 1978 Wolfgang Russ, 1979 Finn-Leonhardt, 1981 Cason. Burnt and wrecked on Dec. 5, 1987.
Chartered by Partenreederei m.s. Finn-Leonhardt, (Leonhardt & Blumberg), Hamburg, to Oy Finnlines Ltd for U.S. Gulf service.

FINNCLIPPER (II)	7,955/79	**1979–1981**

ex Gulf Express -79. Later 1981 Gulf Express, 1982 Atlantic Stream, 1991 Anglebury, 1992 Jolly Oro, 1993 Anglebury, 1994 Und Denizcilik.
Chartered by AB Skärhamns Oljetransport, Skärhamn, to Atlantic Cargo Services AB for U.S. Gulf service.

FINNEAGLE (IA)	8,708/79	**1979–1981**

Later 1981 Qatar Express, 1982 Nordic Stream, 1992 Exonbury, 1992 Jolly Argento, 1993 Exonbury, 1994 Und Hayri Ekinci.
Chartered by AB Skärhamns Oljetransport, Skärhamn, to Merivienti Oy and sublet to Atlantic Cargo Services AB for U.S. Gulf service.

FINNROSE (IA)	5,466/78	**1979–1980**

ex Stena Transporter -79. Later 1980 Stena Transporter, 1980 Baltic Ferry, 1992 Pride of Suffolk.
Chartered by Stena Cargo Line Ltd., London, to Atlantic Cargo Services AB for U.S. Gulf service.

FINNORIENT	1,599/78	**1979–1981**

ex Eleanora -79. Later 1981 Santa Cruz, 1981 Eleanora, 1984 San Juan II, 1987 Isla Serrana, 1988 Don Faustino.
Chartered by Deckships 4 Ltd., Monrovia, to Oy Finnlines Ltd for Khor al Fakkan – Karachi feeder service of Mideastcargo.

FINNCLIPPER (III)	15,636/81	**1981–1982**

Later 1983 Zenit Clipper, 1986 American Falcon.
Chartered by AB Skärhamns Oljetransport, Skärhamn, in 1981–1982 and in 1982 by Kockums AB, Malmö, to Atlantic Cargo Services AB for U.S. Gulf service.

FINNEAGLE (IB)	15,632/81	**1981–1982**

Later 1983 Zenit Eagle, 1983 American Eagle, 1993 Cape Orlando.
Chartered by AB Skärhamns Oljetransport, Skärhamn, to Atlantic Cargo Services AB for U.S. Gulf service.

FINNSAILOR (IIA)	15,780/81	**1983–1983**

ex Paloma -83. Later 1983 Paloma, 1983 Mira, 1987 Split.
Chartered by Partenreederei m.s. Paloma, (F. Laeisz), Hamburg, to Atlantic Cargo Services AB for U.S. Gulf service.

FINNBIRCH (II)	14,059/78	**1997–**

ex Bore Gothica -97, Stena Gothica -88, Stena Ionia -85, Merzario Ionia -82, Stena Ionia -81, Atlantic Prosper -81.
Chartered by Bore Lines AB, Stockholm, to Finncarriers Oy Ab.

FINNFOREST (IV)	15,525/78	**1997–**

ex Bore Britannica -97, Stena Britannica -88, Stena Hispania -86, Kotka Violet -85, Stena Hispania -84, Merzario Hispania -83, Atlantic Project -81.
Chartered by Bore Lines AB, Stockholm, to Finncarriers Oy Ab.

ms FINNSAILOR in 1983 on Atlanticargo service
Photo by FotoFlite

ms FINNFOREST ex BORE BRITANNICA in 1997
Photo by Matti Pietikäinen

ms FINNOAK ex AHTELA in 1997
Photo by Matti Pietikäinen

FINNRIVER ex CELIA in 1997
Photo by Matti Pietikäinen

FINNOAK (III)	6,620/91	1997– ex Ahtela -97. Chartered by Laivanisännistöyhtiö (Part Owners) Ahtela, Rauma /Raumo, to Finncarriers Oy Ab.
FINNRIVER (II)	20,172/79	1997– ex Celia -97, Hesperus -86, Vasaland -83. Chartered by B & N Rederi AB, Skärhamn, to Finncarriers Oy Ab.
FINNROSE (III)	20,169/78	1997– ex Cortia -97, Hektos -86, Timmerland -84. Chartered by B & N Rederi AB, Skärhamn, to Finncarriers Oy Ab.
FINNSEAL (II)	7,395/91	1997– ex Bore Nordia -97. Chartered by Oy Rettig Ab, Turku /Åbo, to Finncarriers Oy Ab.
FINNBEAVER (II)	5,972/91	1997– ex Ann-Mari -97. Chartered by Oy Rettig Ab, Turku /Åbo, to Finncarriers Oy Ab.

ms FINNBEAVER
Photo by Pär-Henrik Sjöström

Sources and Bibliography

Archival Sources
FG-Shipping Oy Ab
    Annual reports
    Ship documents
    Ship statistics
Finnish Maritime Administration – Ship Register
    Ship documents
    Ship statistics
Finnish National Archives
    Ship documents
Finnish National Board of Patents and Registration – Register of
    Companies
    Company documents
Finnish Provincial Archives
    Ship documents
Guildhall Library
    Lloyd's Voyage Records
    Lloyd's Weekly Casualty Reports
Helsinki Magistrate – Archives
    Ship documents
Information Group at Lloyd's Register of Shipping
Kotka Magistrate – Archives
    Ship documents
Maritime Museum of Finland
Maritime Museum of Åbo Akademi
Port of Helsinki – Archives
    Port diaries
Porvoo Magistrate – Archives
    Ship documents
Swedish State Archives
    Ship documents
Turku Magistrate – Archives
    Ship documents

Printed Sources
Ship Registers
Det Norske Veritas – Register
Eesti Laevaregister – Estonian Ship Register
Lloyd's Confidential Index
Lloyd's Register of Shipping
    Registers of Ships
    Lists of Shipowners
    Appendices
    Supplements and New Entries
Suomen Kauppalaivasto – Finlands Handelsflotta – Finnish
    Merchant Marine – Register
Sveriges Skeppslista

Literature
British Standard Ships of World War I by W.H. Mitchell & L.A. Sawyer
Costa Liners by Eliseo & Piccione
DFDS 1866–1991 by Søren Thorsøe & others
Dictionary of Disasters at Sea during the Age of Steam 1824–1962 by Charles Hocking
Die deutsche Handelsflotte im zweiten Weltkrieg by Günther Steinweg
Die deutsche Handelsschiffahrt 1919–1939 by Reinhart Schmelzkopf
Die Handelsflotten der Welt 1942 by Erich Gröner
Empire Ships by W.H. Mitchell & L.A. Sawyer
En man och hans linje – Gunnar Eklund och färjetrafiken
Enso-Gutzeit Osakeyhtiö 1872–1958 by Victor Hoving
Enso-Gutzeit Oy laivanvarustajana – Oy Finnlines Ltd ja Merivienti Oy vuosina 1947–1982 by Petri Karonen
Finnlines – matkustajaliikenne 20 vuotta
From America to United States by L.A. Sawyer & W.H. Mitchell
Från Crichton till Åbovarven by Nils von Knorring
Illustrert norsk skipsliste
J. Lauritzen 1884–1984 by Søren Thorsøe
Laiva saapui Helsinkiin – A Ship Sailed to Helsinki by Riitta Blomgren & Peter Raudsepp
Lloyd's Maritime Atlas
Matson's First Century in the Pacific by Willam L. Worden
Meidän isä on töissä telakalla – Rauma-Repolan laivanrakennus 1945–1991 by Mikko Uola
Modern Shipping Disasters 1963–1987 by Norman Hooke
Navis Fennica I–IV by Erkki Riimala
Olje-Lars – Berättelsen om Johansson Gruppen by Göran Littke
Oy Finnlines Ltd 1947–1967
Oy Vaasa-Umeå Ab 1948–1973
Review of Oy Finnlines Ltd's Activities 1947–1977
Sailing into Twilight – Finnish Shipping in an Age of Transport Revolution by Yrjö Kaukiainen
Ships of our First Century – Effoa Fleet 1883–1983 by Matti Pietikäinen & Bengt Sjöström
Sjöhistorisk årsskrift för Åland
Steam Collier Fleets by J.A. MacRae & C.V. Waine
Stena 1939–1989 by W.J. Harvey
Suomalaiset matkustajalaivat 1960–1996 – Finnish Passenger Ships 1960–1996 by Hannu Vapalahti
Suomen Kauppamerenkulku ja erityisesti linjaliikenteen osuus siinä by Jorma Pohjanpalo
Suomen Kuvitettu Laivaluettelo – Finnish Illustrated List of Ships by Hannu Vapalahti
Svenska Lloyd genom etthundra år by Ture Rinman
Svensk illustrerad skeppslista
Wärtsilä 1834–1984 by Paavo Haavikko

Periodicals
Belgian Shiplover
Båtologen
Enso-Gutzeit
Effoa-uutiset – Effoa-nytt
Finnlines
Full Ahead
Lloyd's Shipping Index
Lloyd's Voyage Records
Lloyd's Weekly Casualty Reports
Länspumpen
Marine News
Navigator
Norwegian Shipping News
Poiju
Sea Breezes
Shipping World & Shipbuilder
Ships Monthly
Skipet
Strandgut
Suomen Kuvalehti
Suomen Laivasto
Suomen Merenkulku – Finlands Sjöfart
Svensk Sjöfartstidning – Scandinavian Shipping Gazette
Søfart
Tornator
Ålands Sjöfart

Newspapers
Aamulehti
Etelä-Suomi
Helsingin Sanomat
Hufvudstadsbladet
Kauppalehti
Lloyd's List
Länsi-Suomi
Satakunnan Kansa
Savon Sanomat
Turun Sanomat
Uudenkaupungin Sanomat
Uusi Suomi
Åbo Underrättelser
Åland

Miscellaneous
Cosfim Oy
Effoa – Finland Steamship Co. Ltd. – Annual Reports
Finncarriers Oy Ab – Annual Reports
Finnlines Ltd – Annual Reports
Oy Finnlines Ltd 1947–1985 by Pasi Järvelin
Oy Wärtsilä Ab – List of Newbuildings
Rauma-Repola Oy – List of Newbuildings
World Ship Society Central Record

Index of Ship Names

Name	Built	First F-name	No.	Page
Aatos	1975	Mega	132	232
Abuja Express	1978	Fosseagle	98	189
Aconcagua	1972	Finnsailor (II)	65	136
Aconcagua 1	1972	Finnsailor (II)	65	136
Aegean V	1958	Airismaa	20	66
Agios Vassilios	1962	Hansa Express	31	81
Ai Shan	1960	Simpele	25	72
AIRISMAA	1958		20	66
Alek	1953	Finnmerchant (I)	12	55
Alexis Taf	1957	Soskua	54	119
Alfa	1983	Para-Alfa	102	194
Alfa-Rock	1983	Para-Alfa	102	194
Alkyon	1950	Isla Finlandia	55	120
Alouette Arrow	1980	Finnarctis	92	181
An Da	1964	Finnseal	35	87
An Guo	1972	Finnpine (II)	66	137
Angelina Maglione	1953	Finnmerchant (I)	12	55
ANNIKA	1965		56	121
ANTARES	1988	Finnforest (III)	123	219
Antares	1972	Jalina	105	196
Ao Jiang	1961	Kaipola (I)	27	75
Apollonia V	1972	Koiteli	73	149
Aquila-I	1971	Kaipola (II)	63	132
ARCTURUS	1982		126	224
ARIEL	1970		121	216
Arona	1972	Farona	129	228
Asian Exporter	1964	Finnenso	38	91
ASTREA	1991		130	230
Astrea	1978	Lapponia	110	203
Atlanta	1978	Walki	83	166
Atlanta Forest	1978	Walki	83	166
Aung Mingala	1979	Walki Paper	87	172
Aura	1923	Wille	1	39
Aurora	1982	Arcturus	126	224
BALTIC	1987		114	208
Baltic Skou	1986	Finntrader (III)	106	199
Baltic Stone	1972	Tuira	71	146
Baltikum	1977	Pollux	118	212
Berga Falcon	1984	Finnfalcon	99	191
Berga Pride	1985	Finnwhale	100	192
Bergen Falcon	1984	Finnfalcon	99	191
Bergen Pride	1985	Finnwhale	100	192
Bernice	1979	Walki Paper	87	172
Besseggen	1958	Finnalpino (I)	28	76
Birgitta	1962	Mälkiä	52	116
Bluebill	1977	Puhos	90	178
BOARD	1987		115	209
Borac	1978	Fosseagle	98	189
BOTNIA	1987	Baltic	114	208
Bradeverett	1963	Finnforest (I)	34	86
Bravaden	1979	Walki Paper	87	172
Brazen Head	1927	Enso	7	48
Bristol	1957	Soskua	54	119
BULK	1987		116	210
Bure	1962	Vaasa	32	83
CANOPUS	1977	Finnforest (II)	88	174
CAPELLA	1972	Hans Gutzeit	69	142
CAPELLA AV STOCKHOLM	1972	Hans Gutzeit	69	142
CARELIA	1972	Finnwood (II)	70	144
Carmencita	1960	Lovisa	58	124
CASTOR	1972	Finntrader (II)	72	148
Central Master	1954	Pamilo	14	58
Charlie	1984	Para-Charlie	101	193
Chimo	1980	Finnarctis	92	181
Cielo di Siena	1986	Finntrader (III)	106	199
Citta di Firenze	1958	Finnalpino (I)	28	76
Citta di Viareggio	1965	Finnbrod	39	93
CLIO	1972	Valkeakoski	67	138
Clipper Fame	1977	Lotila (II)	82	165
Clipper Forest	1978	Walki	83	166
CONCORDIA AMER	1971	Finn-Amer	62	131
CONCORDIA BUILDER	1971	Finnbuilder	64	134
CONCORDIA FINN	1965	Finnbrod	39	93
Concordia Maria	1953	Finnmerchant (I)	12	55
CONCORDIA SAILOR	1972	Finnsailor (II)	65	136
Condor	1965	Finnmaid (II)	43	100
Conemaugh	1909	Pankakoski	5	44
Copiapo	1971	Finnbuilder	64	134
Cordillera	1965	Finnarrow (I)	42	98
CORONA	1972	Finnmaster (II)	68	140
Corral	1965	Finn-Enso	44	101
Costa Playa	1967	Finlandia	78	158
Costis Taf	1957	Pälli	53	117
Cowboy	1919	Kalle	2	40
Cupria	1977	Finnforest (II)	88	174
Dana Corona	1972	Jalina	105	196
Danaos	1958	Finnalpino (I)	28	76
Delfini	1975	Finnbeaver	84	168
Dominion Trader	1958	Finnpine (I)	24	71
Dover	1957	Pälli	53	117
Du Shan	1964	Rekola	37	90
Ebbella	1956	Finnwood (I)	21	67
EERO	1919		3	42
Elise	1919	Eero	3	42
Emirates Express	1978	Fosseagle	98	189
Empire Concession	1927	Enso	7	48
ENSO	1927		7	48
ENVIK	1983		128	227
Eolos	1962	Hansa Express	31	81
Equus	1951	Finntrader (I)	9	50
Ernst Brockelmann	1927	Enso	7	48
Esso Finlandia	1950	Isla Finlandia	55	120
FARONA	1972		129	228
Feiyu	1975	Finntimber	77	157
Feng	1964	Finnenso	38	91

248

Feng Ning	1964	Finnenso	38	91	**FINNPINE (I)**	1958		24	71
FENNIA	1973		112	205	**FINNPINE (II)**	1972		66	137
Fernandoeverett	1965	Finnhawk (I)	41	96	**FINNPINE (III)**	1984		135	235
Festos	1966	Finnpartner (II)	74	151	**FINNPOLARIS**	1981		94	183
Fidaa	1967	Tyysterniemi	48	109	**FINNPULP**	1953		11	53
FINLANDIA	1967		78	158	**FINNREEL**	1965	Annika	56	121
FINN	1987		113	206	**FINNRIVER**	1959	Taina	60	128
FINN-AMER	1971		62	131	**FINNROSE (I)**	1960	Lovisa	58	124
FINN-ENSO	1965		44	101	**FINNROSE (II)**	1980		96	186
FINNALPINO (I)	1958		28	76	**FINNROVER (I)**	1963	Nina	59	126
FINNALPINO (II)	1973		75	154	**FINNROVER (II)**	1972	Jalina	105	196
FINNARCTIS	1980		92	181	**FINNRUNNER**	1963	Lauri-Ragnar	57	123
FINNARROW (I)	1965		42	98	**FINNSAILOR (I)**	1953		10	52
FINNARROW (II)	1996		139	239	**FINNSAILOR (II)**	1972		65	136
FINNBEAVER	1975		84	168	**FINNSAILOR (III)**	1987		122	217
FINNBIRCH	1953		23	70	**FINNSEAL**	1964		35	87
FINNBOARD	1958		18	63	**FINNSTAR (I)**	1955		22	68
FINNBOSTON	1964	Finnenso	38	91	**FINNSTAR (II)**	1967	Finlandia	78	158
FINNBROD	1965		39	93	**FINNSTRIP**	1964	Rekola	37	90
FINNBUILDER	1971		64	134	**FINNTIMBER**	1975		77	157
FINNCARRIER	1969		51	114	**FINNTRADER (I)**	1951		9	50
FINNCLIPPER	1962		30	79	**FINNTRADER (II)**	1972		72	148
FINNDANA	1962	Hansa Express	31	81	**FINNTRADER (III)**	1986		106	199
FINNEAGLE (I)	1962		29	78	**FINNTRADER (IV)**	1995		138	238
FINNEAGLE (II)	1978	Fosseagle	98	189	**FINNTUBE**	1964	Lotila (I)	36	88
FINNELM	1972	Koiteli	73	149	**FINNWHALE**	1985		100	192
FINNENSO	1964		38	91	**FINNWOOD (I)**	1956		21	67
FINNFALCON	1984		99	191	**FINNWOOD (II)**	1972		70	144
FINNFELLOW	1973		76	155	**FINNWOOD (III)**	1989		124	221
FINNFIGHTER (I)	1965		40	94	Firenze	1919	Eero	3	42
FINNFIGHTER (II)	1978	Kaipola (III)	86	171	Flag Adrienne	1968	Kotkaniemi	49	110
FINNFOREST (I)	1963		34	86	Fokus Barge	1983	Para-Alfa	102	194
FINNFOREST (II)	1977		88	174	Folkliner	1966	Finnpartner (II)	74	151
FINNFOREST (III)	1988		123	219	Forano	1975	Finnfury	85	169
FINNFURY	1975		85	169	**FOSSEAGLE**	1978		98	189
FINNHANSA (I)	1966		46	105	Frengenfjord	1979	Walki Paper	87	172
FINNHANSA (II)	1994		136	236	Gagich	1975	Finntimber	77	157
FINNHAWK (I)	1965		41	96	Gambia	1956	Finnmaid (I)	15	59
FINNHAWK (II)	1980		95	184	Gelinda	1960	Lovisa	58	124
FINNJET	1977		81	163	Gina	1953	Finnpulp	11	53
FINNKRAFT (I)	1956		16	60	Golden Hill	1965	Finn-Enso	44	101
FINNKRAFT (II)	1972	Valkeakoski	67	138	Good Faith	1975	Finntimber	77	157
FINNLARK	1966		45	103	Gotland	1996	Finnarrow (II)	139	239
FINNMAID (I)	1956		15	59	Gracia	1953	Finnsailor (I)	10	52
FINNMAID (II)	1965		43	100	Great Trans	1983	Taurus	117	209
FINNMAID (III)	1972	Hans Gutzeit	69	142	Gryf	1962	Hansa Express	31	81
FINNMASTER (I)	1954	Pamilo	14	58	H.A. Scandrett	1909	Hamina	6	46
FINNMASTER (II)	1972		68	140	Hai Pung	1923	Wille	1	39
FINNMASTER (III)	1973	Fennia	112	205	Hakuni	1927	Enso	7	48
FINNMERCHANT (I)	1953		12	55	**HAMINA**	1909		6	46
FINNMERCHANT (II)	1982		97	188	**HANS GUTZEIT**	1972		69	142
FINNMILL	1965	Finnbrod	39	93	**HANSA EXPRESS**	1962		31	81
FINNMINI	1965		50	112	Harbour	1965	Finn-Enso	44	101
FINNOAK (I)	1971	Kaipola (II)	63	132	Helmwood	1923	Wille	1	39
FINNOAK (II)	1972	Tuira	71	146	Helsinki	1975	Finntimber	77	157
FINNOCEANIS	1978	Walki	83	166	Henry Deutsch de la Meurthe	1921	Neste	8	49
FINNPARTNER (I)	1966		47	106	Honfleur	1919	Kalle	2	40
FINNPARTNER (II)	1966		74	151	Huang Long	1964	Finnseal	35	87
FINNPARTNER (III)	1995		137	237					

249

Hue Lu	1964	Finnenso	38	91	Makena	1919	Kalle	2	40
Ialyssos	1966	Finnpartner (I)	47	106	Maldive Merchant	1956	Finnmaid (I)	15	59
Ice Lark	1966	Finnlark	45	103	Maldive Star	1955	Finnstar (I)	22	68
Imperial	1971	Finn-Amer	62	131	Malmö Link	1980	Finnhawk (II)	95	184
Infanta	1983	Taurus	117	209	**MALTESHOLM**	1965	Finnhawk (I)	41	96
Innstar	1967	Finlandia	78	158	Man Cheong	1958	Finnboard	18	63
Irving Forest	1973	Finnalpino (II)	75	154	Manja Dan	1959	Taina	60	128
Isla del Rey	1927	Enso	7	48	Mar del Nord	1956	Finnwood (I)	21	67
ISLA FINLANDIA	1950		55	120	Maria D	1953	Finnmerchant (I)	12	55
J. Sister	1972	Finnwood (II)	70	144	Maria di Maio	1953	Finnmerchant (I)	12	55
JALINA	1972		105	196	Mark VII	1958	Airismaa	20	66
Ji Xi	1972	Finnwood (II)	70	144	Martti-Ragnar	1953	Finnbirch	23	70
Jia Fa	1972	Finnmaster (II)	68	140	Master	1954	Pamilo	14	58
Jin Tai	1972	Finnmaster (II)	68	140	Matai	1975	Finnbeaver	84	168
Jin Yue	1961	Kaipola (I)	27	75	Maurice Desgagnes	1963	Lauri-Ragnar	57	123
John P	1953	Finnbirch	23	70	Mayssa Junior	1967	Tyysterniemi	48	109
JURMO	1954		26	74	Mediterranean Sun	1972	Tallink	125	222
Jussara	1963	Tervi	33	85	**MEGA**	1975		132	232
KAIPOLA (I)	1961		27	75	Milagro	1975	Finnfury	85	169
KAIPOLA (II)	1971		63	132	Mini	1965	Finnmini	50	112
KAIPOLA (III)	1978		86	171	Monsun	1975	Finnfury	85	169
KALLA	1986		108	201	**MOTTI**	1993		133	233
KALLE	1919		2	40	Mount Delphi	1919	Eero	3	42
Kamari	1977	Puhos	90	178	**MÄLKIÄ**	1962		52	116
Kamari I	1977	Puhos	90	178	Nada	1919	Kalle	2	40
Kamsa	1919	Eero	3	42	Nada D	1956	Finnkraft (I)	16	60
Kaptanikos	1958	Finnboard	18	63	Nanoula	1963	Nina	59	126
Karla Dan	1916	Tornator	4	43	Nassiouka	1959	Taina	60	128
Katingo H	1954	Jurmo	26	74	**NB AESA 78**	1998		140	240
KEMIRA	1981		93	182	**NB AESA 79**	1998		141	241
Kent Forest	1978	Walki	83	166	Nedlloyd Rockanje	1972	Jalina	105	196
Kimolos	1971	Kaipola (II)	63	132	Nelli	1958	Airismaa	20	66
KOITELI	1972		73	149	Neni	1959	Taina	60	128
Kotka Lily	1972	Jalina	105	196	Nesshorn	1958	Finnboard	18	63
KOTKANIEMI	1968		49	110	Nesshörn	1958	Finnboard	18	63
Kun Shan	1964	Finnseal	35	87	**NESTE**	1921		8	49
KUURTANES	1976		80	162	New Dalia	1963	Nina	59	126
Lacerta	1975	Finnfury	85	169	Nikolas II	1953	Finnmerchant (I)	12	55
Lagoa	1962	Vaasa	32	83	**NINA**	1963		59	126
LANKA ABHAYA	1989	Finnwood (III)	124	221	Nomadic Patria	1978	Patria	120	215
LAPPONIA	1978		110	203	Nomadic Pollux	1977	Pollux	118	212
Largo	1972	Farona	129	228	Norcove	1977	Finnforest (II)	88	174
Larona	1972	Farona	129	228	Norden	1976	Rautaruukki (I)	79	161
LAURI-RAGNAR	1963		57	123	Nordlys	1916	Tornator	4	43
Leonoreverett	1962	Finnclipper	30	79	Norse Mersey	1969	Finncarrier	51	114
Lily	1964	Lotila (I)	36	88	North Star	1909	Hamina	6	46
Ling Jiang	1960	Simpele	25	72	North Viscountess	1986	Finntrader (III)	106	199
Lisa	1960	Simpele	25	72	Northern Sapphire	1971	Finnbuilder	64	134
LOTILA (I)	1964		36	88	Ntabeni	1984	Tellus	111	204
LOTILA (II)	1977		82	165	**NUNNALAHTI**	1957		17	62
LOVISA	1960		58	124	Nyhammer	1954	Jurmo	26	74
Lu Shan	1972	Valkeakoski	67	138	Nyx	1958	Finnpine (I)	24	71
Lübeck Link	1980	Finnrose (II)	96	186	Ocean Mercury	1972	Finnmaster (II)	68	140
Lun Shan	1965	Finnfighter (I)	40	94	Ocean Pearl	1967	Finlandia	78	158
Madzy	1976	Kuurtanes	80	162	Odysseas Elytis	1972	Tallink	125	222
Mago	1962	Vaasa	32	83	**OIHONNA**	1984		127	226
Magos	1962	Vaasa	32	83	**OLAU FINN**	1966	Finnpartner (II)	74	151
Mah	1965	Finn-Enso	44	101	Orizaba	1956	Finnwood (I)	21	67
Maid	1956	Finnmaid (I)	15	59	**OUTOKUMPU**	1958		19	65

Pacific Sky	1959	Taina	60	128	Sara	1919	Eero	3	42
Palladia	1965	Finnmaid (II)	43	100	Saronikos	1919	Kalle	2	40
PALLAS	1971		119	214	Scandinavia	1969	Finncarrier	51	114
PAMILO	1954		14	58	Scandinavia Link	1969	Finncarrier	51	114
PANKAKOSKI	1909		5	44	Scandinavian Sky	1972	Tallink	125	222
Panorea	1953	Finnbirch	23	70	Scaplake	1953	Finnpulp	11	53
Paoletta	1962	Mälkiä	52	116	Seahorse	1972	Jalina	105	196
PARA-ALFA	1983		102	194	Searider	1969	Finncarrier	51	114
PARA-BRAVO	1984		103	195	Seatra	1958	Finnboard	18	63
PARA-CHARLIE	1984		101	193	Seng Soon Chew	1959	Taina	60	128
PARA-DELTA	1985		104	196	Sfakia	1957	Soskua	54	119
PARA-DUO	1984	Para-Bravo	103	195	Shouragallus	1919	Eero	3	42
PARA-UNO	1992		131	231	Silja Dan	1951	Veli	61	129
Parthenon	1956	Finnkraft (I)	16	60	Silver Faith	1975	Finntimber	77	157
Passad	1975	Finnbeaver	84	168	Silverlark	1966	Finnlark	45	103
PATRIA	1978		120	215	**SIMPELE**	1960		25	72
Pearl	1967	Finlandia	78	158	Sin Hock Chew	1959	Taina	60	128
Pearl of Scandinavia	1967	Finlandia	78	158	Sirius	1973	Fennia	112	205
Peer Gynt	1966	Finnpartner (I)	47	106	Solano	1984	Finnpine (III)	135	235
Ping Shan	1964	Lotila (I)	36	88	**SOSKUA**	1957		54	119
Pinocchio	1965	Finnmini	50	112	Sovereign Sapphire	1951	Finntrader (I)	9	50
Pisces Venturer	1989	Finnwood (III)	124	221	Sri Lanka	1956	Finnwood (I)	21	67
Po Sea	1961	Kaipola (I)	27	75	**STEEL**	1987	Finn	113	206
POKKINEN	1980		91	179	Stena Atlantica	1966	Finnpartner (II)	74	151
Polaris	1969	Finncarrier	51	114	Stena Baltica	1966	Finnpartner (I)	47	106
POLLUX	1977		118	212	Stena Paper	1957	Pälli	53	117
Poyang	1964	Finnenso	38	91	Stena Searider	1969	Finncarrier	51	114
Prairial	1919	Eero	3	42	Stena Wood	1957	Soskua	54	119
Princesa Marissa	1966	Finnhansa (I)	46	105	Stern	1967	Tyysterniemi	48	109
Prinsessan	1966	Finnhansa (I)	46	105	Strilberg	1978	Lapponia	110	203
Puerto de Vita	1951	Finntrader (I)	9	50	Su Lin	1972	Finntrader (II)	72	148
PUHOS	1977		90	178	Sunnanhav	1962	Mälkiä	52	116
Pygmalion Jupiter	1951	Finntrader (I)	9	50	Susan. C	1967	Tyysterniemi	48	109
PÄLLI	1957		53	117	Svanö	1961	Kaipola (I)	27	75
RAILSHIP I	1975		134	234	Svea Regina	1972	Tallink	125	222
Raimo-Ragnar	1955	Finnstar (I)	22	68	Sveaborg	1966	Finnpartner (I)	47	106
RAUTARUUKKI (I)	1976		79	161	Syros	1962	Mälkiä	52	116
RAUTARUUKKI (II)	1986		107	200	Tacamar VII	1965	Finnbrod	39	93
Recife	1984	Tellus	111	204	**TAINA**	1959		60	128
Red Sky	1956	Finnkraft (I)	16	60	**TALLINK**	1972		125	222
Regina	1954	Jurmo	26	74	Tamanaco	1965	Finnbrod	39	93
Regina	1972	Tallink	125	222	Tamaris	1963	Nina	59	126
REKOLA	1964		37	90	Tara Rose	1967	Tyysterniemi	48	109
Resalla	1979	Walki Paper	87	172	**TASKU**	1986		109	202
Resolute Spirit	1953	Finnmerchant (I)	12	55	**TAURUS**	1983		117	211
Rex	1956	Finnwood (I)	21	67	**TELLUS**	1984		111	204
Rheinfels	1972	Jalina	105	196	**TERVI**	1963		33	85
Rimja Dan	1960	Lovisa	58	124	Teuvo	1975	Mega	132	232
Roine	1919	Eero	3	42	Tian Shan	1965	Annika	56	121
Rolita	1977	Finnforest (II)	88	174	Toftön	1980	Pokkinen	91	179
Rosseverett	1962	Finneagle (I)	29	78	Torborg	1921	Neste	8	49
Royal Paper	1957	Pälli	53	117	**TORNATOR**	1916		4	43
Royal Wood	1957	Soskua	54	119	Tramarco Carrier	1971	Kaipola (II)	63	132
S.M. Spiridon	1967	Tyysterniemi	48	109	Tramarco Trader	1979	Walki Paper	87	172
Saga	1966	Finnpartner (II)	74	151	**TRANSESTONIA**	1972	Farona	129	228
Sagar Tarani	1965	Finnmini	50	112	Triton Ambassador	1951	Finntrader (I)	9	50
Salama	1972	Koiteli	73	149	**TROLLEHOLM**	1962	Finneagle (I)	29	78
Salla	1979	Walki Paper	87	172	Tropique	1919	Eero	3	42
Sandlark	1966	Finnlark	45	103	**TUIRA**	1972		71	146

Tumi	1953	Finnsailor (I)	10	52	W.W. Atterbury	1909	Pankakoski	5	44
TUPAVUORI	1954		13	57	**WALKI**	1978		83	166
TYYSTERNIEMI	1967		48	109	**WALKI PAPER**	1979		87	172
Ukraina	1978	Patria	120	215	Wan Fu	1965	Finnfighter (I)	40	94
United I	1963	Nina	59	126	War Racoon	1919	Eero	3	42
VAASA	1962		32	83	Westön	1979	Varjakka (II)	89	177
Vaasa Provider	1963	Lauri-Ragnar	57	123	**WILLE**	1923		1	39
VALKEAKOSKI	1972		67	138	Wspolpraca	1921	Neste	8	49
VARJAKKA (I)	1961	Kaipola (I)	27	75	Xian Ren	1965	Annika	56	121
VARJAKKA (II)	1979		89	177	Yi Feng	1964	Lotila (I)	36	88
VASAHOLM	1965	Finnarrow (I)	42	98	Yue Lu Shan	1972	Valkeakoski	67	138
VELI	1951		61	129	Zhe Hai 319	1960	Simpele	25	72

THE COMPANY FLAG

THE COMPANY JACK